Kentuckian in Blue

Major General Lovell Harrison Rousseau (Library of Congress).

Kentuckian in Blue

A Biography of Major General Lovell Harrison Rousseau

by DAN LEE

McFarland & Company, Inc., Publishers
Jefferson, North Carolina, and London

LIBRARY OF CONGRESS CATALOGUING-IN-PUBLICATION DATA

Lee, Dan, 1954–
    Kentuckian in blue : a biography of Major General Lovell Harrison Rousseau / by Dan Lee.
       p.   cm.
    Includes bibliographical references and index.

    ISBN 978-0-7864-4818-0

    1. Rousseau, Lovell Harrison, 1818–1869. 2. Generals — United States — Biography. 3. United States — History — Civil War, 1861–1865 — Biography. 4. United States — History — Civil War, 1861–1865 — Campaigns. 5. Kentucky — History — Civil War, 1861–1865 — Campaigns. 6. Tennessee — History — Civil War, 1861–1865 — Campaigns. 7. United States. Army — Biography. 8. Soldiers — Kentucky — Biography. I. Title.
E467.1.R77L44   2010
    355.0092 — dc22 [B]   2010006522

British Library cataloguing data are available

©2010 Dan Lee. All rights reserved

No part of this book may be reproduced or transmitted in any form or by any means, electronic or mechanical, including photocopying or recording, or by any information storage and retrieval system, without permission in writing from the publisher.

On the cover: Major General Lovell Harrison Rousseau, between 1860 and 1870 (Library of Congress); background ©2009 Shutterstock and Clipart.com

Manufactured in the United States of America

McFarland & Company, Inc., Publishers
  Box 611, Jefferson, North Carolina 28640
    www.mcfarlandpub.com

To J.F.L. and S.E.L.

"The past is a foreign country."
— L. P. Hartley (in *The Go-Between*, 1953)

Table of Contents

Preface 1

1. From a Boy to a Man in Kentucky 5
2. A New Home in Indiana 11
3. Captain Rousseau in Mexico 16
4. Louisville and the Know-Nothing Riots 28
5. Kentucky's Secession Crisis of 1861 37
6. Camp Nevin and the Federal Advance in Kentucky 45
7. The Battle of Shiloh 54
8. The Corinth Campaign 62
9. Following General Bragg to Kentucky 67
10. The Battle of Perryville 83
11. The Battle of Stones River 93
12. The Tullahoma Campaign 106
13. Chickamauga and Chattanooga 117
14. The Great Alabama Raid 130
15. The Defense of Middle Tennessee 153
16. Nashville and the End of the War 170
17. In and Out of the House of Representatives 177
18. Rousseau and an American Alaska 190
19. The Department of Louisiana 203

Afterword 213
Chapter Notes 217
Notes on Selected Sources 225
Bibliography 231
Index 239

Preface

There was once a class of men in America who slipped gracefully between military service, political office, and the private business world where they earned their living. They were excitable by nature, and their energies overflowed. One life was not enough for them. Their spirits ran too high for them to sit quietly at home when the war trumpets sounded. Their vision of the country's rightful direction was too strong for them to refuse political office, and their ambition too restless for them not to reach for the wealth to be made in a young country that offered so many opportunities.

They were self-made men, and they excelled with such seeming ease at each endeavor that others responded to them and imagined that they, too, could excel like these men they admired. These men are admired even today.

Yet, they would not belong in the 21st century. They were too bold, too scrappy. They were courtly, but not delicately genteel and they would resort to physical solutions when other remedies failed. They fought duels and administered beatings. Their behavior would offend modern etiquette and their attitude afterward even more so, for they were unrepentant. They would not fit the sensitivities of a time when a tearful, televised apology and a brief stint in rehab will expunge almost any deed from the record. These men took responsibility. They were not sorry.

Andrew Jackson was the epitome of this class of men, but there were others. Sam Houston was one, and, a half-generation later, so was Lovell Harrison Rousseau.

* * *

These men had something else in common. Each came from difficult, if not tragic, early circumstances. Having lost a parent at an early age, and forced to deal with the most grinding poverty, these men learned early that the world was antagonistic. The fight was on and their fate was in their own hands.

Rousseau was at war his entire life. He buried his father beside the Mill Springs Road and from that time forward fought to overcome poverty and ignorance. He fought his way to the top of the legal profession and afterward won political office, sometimes as the candidate of both parties at once. And he made war against the enemies of his country during the Mexican War and in the Civil War. The war of 1861–1865 was the best showcase of his talents. He was no West Pointer, which made his rise to Major General all the more impressive. Rousseau advanced by virtue of his native intelligence, his talent for learning from experience, and his very visible courage. Rousseau did not try to lead from behind; he was a cheerful warrior on horseback who seemed to be inspired by danger—and inspired his men, in turn. In this way, too, Rousseau reminds one of Jackson and Houston. They were all born to command.

* * *

Most difficult to admire about these men is their racial attitude. They were comfortable in their belief that the white race was superior, and it led them to be paternalistic on the one hand and cruelly dismissive on the other. If it was in their power to pet, it was also in their power to punish and to buy and sell.

Rousseau shared the racial biases of Jackson and Houston, and of a great many others whose names are remembered as heroes of war and of politics. Rousseau was raised in a slave-owning family and it inevitably shaped his outlook. However, he grew beyond a casual acceptance of slavery as a good and proper institution. He defended and won acquittals for blacks in a Louisville courtroom in the 1850s—and when a crowd threatened his defendants, he physically protected them from their white assailants until they could be gotten to safety. In 1863 he said in the presence of the correspondent W. F. G. Shanks, "No law, human or divine, justified slavery." And, in a political speech near the war's end, he exclaimed before a Kentucky crowd, "Slavery, thank God! is dead." He criticized his home state for being slow to ratify the 13th Amendment.[1]

During the war, he had no personal qualms about blacks serving in uniform and thought they should be armed, which was an attitude that went far beyond the thoughts of some of the other officers in blue. In 1863, he advised fellow officers who were on the verge of insubordination over the question of black enlistment to be calm and not take actions they would regret. He had black regiments in the department he commanded in Tennessee in 1864 and 1865.

Yet, he willingly followed the early war policy of returning runaway slaves to their masters, and continued to do so longer than many Union officers. He believed in a segregated army, and he had little faith, later on, in the fighting ability of the black troops in his department, an attitude that hardened after black soldiers retreated precipitously from a strong position behind blockhouse walls at Elk Creek, Tennessee, in 1864. He sometimes used racial epithets in conversation and in his speeches.

As a U.S. congressman, Rousseau opposed the renewal of the Freedman's Bureau, and, as commander of the Department of Louisiana in 1868, he arguably did too little to insure the rights of black voters.

His attitudes may be difficult to understand, but Rousseau was not alone, among the Civil War generation, in his contradictory behavior insofar as race was concerned. President Lincoln worked to free the slaves — but he wanted to colonize them in South America or the Caribbean and believed that only the intelligent of those who remained should be allowed to vote. U.S. Grant had owned slaves and William Tecumseh Sherman was so harsh in his disdain for blacks that he was chastised by his superiors and warned by the Washington authorities that many Northerners considered his actions criminal. And if Rousseau's vocabulary contained racial slurs, he was no different than Robert Gould Shaw, the Massachusetts-born commander of the all-black 54th Massachusetts, who peppered his letters with words like darkie and nigger.

How does one reconcile the many venerable qualities of Rousseau, and others who were loyal to the North, with their insensitive racial beliefs? The answer is to judge them not by the standards of our time but by the standards of their own. If Rousseau's attitudes were not perfect by our principles, they were still ahead of those of millions of his fellow Americans in the middle 1800s. Other men of that period must be judged individually through the records of their actions. In the specific case of Rousseau, it must be fairly said that his personal interactions with African Americans, and the efforts he made on their behalf, helped to counterbalance the darker strains of his personal prejudices.

* * *

This is not the last word on Rousseau. Rather, it is only a beginning, an introduction to the life of a man who has been the subject of very few written pages considering that he was a soldier, a state and national legislator, a special envoy for the State Department, and a departmental commander during Reconstruction. That he has not been the subject of a biography until now may be attributed to the fact that there is such a scarcity of primary sources regarding Lovell Harrison Rousseau. There is no comprehensive (or even sizable) archive of his papers, only small, scattered collections — sometimes containing a single document — that pertain to him. Two of the best of those collections that do exist are found at the Library Company of Philadelphia and at the Filson Historical Society in Louisville, Kentucky. The author thanks both of these, as he does the helpful and friendly staff at the Eugene and Marilyn Glick History Center of the Indiana Historical Society in Indianapolis, James Simard and Damon Stuebner at the Alaska State Library, and the family researchers who have painstakingly gathered material and anecdotal information about General Rousseau. The author is grateful to Linda Smetzer, who was extremely generous with both her research and her encouragement. Above all, the author wishes to thank his wife, Linda Akins Lee, for her computer expertise and for her patience in listening endlessly to the stories of Lovell H. Rousseau's adventurous saga.

Future scholars are invited to pick up the standard and carry on the effort to find the hidden chapters of Rousseau's life, to interpret them, and to help complete the portrait of this remarkable man.

And readers are invited now to read the life story of Rousseau the Kentuckian, an uncelebrated American hero.

1

From a Boy to a Man in Kentucky

A newcomer to Kentucky in the summer of 1833 could have been excused for believing that war had come to the Commonwealth, for every road and turnpike was crowded with refugees struggling along, worried, their clothes and other necessities piled into carts or wagons or laced onto the backs of pack horses.

The upheaval our newcomer would have witnessed along his way was not war, however. It was an epidemic of Asiatic cholera. Cholera was a dreadful disease and a fast acting one. It was said that a person could feel fine at breakfast, fall ill by noon, and be dead by suppertime. Near the end, the vomiting, sweating, diarrhea-stricken victim turned blue from the relentless gush of bodily fluids.

The first cholera cases of 1833 appeared in late May, when a dozen victims were reported in Maysville. Maysville was an Ohio River town and the disease may have arrived on a river packet. The still-healthy citizens of the handsome old town quickly made plans to flee. No more than two days after the first death, nine-tenths of Maysville's white population had left the town — and in their flight spread the disease throughout the region. Many of them fled to Lexington, reputed to be the most healthful town in the Bluegrass. Others hedged their bets by making for the health resorts at Blue Licks and Harrodsburg. It was of no use; the disease caught up with them wherever they went and spread further. Seven percent of the population of Paris died, and 4 percent of the population of Cynthiana — and the survivors packed up to leave, repeating the pattern and accelerating the spread of cholera.

When torrential rains came in June and caused the creeks to overflow, the incidents of illness quickened. In Lancaster, 116 citizens died and in healthful Lexington the people began dying at a rate of fifty a day. The safest places in the region seemed to be further south, in Wayne and Pulaski counties. It was to Mill Springs in Wayne County that David Rousseau, a Lincoln County farmer, decided to take his family — a wife and nine of his eleven children.

David Rousseau's brother John lived in Wayne County, along with other relatives, so the Lincoln County brood would be welcome there.

The Rousseau family was scattered throughout Central Kentucky. They had come to Kentucky from Culpeper County, Virginia, in the 1790s, steering flatboats down the Ohio River to Maysville, Mason County, where they stayed for several years before they began to spread through the Bluegrass and Pennyroyal regions of the state. Their break from Virginia was not a clean one, and members of the family traveled back and forth between their new home and their old one for years to come. David Rousseau is said by some not to have settled permanently in Kentucky until 1814. That may be so, but the 1810 census shows him as a resident of Pulaski County. He finally settled in Lincoln County, near Stanford.

Many families experienced an economic dislocation in their move west of the Appalachians, and it sometimes took years for them to get back on a solid financial footing. So it was with David Rousseau. He was sixty-one years old; time was running short. Though he owned considerable undeveloped acreage and was a slave owner, he was not as far along in the accumulation of wealth as a man of his age should have been when the cholera epidemic persuaded him to leave Lincoln County for Wayne County and safety.

It was too late. Along the way, David Rousseau became sick and died. Neither the settlers living nearby nor any of the travelers passing on the pike would stop to help the family. They saw the corpse, recognized the signs, and scurried away in dread. The oldest Rousseau sons, John and Richard, had already left home by 1833 and were not with the family when the father died, so it fell to the second oldest son, Lovell Harrison Rousseau, with the help of his two younger brothers to dig their father's roadside grave. It was night before the body was lowered into the ground.

The children's mother, Catherine Gaines Rousseau, for reasons unknown, did not proceed to Wayne County. Or, if she did, it was only for a brief time. She turned back to Lincoln County and her own home and farm.

David Rousseau had died and left his family stranded in poverty. Now, Lovell Harrison Rousseau was the family's principal breadwinner. He was fifteen years old.

* * *

Lovell Harrison Rousseau was born in Lincoln County on August 4, 1818. It was one of the three oldest counties in the commonwealth, along with Jefferson and Fayette, created in 1780 when Mother Virginia divided her western lands. Lewis Collins, in his *History of Kentucky,* described Lincoln County as a good land for "horses, mules, cattle, hogs, and wool; while wheat, corn, oats, and rye are extensively cultivated."[1]

Growing up there, Lovell would have heard stories of the pioneer leader Benjamin Logan, whose 1775 fort, St. Asaph's, became Stanford, the county seat. The remains of the old fort could still be seen. The Shawnee had called St. Asaph's the Standing Fort because they could never reduce it by storm or siege. Benjamin Logan was a militia leader and legislator who led a company of riflemen against the Indians one week and traveled to Danville to make laws the next. The combination of soldier and lawmaker must have appealed to the imagination of the boy.

He would have heard the story of the capture of Samuel Daviess' wife and seven children by the Indians and how, at the moment of their rescue, the oldest boy was scalped by a warrior who escaped through a hail of rifle balls with the boy's top-knot as his trophy. The boy struggled to his feet and made only one mild complaint: "Curse that Indian, he has got my scalp."[2]

He would have heard the story of Mrs. Woods and her slave, a lame Negro man, who were chased into the family cabin by Indians. One brave burst into the cabin before the door was slammed shut. As the slave and the Indian wrestled on the floor, Mrs. Woods held the door closed against the rest of the war party while her daughter hit the inside Indian on the head with an axe, killing him. The Negro proposed to let the rest of them in one at a time and they could dispatch the whole war party the same way, one by one. The arrival of a party of men from the nearby fort frightened the Indians away and prevented the Woods women and the slave from carrying out their plan.

And Lovell would have heard thrilling stories of the settler William Whitley, whose brick house was a landmark on the Wilderness Road, which ran through the county. Whitley's plantation was called Sportsman Hill and featured the first oval race track in Kentucky. Whitley was an unrepentant enemy of the British and, because he did not want to do anything in the style they did, he decreed that the races on his track would run opposite to the British horses — races at Sportsman Hill were run counterclockwise, beginning the custom that still endures on American tracks. The race-day barbeques at Sportsman Hill were legendary, but life was not all joviality. Lovell would have heard, too, of how old Whitley had fought the Indians through the Revolution, had lost the tip of his nose to an Indian arrow, and had vowed to take thirteen scalps, one for each colony, before he was done. He was killed at the Battle of the Thames in 1814, aged sixty-four years and going after that thirteenth scalp.

These were the kind of people Lovell Harrison Rousseau grew up among: determined, resourceful, calm in the face of danger and accepting of hardship, respecters of the law who were ready to go to war when their way of life was threatened and, when the fighting was done, to take a moment to enjoy life, a horse race, maybe, or a sip of bourbon whiskey.

* * *

The death of his father was certainly the pivotal moment of Lovell Harrison Rousseau's young life. It forced upon him prematurely the heavy responsibilities of manhood and propelled him into a life of work so never-ending that it became habitual, to the detriment of his own children in later years.

Yet, until he buried his father, the evidence suggests that Lovell's life was a happy one. There were eleven children in the family. Some scholars have stated that David and Catherine Rousseau had twelve children, and some family historians have counted only ten, but a deed for a sale of 382 acres of land to John Rousseau of Wayne County, dated October 20, 1834, names eleven children: John A., Richard H., Elizabeth B., Lucy Anne, Lovell H., Nancy M., Mary G., Edmund P., William C., David Q., and Samuel D. With so many brothers and sisters, there must have been a great deal of hilarity and, no doubt, some pitched battles. The siblings made alliances among themselves; Lovell and Richard seem to have been especially close, if their adult years are an indication. The routine of farm chores was punctuated by services at the Presbyterian Church and during the winter there was school — but never too much, it appears. In an 1866 autobiographical sketch Rousseau said, "I never attended a school or institution of learning three months in my life."[3]

Adding to the lively life on the Rousseau farm was a slave family of three: Sampson, Aggie, and, after 1820, their child, Thomas. A sketch of the little slave family is one of the few glimpses of early life on the Rousseau farm. In an undated, unpublished piece called "A Bluegrass Lassie," Edmund Thickstun (the son of Mary G. Rousseau and Lovell's nephew) told that the slave child Thomas and the white child Mary were born only two days apart, Mary on December 30, 1819, and Thomas on New Year's Day 1820. It was soon discovered that Catherine Rousseau could not nurse her daughter, so David Rousseau carried the two-day-old infant from the main house down to the slave cabin, to Aggie, who was expected now to nurse the white child along with her own son. In Thickstun's account, Aggie was happy to take on the extra baby, saying, "I'se shore glad you brung her, Marse David."[4]

Aggie's joy at another mouth to feed seems too good to be true, but, judging by the bits of evidence that exist, the Rousseaus did try to be kind slave owners and relations between the whites and the blacks were friendly. Yet, slavery was by its nature a severe institution. Even people who were generally well-intentioned slid into cruel behavior and there is a troubling postscript in the tale of Aggie and the newborns. Before he left the slave cabin, David Rousseau reminded Aggie in a powerful though polite way of her status. According to Thickstun, Rousseau picked up the black child and asked, "What have you named your baby, Aggie?"

"Thomas will be his name."

"All right, Aggie, and when he grows up he shall be Miss Mary's servant."[5]

Thus, on the day he was born, the fate of Aggie's son was decided by another; he was given away to be the servant of the master's white child.

The slaves may have gone toward Wayne County with the Rousseaus in 1833 — some accounts say they helped bury David Rousseau — but, if so, it was an uncommon arrangement. More often, the slaves were left behind to watch over the abandoned home and property until the cholera passed and their white masters returned.

In any case, the slaves were back with the Rousseaus in Lincoln County after David's death. One evil consequence after another followed the fatal decision to go to Mill Springs. The Rousseaus struggled along for a few years on the Lincoln County farm, but their private war on poverty was a lost cause. Edmund Thickstun's account of the Rousseau family, though long on dialect, was short on dates; however, from independent evidence, it seems that about 1837 or '38, the family was ordered to settle the estate by means of an auction sale. Thickstun mentioned "scores of slaves," which seems unlikely. The 1820 Lincoln County census shows that the Rousseaus owned only one slave, a female; it would have been an unusual streak of prosperity if they were able to add nineteen or more slaves to their inventory in so few a number of years. Unfortunately, the family does not appear in the 1830 Lincoln County census, which would have shed light on the question.[6]

Furthermore, a family who owned twenty slaves would not have been in such desperate straits as to suffer a forced auction.

The auction was tragic for both blacks and whites and, in this instance, both the slaves and their owners were equally helpless to control events. Insofar as the blacks were concerned, Thickstun had this to say:

> Sampson and Aggie, I think, were sold to a man in Lincoln County, who could appreciate their intrinsic value, though their market value was low, just like a horse past fifteen is low in price. But Tom was spotted by a Negro trader from the south as a profitable investment, just as a gelding of two years is a likely bargain. He got the boy and was starting away with him. Here is where Mary went frantic. She rushed between the boy and the speculator with the fury of a tiger. "You shall not take Tom to Mississippi, he belongs to me."
>
> "Indeed Miss? Show your papers. If he is yours, then I am done."
>
> "Pappy and Aunt Aggie always said that he is my servant. Pappy gave him to me when I was only two days old."

"I would require more substantial proof. Your father is dead, Aunt Aggie is a Negro, and I guess that your memory of the event must be rather hazy. I have a bill of sale, made to me by the order of the court. Come honey, calm yourself. The boy is my property, legally transferred, as I know." ...

Her anguish was heightened by Aunt Aggie, who wailed: "O, dey aguine to take my Tommy down to Missip, and kill him off on de cotton plantation." But all the expostulations of Mary and Aggie did not count.[7]

The results of the auction were far-reaching and, in some respects, surprising. Mary Rousseau became a "rampant, red hot, radical Abolitionist." Aggie's Tom survived Mississippi and returned to Kentucky sometime during the Civil War. Edmund Rousseau, Lovell's younger brother and a master brickmason in Louisville, built a home for him. Tom married and had a daughter whom he named Georgia, after Edmund's daughter.[8]

The effect of the auction on Lovell Harrison Rousseau is unknown, in any long-term emotional sense, but the immediate impact was that he was deprived of property of his own to work. The Rousseaus were no longer freeholders and Lovell, like the slave Tom, was forced away from Lincoln County and into a life of hard physical labor.

2

A New Home in Indiana

Kentucky was experiencing a boom in road building during the 1830s. After Andrew Jackson refused Henry Clay's request to let Federal funds be used to build an in-state road between Maysville and Lexington, the commonwealth took it upon itself to construct and improve roads. Everyone recognized adequate transportation as one of the keys to prosperity. A highway department (the first in the Union) was created in 1835 to commission the improvement of old roads and the construction of new ones. Financial oversight was also needed. The new roads cost up to $8,000 per mile.

The roads which the highway department mandated were to be between thirty and fifty feet wide, ditch to ditch, and they were slightly higher in the center as an aid to drainage. A layer of gravel ten inches deep made a fine, smooth surface, much better than the buffalo traces and corduroy roads Kentucky's travelers were accustomed to. The state's determination to build good roads was genuine. James Klotter and Lowell Harrison, in their *New History of Kentucky*, observe that, before the end of 1836, "approximately 343 miles of stone surfaced roads had been completed and 236 miles more were under construction."[1]

Such modern roads were labor intensive, and virtual armies of men were hired to break rocks for surfacing gravel and chop down trees to clear the right of way. This was the kind of unskilled work Lovell Harrison Rousseau found when he left home. He hired on with the gang that was building the turnpike between Lancaster and Lexington.

The young man may have, by this time, attained his adult height of 6 foot 2 inches, and swinging a sledgehammer or an axe ten hours a day no doubt transformed his physique into solid muscle. Almost everyone who saw Rousseau as an adult described him using the same adjective: Herculean.

Working on the road crew was Rousseau's introduction into the male-dominated world where he would spend most of his life. The law, the military, and the halls of the legislature were domains where a woman was rarely seen. However, these were professional endeavors, decidedly rarified in contrast to the road gang where every sort of rough and tumble man worked shoulder to shoulder with the young Rousseau. He had to learn to get along with them and, probably, to defend himself against bullies with his fists.

This was where Rousseau started, but it was already in his mind that this was not where he would end. He gathered books on grammar, math, and even a French language text, and at night, while his fellow rock-breakers drank or gambled or slept, he would copy out his lessons and the next day, as he swung the sledge, he propped his book up against a boulder so he could study while he worked.

At some point during this period, Rousseau went to Michigan to work. Little is known about his brief time there, only that he continued as a manual laborer and that he pursued his self-education. William Sumner Dodge in his *History of the Old Second Division, Army of the Cumberland* (written in 1864), said that Rousseau "applied himself with necessary attention to the acquirement of that which he so sensibly lacked, and his subsequent career has proved how sound and how practical was his patient self-teaching."[2]

Although his handwriting was never more than a bold scrawl, Rousseau developed a talent for expressing himself with perfect clarity. For some, words are a way to obscure the true man; in Rousseau's case, the words reveal perfectly well what sort of man he was. His powerful logic, often leavened with generous doses of humor, is a trademark of his writing and speeches. A facility for language pointed one toward certain professions. Rousseau chose the law.

In March 1840, he returned to Kentucky. His mother and older siblings were now living in Louisville, Jefferson County, but Rousseau did not lodge with them. Mindful of his limited and painfully-earned savings, the young man moved eight miles out of town to save the expense of city living. Reading law may have been the most demanding course of study that he had ever undertaken. He applied himself with such intensity that he nearly ruined his health. Quoting Dodge again, "His health became seriously impaired and resulted in a severe sickness." He was incapacitated for months.[3]

When he recovered, he moved away from the City at the Falls to Bloomfield, Greene County, Indiana, a town on the prairie southwest of Bloomington. He had a head full of law and $5.50 in his pocket.

In February of 1841, only eleven months after he had resolved upon a legal profession, Rousseau passed the casual oral interview that, in those days, represented the bar exam and received his license to practice law. He continued to study to perfect his knowledge and took on any work that would earn him money until paying clients began to find him.

It happened that his older brother, Richard Hilaire Rousseau, had also been reading law and was admitted to the bar at about the same time as Lovell. The brothers became junior partners in the Bloomfield law firm headed by James I. Dozier, another Kentuckian who had gone north.

Greene County, Indiana, had been surveyed in 1810. Until then, none but Indians and white hunters had seen it. The first settlers came seven years later. Isaac Stalcup was one of the earliest. The father of twenty-one children, Stalcup was a man so primitive that he was said to have gotten rid of his first wife by swapping her for a new hat and ten gallons of whiskey.

Of a more refined sort was Peter Vanslyke, who settled on the site of future Bloomfield. Like Stalcup, Vanslyke arrived in 1817, followed shortly by Daniel Carlin and John Vanverse. They built cabins and cleared fields for crops and, the next spring, brought their families out. The farmers discovered that the gently rolling prairie west of the White River was especially good for corn, wheat, oats and hay. East of the White River the land was hilly and timbered. There was a landmark sycamore tree over there that some claimed was one thousand years old.

When Greene County was created out of Sullivan and Daviess counties in 1821, there was competition between Fairplay and Bloomfield. Bloomfield sat on a handsome bluff above a spring of good water, but what decided the question was Vanlyke's donation of sixty-two acres of land. The decision made on the basis of this incentive, the town site was next surveyed into lots, the sale of which was advertised in the Salem and Indianapolis newspapers. The first sale was held in November 1824 and cleared $1,262 in profit. Bloomfield was on its way.

Attracted by the opportunity of a fresh start in a new town, the businessmen and artisans soon began to arrive. Augustine Passmore built a tavern and a grocery the first year of the town's history, and Otis Hinkley came the next year to open a store stocked with $800 worth of goods. He sold linen and needles and boots, and when the second courthouse was built in 1825, the county bought the hardware and glass from Hinkley. (The Rousseau brothers would practice in the third courthouse, built in 1836.)

Regrettably for the issues-minded citizens of Bloomfield (and also for later students of the town and its residents), the town's one newspaper, the *Comet*, folded in 1840, but there was a library. Bloomfield boasted a brick school and two churches, as well as a distillery and a tannery. It also had a carding mill, a grist mill, and not too far away, a small iron furnace on Richland Creek.

There were doctors and mechanics in town, coopers and carpenters, and, as of 1841, two new professional men — Richard and Lovell Rousseau. The Rousseaus soon attracted attention for their skill as defense attorneys and their persuasive powers before a jury.

The sequence of events is speculative, but it may be that the move to Bloomfield had been Richard's idea. In November 1839, he had married James Dozier's daughter Mary. It was reasonable that he should move to Bloomfield to practice in his father-in-law's firm and reasonable, too, that Lovell, needing a step up, should follow his older brother there. It turned out to be a fortunate private as well as professional move, for Lovell found a wife of his own in Bloomfield. She was Marie Antoinette Dozier, another daughter of James Dozier. They married in July 1843. It was a good match, evidently, for the couple remained together until Lovell's death twenty-six years later.

Now the Rousseau brothers were even closer, connected by blood, by profession, and by law.

* * *

The law practice, though profitable, was unexceptional. There were both civil and criminal cases; the most florid of these was the case of a man who was accused of drowning his wife in a well. Lovell Rousseau defended the man and won an acquittal. He was well known for his persuasive skills in front of a jury. He later admitted, "I am a lawyer by profession, and my friends think a pretty good one. Of course, I agree with them in the opinion."[4]

Still, the evidence is that the practice did not satisfy the younger Rousseau for, in 1844, he entered the race as the Whig candidate for the Indiana House of Representatives. Greene was a Democratic county and his opponent was well funded, but Rousseau won when the votes were tallied on the first Monday of August 1844.

The following December 2, he was present for the opening of the 29th session of the Indiana House of Representatives and was assigned to serve on the Joint Committee on the State Library. The early days of the session were occupied with electing House officers, the clerk and the speaker, and, on December 4, Governor James Whitcomb addressed the legislators on various topics: the number of arms reported by the Quartermaster General, and the financial issues that confronted the state, especially the accounts of the Wabash and Erie Canal and of the Madison and Indianapolis Railroad, and certain bond issues.

As a member of the House, Rousseau was asked to help decide such chewy issues as whether or not there should be a review of the law that required county boards to levy road taxes. Preferring local discretion in the assessment of taxes, Rousseau voted "Yea."

But, regarding a bill to mandate an Indiana constitutional convention, he voted "Nay."

Naturally, there were the demands of his constituents to attend to, as well. Late in the session, on December 31, Rousseau presented a petition from the citizens of Greene County to allow Thomas Carrico to erect a dam across Black Creek. Since the legislature had declared Black Creek as navigable, it had to decide whether the proposed dam would be an insufferable obstacle on the creek. The select committee which studied the question recommended that the petitioners' request be approved, which it was.

Most portentous, though it may not have seemed so at the time, was the passage of a resolution encouraging the citizens of the Republic of Texas to resist Mexican incursions inside the Lone Star's boundaries. Before many months passed, the issue of Texas would come to bear more directly on the lives of some of these legislators.

On January 13, 1845, the House informed the Senate that they were now ready to adjourn, and soon Rousseau was back at home in Bloomfield.

A second term in the House followed in late 1845, when the lawmakers considered bills for preserving wild game, authorizing a bounty on wolf scalps, and the issue of whether canoes and pirogues should be allowed to travel on the Wabash and Erie Canal. But the question of Mexican trespass into Texas had not gone away. The issue had, in fact, grown sharper since December 29, 1845, when Texas had entered the Union as the 28th state.

When the next session of the Indiana House met, the representative from Greene County would not be there. Rousseau would be away at war.

3

Captain Rousseau in Mexico

In the fall of 1845, President James K. Polk offered Mexico $25 million and a cancellation of all claims for damages, in return for a peaceful acknowledgement of Texas as a U.S. state with the southern boundary at the Rio Grande. From the point of view of Mexico, Texas statehood might be an accomplished (though regrettable) fact, but the true southern boundary was still to be decided. They believed that the southern boundary of Texas should be the Nueces River. They rejected Polk's offer and President Jose´ Herra ordered cavalry patrols north to protect Mexican interests in the region between the two rivers. At the same time, President Polk sent four thousand troopers under General Zachary Taylor to roam between the Nueces and the Rio Grande. A bloody clash was inevitable. It came on April 25, 1846, when a Mexican patrol sent a group of American cavalrymen scampering, leaving behind sixteen dead, with several more wounded or captured. It was the incident that Polk had been waiting for; now he could claim that American blood had been spilled on American soil. On May 13, Congress declared war. The president immediately called for volunteers. The *Indiana Democrat* responded enthusiastically — its May 22 headline blared "To Arms! To Arms!" Indiana's quota was three regiments, each man to furnish his own clothing and to receive $13.50 a month for twelve months' service.[1]

Within two weeks, Lovell Harrison Rousseau was commissioned as a captain and authorized to raise a company. War fever was running high in all regions of the country and, it seems, in all corners of Greene County, for Rousseau's company was complete by the 8th of June and on the 22nd it was mustered into U.S. service as Co. E, 2nd Indiana Volunteer Infantry.

Lovell and Marie Rousseau were the parents of a child, by this time; a daughter named Mary, born in 1844. Marie was pregnant at the time that her husband raised his company and the evidence is that she went to stay with either his relatives or hers in Kentucky while he was gone away to war, for the Rousseaus' second child and first son, Richard, was born in 1846 in Kentucky.

It was arranged that Rousseau's new volunteers would rendezvous at Owensburg. Just before they left that place to join the other companies of their regiment, the ladies of Owensburg and Springfield presented them with a bright silk flag. Rousseau replied with some appropriate remarks. It is a loss to history that there is no record of what he said, but it was no doubt both patriotic and sadly poetic in the oratorical manner of the time. The ceremony concluded, the boys of Co. E piled into wagons or climbed into the saddle and moved out for Camp Whitcomb.

Camp Whitcomb was near the mouth of Silver Creek, about a mile above New Albany, Indiana, on the Ohio River opposite Louisville. If Captain Rousseau was given a furlough to cross the river and visit his brothers and sisters living in the city, there is no account of it. What is known is that learning the trade of soldiering was hard, unfamiliar work and the boys in Co. E, 2nd Indiana were kept busy responding to a dizzying sequence of commands barked at them by no-nonsense drillmasters. Their officers, like Rousseau, were kept busy as well, studying the manual of arms and learning their own responsibilities as leaders of men.

There was also the matter of regimental elections. Colonel Joseph Lane first commanded the 2nd Indiana, but he was promoted to brigadier general, so a new colonel had to be elected. Lane's successor was Captain W. L. Sanderson, formerly the captain of Co. A (the Spencer Greys), but when it was discovered that some votes had not been counted, the results were voided and a second election was ordered. In the meantime, Captain W. A. Bowles took command of the regiment. The new election would not be held at Camp Whitcomb, however. On July 11, the regiment was ordered south. Five companies (including, it is believed, Co. E) boarded the riverboat *Uncle Sam* and steamed down the Ohio River away from New Albany.

It was a rainy trip, but spirits were high among these young men who were on the adventure trip of their lives. They disembarked at Baton Rouge long enough to be armed from the arsenal there; each man got a musket and accoutrements, forty cartridges, and two flints. On July 17, they arrived in New Orleans and were ordered to bivouac on the old Chalmette Plantation. Here, on the 8th of January 1815, Andrew Jackson with an army of recruits almost as green as these, had defeated Sir Edward Pakenham's battle-hardened British regulars. Perhaps this site was selected to inspire valor among the young troops. Certainly, it was not picked for comfort. Clouds of mosquitoes filled the muggy air and the ground was like a saturated sponge. The boys corduroyed the floors of their tents by laying down lengths of firewood like a rough parquet floor. They could not have been sorry when, on July 18, they struck tents and boarded the *Governor Davis* and the *Partheon* for the trip down to the mouth of the Mississippi and across the Gulf of Mexico to Brazos Santiago on the Texas coast.

This leg of their journey was much different. The men became violently seasick crossing the Gulf and spirits plummeted. Lovell H. Rousseau was especially vulnerable to seasickness and one can imagine that he was among the sickest of the sick. A thunderstorm on the night of July 19 only made a bad situation worse. Nauseous men below decks could not have taken much interest when a school of porpoises was spotted on July 22, and when a soldier was buried at sea on the 23rd, many of the suffering, groaning men must have felt that they would soon be joining their comrade in the deep.

On July 24, the ship drew near Brazos Santiago. The men undoubtedly took comfort in the sight of solid land, even this narrow sliver of a barrier island, but their ordeal was not quite over. It was not until three days later that tenders arrived to ferry the soldiers to shore.

On August 1, the postponed election for Colonel of the 2nd Indiana was held at last. Captain Sanderson was again a candidate and, the habit of politics dying hard, so was Captain Rousseau. W. A. Bowles, who had been acting colonel since Camp Whitcomb, outcanvassed them both and continued in command, now officially. It was Bowles who led the 2nd Indiana up the Rio Grande when the order came to move out on August 3. The Rio Grande valley was scrub country, with needle-bearing underbrush beneath the mesquite trees, quite unlike anything the Indiana boys had seen before.

They reached Camp Belknap, fourteen miles below Matamoros, on the night of the 3rd and made a comfortable camp on a grassy ridge above the river. There, they settled in for several weeks of camp life. The drill that had begun at Camp Whitcomb in June and continued sporadically since then became routine at Camp Belknap. The men were roused for regimental drill every morning at five o'clock. There was also company drill and guard duty was another obligation, but it rotated among different squads of men in the regiment. Free time was filled with camp chores such as gathering wood, cooking, and washing clothes. Occasionally, there were burials to attend.

The long bivouac at Camp Belknap was a welcome one in the sense that it gave time for the men's back pay to arrive and for the mail to catch up. Captain Rousseau surely must have received letters from his wife and his brother, but if they exist, their location is unknown.

Benjamin F. Scribner of Co. A received a letter from his friend Ulysses that said, "Frank, when you get to them halls of Montezuma that I hear so much talk about, just take out your jack knife and cut me a chip off the front door if you please and pocket it for me."[2]

As September faded into October with no move upriver toward the action, the seven hundred boys of the 2nd Indiana must have wondered if they ever were going to see "them halls of Montezuma."

* * *

By the time the 2nd Indiana Volunteer arrived at Camp Belknap, a lot of the war had already been fought. General Taylor, after that initial incident that started the war, had defeated the Mexicans at Palo Alto and Resaca de la Palma, had seized Matamoros and built Fort Brown on the opposite bank of the Rio Grande. From there, he moved 120 miles upstream to Camargo, which would be the stepping off point for an assault on Monterrey.

In mid–August, the first of Taylor's troops moved out of Camargo for Cerralvo, a seven-day march. Along the way, they were kept busy by Mexican dragoons, but they were just an annoyance. A worse threat was waiting at Monterrey — 7,300 of the enemy arrayed in a good defensive position, protected by high hills and a river on the south and west and by battlements bristling with artillery on the north and east. Inside the city proper were additional defenses.

The Americans first saw what awaited them on the morning of September 19. The Mexican gunners welcomed them with a few well-aimed artillery rounds — one twelve-pound solid shot came to rest at General Taylor's feet. A party of Mexican cavalrymen came out in an apparent attempt to lure the army into musket range, but Taylor was too old a fox to step into that trap. Instead, he had his army camp in a grove of oak and pecan trees, while he contemplated the challenges of attacking a fortified position. This was something new to a man more used to fighting Seminole Indians or Mexican horsemen out in the open, where an army could maneuver.

Taylor decided to divide his forces. Two thousand men led by General William Worth would attack the two well-defended hills west of Monterrey. Taylor would make a demonstration on the east and the two forces would then converge on the Mexicans in a pincer movement. The attack would commence on September 21.

On the day of battle, Texas Rangers, the 5th U.S. Regulars, and a battery of artillery were able to take one of the two hills, half of the expected gain, but Taylor on the east had an even harder time. His men were caught in a crossfire, turning this way and that, trying to find a way forward. A charge of the reserve troops failed to drive the Mexicans back, but a second attempt finally broke the Mexican resistance on Taylor's front and the Americans gained a fragile hold on the edge of Monterrey. A probing force was sent forward to see if the small victory could be improved upon, but they were forced back by artillery fire and the day's fighting ended.

The next morning, in a cold rain, Worth's command took the second hill on Monterrey's west. Taylor's column, on the east, was not very involved this day. The Mexicans pulled back into the city's interior defenses. Here would be the third day's fight.

This concentrated force in Monterrey's center fought viciously to keep the Americans back on September 23. The roofs of Monterrey were flat, and every one was heavy with Mexican infantry, who stung the Americans with a deadly storm of lead. Still, the Americans inched painfully forward. As Taylor's men fought their way up the narrow streets from one direction, Worth directed his Texans and Regulars to forsake the streets and to advance *inside* the buildings by digging their way forward through the soft adobe walls.

Near dusk, with their enemies converging, their one stronghold reduced to the area of the city plaza, and their ordnance and ammunition running out, the Mexicans surrendered, but with the demand that they could march out of Monterrey with their arms and that an eight-week armistice would follow. In order to avoid a bloodbath, Taylor agreed.

The soldiers were proud of their victory in what they felt, incorrectly as it turned out, was the toughest fighting they would ever see. Taylor was glad for an agreement that would give his army time to rest and reinforce. And the American public was joyful at the news of another American victory. But, in Washington, D.C., President Polk was beside himself. Polk, a Democrat, was growing alarmed at the increasing possibility of Zachary Taylor as a Whig presidential candidate in 1848 and, unhappy that the war was dragging on longer than he had intended, the president was annoyed with Taylor's unilateral two-month long interruption of American progress.

The answer to both problems was to send another force into Mexico. Consequently, Polk ordered General Winfield Scott to invade Mexico from the Gulf Coast and bring pressure to bear against Mexico City. Not only would this hasten the end of the war, but since Scott was another Whig, it would split that party's enthusiasm between two heroes. In a political version of the old military maxim "divide and conquer," Polk would tear the Whigs in two and cost them the 1848 election. The flabbergasted Taylor was ordered to dismember his army, to send the bulk of it south to join Scott, and to remain at Monterrey with the diminutive command left to him.

Taylor sent the troops as ordered, but he did not remain in Monterrey. He pushed forward to Saltillo, for he was in no mood to obey orders from either a president who was plainly his enemy or from an "Old Fuss and Feathers" general who might prove to be his superior in rank only.

But, this small insubordination notwithstanding, there was little more that Taylor could do until reinforcements arrived.

* * *

The Indiana Volunteers were disappointed that they had arrived in the theater of operations too late for the fighting at Monterrey, and there was little need for them during the armistice, but on December 5, they were ordered to break camp and join "Old Rough and Ready" Taylor at Saltillo. Seven companies steamed up the Rio Grande on the *Enterprise*; the three remaining companies soon followed on the *Whiteville*. The regiment arrived at Camargo on December 18 and marched for Monterrey about noon of the next day. Their haversacks were heavy with four days' rations of coffee, salt, pickled pork, and bread. Along a road whose surface was described as "ankle deep" in dust, they made nine miles before they camped. As their legs limbered up over the next few days, they would make marches twice or even three times as long.[3]

The start of the new year saw the regiment at Saltillo. Benjamin F. Scribner, whose friend wanted a chip off of Montezuma's door, kept a wartime diary that was later published as *Camp Life of A Volunteer*. In it, he detailed his impressions of the town:

> The city of Saltillo is situated on the side of a hill. It has narrow streets and sidewalks, which are roughly paved with stone. The houses are built of stone and mud bricks, whitened over on the outside with plaster. They have flat roofs ... [there are] two cathedrals, a nunnery, and four plazas. In the center of the plazas are fountains.
>
> The church and plaza Santiago are truly magnificent, covering a whole square.[4]

Scribner was intrigued with the church, which did not resemble the Baptist and Presbyterian sanctuaries back home in Indiana, bedecked as it was in silver and decorated with paintings and images set in glass cases.

For Lovell Harrison Rousseau, too, the churches and plazas must have been exotic and interesting, but the most fascinating sight may have been of his fellow Kentuckian and Whig hero, General Taylor. At first, Rousseau may have made the same mistake of a wet-behind-the-ears lieutenant who mistook the plain-dressed Taylor for an orderly and offered him a dollar to clean his sword. Characteristically, Taylor took the dollar and did the chore.

Certainly, Taylor was no show pony. He was a short and heavy-set tobacco chewer, slovenly dressed and looking like the farmer he was. Generally, he wore a wide-brimmed straw hat, a faded gray coat of sackcloth, and a blue neckerchief. Even mounted on horseback, he did not look like a general; he was said to sit astride his war-horse, Old Whitey, like a toad. But, Taylor had proven that he could win battles and, Polk or no Polk, he was about to go south and win another one.

While still at Saltillo, General Taylor was reinforced by General John E.

Wool and his column, who had marched down from Chihuahua to join him. With the addition of Wool's troops, Taylor had six thousand men (nine-tenths of them volunteers) as he pushed down to Agua Nueva, a ranch south of the hacienda Buena Vista. There, Taylor received a reliable report that a large Mexican force was only thirty miles away and moving north toward him on the road between Buena Vista and San Luis Potosi. The Mexicans were led by the new president of Mexico, Santa Anna, the infamous conqueror of the Alamo.

The position at Agua Nueva was not a strong one, so Taylor fell back eleven miles to a narrow pass called La Angostura. Here, the Mexicans would have to use the road, because the rocky ridges on either side would be impossible for their cavalry and artillery to navigate. On the west of the road was a solid ridge crowned by an even higher peak; on the east was a successive series of ridges and ravines resembling a right hand, palm turned up, with the thumb and fingers pointing northwest.

The position selected, General Taylor went back to Saltillo to see about the defenses of the town; reports were that a Mexican cavalry force was scouring that area behind the Americans, a threat that Taylor could not abide. General Wool was left in command of La Angostura and it was he who placed the troops.

In the defile between the hills, pointing south in the direction Santa Anna would be coming, Wool placed Captain John Washington's artillery battery. Behind Washington and to the left, on the crest of a high ridge, were the 1st and 2nd Illinois and the 2nd Kentucky. Three artillery batteries, Thomas W. Sherman's, Braxton Bragg's, and John Paul Jones O'Brien's, were next in line; then the 2nd Indiana (390 men present). The American line was oriented from the fingertips to the heel of our imaginary hand, facing southwest. In his report of the battle, Zachary Taylor called it a line of "remarkable strength."[5]

On the morning of February 22, the Mexicans came into view. Within minutes, they deployed and began directing fire at the Americans. The Americans fired back. After a few hours of this commotion, Santa Anna sent forward a flag of truce, boasting of twenty thousand men and demanding surrender. The accounts of Taylor's reply range from the formal ("I beg leave to say that I decline acceding to your request") to the plain-spoken ("If you want us, come and take us!"), but either way, the meaning was clear. Taylor was not intimidated and intended to fight. The skirmish of the 22nd ended at dark. No Americans were killed, but General Wool insisted in his report that the Mexicans lost heavily. Everyone knew that the enemy would attack at dawn, so the men slept on their arms. The weather was cold, there had even been a snowstorm a few days earlier, but because this wasteland was barren of wood, there were no fires.[6]

Taylor went back to Saltillo during the night, still worried about the mischief that the Mexican cavalry might make in the rear, so he was not at La Angostura the next morning when the enemy attacked.

At the hour that would have been dawn, if there had been one to be seen on this drizzly morning, the Mexican cannons spoke. An enemy division charged up the road toward Captain Washington's artillery and was repulsed, but the Mexicans enjoyed more success in their attack on the American left flank. During the night, while the Americans tried to rest, the Mexicans had crept up the sides of the arroyos and were in place to attack *en masse* the American left, just where the 2nd Indiana was positioned. Wool responded quickly when seven thousand Mexicans advanced. To drive them back, he ordered Brigadier General Lane (who commanded the 2nd Indiana before his promotion) to send Lt. O'Brien and his three small field pieces forward, supported by the infantrymen of the 2nd Indiana. The Mexicans fired two rounds into them before they could get into place, but they advanced through the barrage to within musket range, and began firing "with great effect," as Taylor reported it.[7]

Nevertheless, the enemy continued to press forward. They had lugged an artillery battery of one twenty-four pounder and two eighteen pounders to the top of the ridge and now, from the left, it sent grapeshot and canister ripping through the American flank. Scribner wrote that the Mexican artillery fire "raked our flank with terrible effect; still we stood front to front.... But the battery on our left galled us exceedingly."[8]

From the first of the fighting around O'Brien's battery, Colonel Bowles, commanding the 2nd Indiana, had behaved in a way that was so shocking as to be noted by his men. A soldier of the regiment later wrote to the *Indiana Sentinel* that "Colonel W. A. Bowles ... acted during the fight in a way but little calculated to inspire his men with confidence in his bravery. He dismounted as soon as the firing commenced and endeavored to shield himself by staying immediately in the rear of his troops and his horse between him and the enemy's battery and while the men were fighting as bravely as men ever fought."[9]

The fight on the left raged for about three hours. Finally, when he was unable to stand it any longer, Colonel Bowles ordered the men to cease fire and retreat. There was later a long argument about whether or not the order was mistakenly given, but whether it was a mistake or not, the boys eagerly obeyed it, and what began as an orderly withdrawal, very quickly dissolved into a frantic footrace to the rear. O'Brien seems not to have heard the order to fall back, but he soon noticed that there was no supporting musket fire coming from his right or left and, looking around, discovered that his battery had been abandoned. He saved two guns; all the horses and men of the third piece were killed.

As the Hoosiers streamed toward the rear, they swept up some nearby companies of Arkansas mounted infantry. The 2nd Illinois collapsed next, along with Sherman's artillery battery. The whole left flank seemed to give away. Only a relative handful of American defenders remained on the ridge. The enemy surged forward, reinforced, and the American line appeared doomed.

Meanwhile, the Mexican cavalry made a wide sweep around the American left and drove hard for Buena Vista. A victory there would not only isolate the defenders on the ridge and set them up for the final kill, but would also deprive the Americans of their supply and baggage trains, which were parked at the hacienda. At just the right moment, General Taylor arrived on the scene, returning from Saltillo and bringing with him Jefferson Davis' Mississippi Rifles, who had scooped up some of the retreating Hoosiers. At Taylor's direction, they flew into the Mexicans. The 2nd Kentucky and Bragg's section of artillery came racing over from the right. The 1st Illinois and the 3rd Indiana added their strength to the American left a moment later, while Bragg's artillery and Sherman's (which had returned to the fight) pounded the enemy with loads of canister. The Mexican assault was stalled, except for Anastasio Torrejon's lancers, who made it past the Americans and charged down on Buena Vista.

Since leaving O'Brien, Captain Rousseau and Major Willis A. Gorman had been trying to stop and rally the routed 2nd Indiana. They finally got them back under control at the hacienda. The boys may have thought that they had left the fighting behind, but the fighting had caught up to them. At least, they had enjoyed a breather. Now, they followed orders and fought as hard as ever to protect the supply train, knowing that to lose it in this stony wasteland would mean disaster. The lancers of the Mexican Army, though they sounded like something out of the Middle Ages, were among the most feared of enemies. The Mexicans had been expert horsemen since before Coronado and, armed with nine-foot-long, steel-tipped spears, they were beyond the reach of sabers or clubbed muskets. The most modern U.S. musket was still only a single shot weapon, and useless for twenty to thirty seconds after each round was fired, but the lancers could ride among their enemies, fending off attacks while inflicting repeated cuts and jabs. The lancers liked to work in pairs or in teams. Once an enemy was down, two or more lancers would swarm over him, stabbing and slashing until he was dead. At the small

Battle of San Pasqual, California, in December 1846, lancers had killed twenty-one Americans in fifteen minutes. It took nerve to stand and face the lancers, but that is who Rousseau's boys of the 2nd Indiana had before them now. The Hoosiers acquitted themselves well. They repulsed Torrejon's charging horsemen and shoved them back and, joined now by the Kentucky and Arkansas cavalry, forced them into a ravine where they were within range of Bragg's field pieces. The storm of iron and lead that poured down on Torrejon's Mexicans soon forced them to raise the white flag. It was a ruse; as the American fire slackened, the trapped Mexicans charged and fought their way through to their main body, and reformed for another attack.

The Americans quickly formed a V, the open end facing the southeast, with the 3rd Indiana on the right leg and the Mississippi Rifles and 150 or more men of the 2nd Indiana on the left. The greenhorns were learning quickly; they held their fire until the Mexicans who were charging into the open mouth of the V were within seventy-five feet. General Taylor sat calmly watching, sitting on Old Whitey, with one leg crossed and thrown casually over the pommel of his saddle, as the infantry fired and the cannons pumped three salvos of canister into the Mexicans, whose charge faltered and failed. This was the climax of the battle. The Mexicans fell back, defeated at the V of Buena Vista. A final, desperate attempt by the enemy was repulsed by American artillery.

Taylor reported, "No further attempt was made by the enemy to force our position." Night fell and the casualties were attended to. Another night without fires increased the suffering of the exhausted and wounded men, but for the others, there was work to keep them warm. The able-bodied were retrieving the wounded and laying them in wagons for transport back to Saltillo, and they were preparing new defensive lines, working alongside the seven fresh regiments that were brought forward. There were alarms throughout the night and everyone expected a renewal of the battle at sunrise.[10]

But there was not going to be any fight on February 24. The Mexicans withdrew south during the night.

In what the Center for Military History called the "hardest battle of the Mexican War," General Taylor reported the American loss to be "two hundred and sixty seven killed, four hundred and fifty six wounded, and twenty three missing." Of that number, 103 of the killed and wounded were from the 2nd Indiana Volunteers. Four were reported as missing, but two of these were later discovered among the dead, raising the number to 105. The number of Mexican casualties was never known, but they left no fewer than five hundred dead behind, and maybe as many as one thousand.[11]

Rousseau's first experience as a combat commander was not unblemished. Three hours of heavy fighting at the start of the battle reflected well on the captain and his untested enlistees, but the rout that followed was dishonorable, if understandable. When, after a time, the fighting came to them, the boys once again performed bravely, and did so in the exact place they were needed, saving the supply trains and helping to drive the enemy back, ultimately, into the mouth of that deadly V. During the fighting at the V, Jefferson Davis of the Mississippi Rifles reported that he noticed "an officer of that regiment [the 2nd], whose gallantry attracted my particular attention, but whose name, I regret, is unknown to me." No one has ever known for a certainty, but more than one scholar has speculated that this gallant but anonymous officer was Captain Lovell H. Rousseau.[12]

After the Mexicans withdrew, Taylor advanced his troops to his earlier position at Agua Nueva. On March 14, the 2nd Indiana was ordered back to Buena Vista and from there, on May 24, to the mouth of the Rio Grande. General Wool issued General Orders No. 295 as his farewell to the regiment. Wool said that he felt "that the moment of parting is not the time to look with a severe eye on the misconduct of a portion of these troops whose companions have merited and will receive the credit which a grateful people always yield to brave men."[13]

General Joseph Lane, however, was on the scene and he knew that it was not the fighting men of the regiment who were to blame for the untimely and disordered withdrawal of the 2nd Indiana at Buena Vista. He preferred charges against Colonel W. A. Bowles, and asked Zachary Taylor to convene a court-martial. General Taylor refused, but said that Bowles could have a court of inquiry, if he desired one. When Bowles did not act, Lane asked for a court of inquiry into his own performance on the basis that *someone* was responsible for the flight of the 2nd Indiana at Buena Vista and that the court would show that *he* was not to blame — that would leave only Bowles. When the court of inquiry exonerated Lane, General Wool took the opportunity to rebuke Bowles in the presence of the other officers. Wool approached Bowles and said, "Colonel Bowles, you have disgraced yourself, your regiment, and your state by giving that order to retreat; you by this act prevented your regiment from achieving one of the most brilliant victories ever achieved by American arms." Bowles did not respond but only bowed his head in shame.[14]

In a belated effort to save face, Bowles did ask for a court of inquiry. The decision did not rebound to his credit. Although he was found to be not guilty of any personal cowardice at Buena Vista, the court did find: (1) that he was ignorant of company, battalion, and brigade drills; (2) he did give the order to cease fire and retreat without the authority from General Lane to do so; (3) that he was ignorant of the duties of a colonel, and (4) that he showed a lack of capacity and judgment as colonel of the 2nd Indiana.

Bowles continued to be a bad character in the years ahead. He seems to have spent a good deal of time in the South during the next few years and, during the Civil War, worked clandestinely on behalf of the Confederates. In 1864 he was accused and convicted of plotting to free Rebel prisoners in Indianapolis and to seize the arsenal, distribute the arms to the Southerners, and lead them in a pro–Confederacy uprising in the heart of the Midwest. The sentence of the court was death. Abraham Lincoln commuted his sentence to imprisonment for life, which the Supreme Court later overturned. Bowles lived the rest of his life in Orange County, Indiana, and died there in 1873. He never lived down the shame of his performance in the fight of February 23, 1847. His obituary spoke of his "miserable bungling, if not his cowardice," and of his having definitely shown the white feather at Buena Vista.[15]

* * *

On July 3, 1847, the 2nd Indiana Volunteers arrived at New Albany to a raucous reception. Scribner remembered, "The cannon roared to welcome us and a flowery arch spanned the street." Crowds cheered them as they entered the city.[16]

When Rousseau and Company E returned to Bloomfield, a public reception was given them at the courthouse. After welcoming addresses, to which Rousseau replied, the throng moved out to Jones' Woods for a barbeque. An ox was roasted and, as they ate, the people crowded around Rousseau to hear stories of the campaign in Mexico.

It was a joyous homecoming, made even sweeter for Rousseau by the news that, while he was gone, he had been elected to the Indiana Senate.

4
Louisville and the Know-Nothing Riots

It took about a week for news from the war in Mexico to reach Indiana. The men who had returned with Rousseau, and Rousseau himself, no doubt eagerly awaited the *Indiana Democrat* or the *Sentinel* to learn what was going on, knowing, as they read it, that the news was already old. Events had moved ahead, gains might have been reversed, acquaintances killed, or, for that matter, Mexico City might have fallen. No one knew.

They knew, even before they left Mexico, that General Winfield Scott had landed successfully on the coast at Veracruz and pushed inland along the same route that Cortez had used in 1519. The rear-echelon strategists feared that Scott had made a fatal error, for how could such a large army as his move through enemy-held territory, living off the land as it went? Then came the thrilling news that the army which the Indiana boys had helped to defeat at Buena Vista in February was defeated again at Cerro Gordo in April. General Winfield Scott had humiliated the proud but unlucky Santa Anna, who had tried to block his way at a narrow mountain pass.

For several weeks following the boys' return to Indiana, there was nothing—no reliable news at all. Then, in late summer, there came a rush of dispatches. At Churubusco, on August 20, General Scott had defeated Santa Anna again, and then at Chapultepec, right at the outskirts of Mexico City, on September 12. Two days later, Scott and his army moved in to occupy the enemy capital until a peace treaty could be arranged. It took five months. The peace treaty was signed on February 2, 1848, at the village of Guadalupe-Hidalgo. The terms were relatively simple: Mexico essentially surrendered its northern half and the U.S. paid Mexico $1.5 million.

By that time, Lovell H. Rousseau was well ensconced as an Indiana state senator. There are no letters known that verify it, but one imagines that he found it hard to concentrate on the minutia of state budgets in some stuffy chamber after all he had seen.

The Mexican War was a terrible expense to the state, which had tried and failed to obtain loans from the Terre Haute Bank, the Vincennes Bank, and the Michigan City Bank, among others. Some, like the Lawrenceburg Branch of the State Bank of Indiana and the Lafayette Branch were more generous. Still, the state had a balance in its treasury of only $694,096.09 as of October 31, 1848. It was belt-tightening time; the state decreased its expenditures from the previous year by $11,488.02. Accountants were ciphering columns of figures right down to the last 2¢ in staid and settled Indiana, and reporting their adventures in arithmetic to the legislators while, in his memory, Rousseau was seeing the wild charge of Mexican lancers across a rocky plateau.

One event of interest that probably did engage Rousseau in 1848 was the presidential election. President Polk's manipulations to deny Zachary Taylor the Whig nomination had failed. Taylor had never voted in a presidential election in his life and stated that the idea of his becoming president would never enter the thinking of a rational person, but now he was in a contest against the Democrat Lewis Cass and former president Martin Van Buren, who was running as the candidate of the Free Soil Party. It was a hard slog for Taylor in Indiana. He had been critical of the Hoosiers' performance at Buena Vista. Asked about it later, he said that he had seen nothing subsequently that would cause him to change his mind. Taylor hurried to add that he nevertheless felt a great fondness for Indiana, that he had seen even veteran troops break and run in battle, and that his confidence in the 2nd Indiana Volunteers was so great that he would have put the regiment into the front lines had there been a third day's fighting at Buena Vista.

Indiana voters were not persuaded. Taylor won the general election but lost Indiana to Lewis Cass by almost five thousand votes.

The presidential campaign was only an interlude. Lovell H. Rousseau's growing dissatisfaction with life in Indiana was so compelling that in 1850, with a year remaining of his term as state senator, he decided to move back to Louisville with his wife, Marie, and their three children (Mary, Richard, and a new daughter known only as B — perhaps Blanche — who was born in 1848). He tried to resign his senate seat, but his constituents would not accept it. Even after he became a resident of Louisville, Kentucky, Rousseau continued to serve Greene and Owen counties until the end of his term in the Indiana Senate. His Democratic opponents ruefully called him "the member from Louisville."[1]

Richard shortly followed Lovell H. to Louisville. They opened the law firm of Rousseau and Rousseau at Court Place downtown and took up residence at the same address in the 6th Ward, on 6th Street between Walnut and Grayson. It was a leafy and level neighborhood and they could see church steeples above the treetops. The Rousseau property must have been lively, for

Richard had four children of his own. The brothers enjoyed having lots of loved ones about. Three female slaves, ages thirty-five, fifteen, and four, were also part of the household.

The same year that Rousseau moved to Louisville, the late Zachary Taylor was brought back for burial. The president had died five days after attending a Fourth of July ceremony at the Washington Monument. It was a hot, bright day. The president became overheated and returned to the White House feeling unwell. He snacked on raw vegetables, fresh fruit, and iced milk, developed severe abdominal pains, and declined steadily until his death on July 9. He was temporarily buried in Washington, D.C., but then his body was shipped home to Louisville, where he had spent the first twenty-three years of his life. He was reburied on November 1, 1850. It would be hard to believe that Rousseau did not visit the grave of his old chief and fellow Whig.

Louisville in the 1850s was a city of 43,000 citizens, one of the most cosmopolitan cities in the West. The gas-lit streets were paved (mostly) and there was a new courthouse with a graceful clock tower under construction. There were thirty churches in the city, including one synagogue. There were five banks, seven bookstores, four daily papers, and twenty-four schools whose graduates might go on to earn a degree in law or medicine at the University of Louisville, the oldest municipal university in the U.S. If going into business was the young graduate's goal instead, there were plenty of opportunities, for Louisville did millions of dollars of annual trade in such commodities as sugar, coffee, tobacco, pork, whiskey, rope, hardware, and sheet iron.

The crowning jewel of the city might well have been the Galt House, a plush-carpeted wonder of the West. No less a personage than Charles Dickens praised its accommodations after his 1842 stay there. Dickens said, "We slept at the Galt House, a splendid hotel; and were as handsomely lodged as though we had been in Paris, rather than hundreds of miles beyond the Alleghenies." The lodgers there could sip their mint juleps and watch the paddle wheelers with names like *The Northerner* and *The Gray Cloud* race on the Ohio River.[2]

The Rousseau brothers threw themselves into the legal life in the city. In no time at all, Lovell H. was adding his support to the effort to win a pardon for an imprisoned man. In a scribbled postscript to a clemency plea to Governor John L. Helm from the prominent Louisville attorney William F. Bullock, Rousseau admitted that the man was rightfully convicted, but his wife was suffering. She was, the lawyer said, "a clean, industrious woman of good standing but *very poor!*" It was common practice for Rousseau to work on behalf of the destitute and the disenfranchised.[3]

Rousseau also remained politically active, on the city level; he was an alderman from the 6th Ward. In more tranquil times, this job might have been considered a sinecure, but the 1850s were not a tranquil time in Louisville. The city was, in fact, becoming badly divided. More than twelve thousand citizens of Louisville were foreign born. The Irish population in the 8th Ward (numbering about 3,100) and the Germans in the 1st and 2nd wards (calculated to be about 7,300) were the two largest blocs. The Germans even had a newspaper in their own language, the *Anzeiger*.

The Irish had fled the potato famine at home and the Germans had exiled themselves because of the failed liberal revolutions in their homeland. There must have been other miscellaneous reasons, but whatever the cause of their emigration, the effect of their arrival was often the same on the native-born Americans in the cities where they made their new homes: dismay that hardened into hatred.

Partly this was because of a fear of radicals. Some of the Germans were socialists or communists. One influential citizen of the German neighborhoods in Louisville, August Willich, had even been a confidant of Marx and Engels in the London Communist League. He arrived in Louisville in 1852.

In the case of the Irish, many of them arrived in such impoverished circumstances that there was a fear they carried disease. Cholera was sometimes mentioned in connection with them — Kentucky had not forgotten the epidemic of 1833 to 1835.

Since the majority of the Irish and Germans were Catholic, there was also a fear of a strengthening Catholic influence over American politics. The 1853 to 1854 American visit of Monsignor Gaetano Bedini, an emissary of the pope, did nothing to allay these suspicions.

The anxiety about foreigners was not a phenomenon in Louisville alone. From New York to St. Louis one would hear the same complaints, which gave way to fears. Finally, those of a like mind turned to the practical solution of creating a political party. It was formally called the American Party, but everyone called it the Know-Nothings.

The new party's nickname came from the response all members were expected to give to nosey questions: "I don't know." There were all manner of strange rituals and signals associated with the Know-Nothings. As a sign of recognition, a member would place a hand between his coat buttons and stick up the thumb. Most bizarre of all was the sequence where a member closed one eye, formed the letter O with his thumb and forefinger, then put the O around the end of his nose. Those in the know recognized this as the physical symbolism of the phrase, "I don't know."

It all sounds ridiculous, like some little boy's club, meeting in a scrap-lumber tree house, but the Know-Nothings were serious in their determination to do something about the foreign threat and were all too ready to resort to intimidation and violence. By 1854, the Know-Nothings boasted one million members.

In Louisville, 1855 was the climactic year. In the mayoral election on April 7, there were some scuffles around the polling places, but when the votes were counted, the Know-Nothing John Barbee had won. There was also some small violence in the May election for county clerk, as the Know-Nothings tried to keep foreign-born citizens from voting. The editor of the *Louisville Daily Journal*, the Connecticut émigré George D. Prentice, was enthusiastically supportive of the new party and so, with two electoral victories behind them and this prominent voice to encourage them, the Know-Nothings planned a complete takeover of the polls in the August elections for governor and a U.S. representative.

On the night of Saturday, August 4, there was a torchlight parade of 1,500 Know-Nothings. The next day, Sunday, was a day of rest, when men could meet, fume over the foreign threat to American freedoms, and make their plans for Monday. It was arranged that Know-Nothings would be given a yellow ticket to carry to the polling place. There, they would enter through a side or a back door to vote. Know-Nothing tough guys would block the main entrance to prevent those who did not display the yellow ticket from voting. Of course, the very sight of these thugs crowding around the front door would discourage some prospective voters from exercising their franchise.

August 6 was a hot, humid day. Each ward had only one polling place and the Know-Nothings got there early, backed by pro–Know-Nothing city cops. The polls opened at 6:00 A.M. Lines began to form. Those Germans and Irish who took their place and stood in line expecting momentarily to vote were manhandled and sent on their way. By lunchtime, the Germans and Irish had quit trying. They stood around in hot, angry knots; at the same time, gangs of cocky Know-Nothings were roaming the streets. Trouble was bound to break out, and it did, when George Bruge was attacked on Jackson Street by some Irishmen. This was all the excuse the Know-Nothings needed. Their response was something like a chemical reaction, and almost as quick; the attack on Bruge was the catalyst that set off the dangerous elements on Jackson Street. A mob numbering five hundred or so suddenly coalesced and headed for the German 1st and 2nd Wards in the eastern part of the city. The Germans took shelter in the buildings along the streets and some random shots were fired at the mob.

The Know-Nothings beat anyone they caught on the street and began setting fire to some buildings and looting others. They broke into Chris Meier's coffeehouse and moved on to Conrad Kitzler's house at Walnut and

Shelby. In the words of the *Daily Courier*, "The property for which he [Kitzler] had laboriously worked was nearly demolished."[4]

A German was killed in the Shelby Street fight and several more were injured before the mob turned toward St. Martin of Tours Catholic Church, where they believed guns and ammunition were stored. Mayor Barbee, the Know-Nothing mayor, now worked frantically to control the forces of hate and fear he had exploited so well in his successful April campaign. He met the mob at the door of the church and told them that the rumor of guns inside was false. The mob was in a burning mood, and reluctant to believe Barbee, but he was one of them after all and, besides, he told them, they had won the election. The mob was temporarily mollified and the church was spared.

Mayor Barbee had come with reinforcements. The 6th Ward neighborhood where Lovell H. Rousseau lived was peaceful that morning and the mayor had called on the former army captain to come help bring some order into the 1st and 2nd Wards. Before arriving at St. Martin of Tours, Rousseau had been in one melee. His friend Thomas Speed wrote a letter to Colonel W. R. Thompson shortly after the riot in which he described what he saw. A small German man was grabbed by the mob and thrown down a flight of steps, then piled upon and beaten with clubs. Speed thought that the Know-Nothings would kill him, but the German got to his feet and began to run. The crowd chased after, pelting him with stones. Then, Rousseau appeared and hurried to the victim through the storm of flying rocks. "Captain Rousseau got up and with three men saved him," Speed said.[5]

Now, Rousseau was at St. Martin of Tours with Mayor Barbee. The mayor told the mob to go with Captain Rousseau and return to their own wards. The *Daily Courier* said, "With much trouble Captain Rousseau marshaled the force and countermarched them to the Lafayette Engine house."[6]

It seemed that conditions were getting back under control when a new mob appeared, fifty men armed with muskets and bayonets, and dragging along a cannon that they had taken from the courthouse lawn. The situation broke wide open again. The mob looted Ambrewster's Brewery and then torched it. There were people hiding inside and the mob shot anyone who ran out of the burning building. As many as eight may have burned alive in the basement. The mob went on to burn Charles Heybach's brewery, and Daniel Smook's confectionary, Charles Becker's bakery, and Charles Drout's barbershop. Joseph Hook's shoe store was demolished, and $1,100 worth of goods was stolen out of out of Fred Burghold's grocery. This was property loss — some lost more. A man named Fritz was shot in the chest. George Edgerton was killed. The German John Feller was stabbed seven times. John Vogt was killed and so was a man named Keiser. German women and children were running for safety while Know-Nothing women and children cheered the rioters on.

Late in the afternoon, the mob turned west toward the 8th Ward where the Irish lived. Passing through the 6th Ward, which had been peaceful in the morning, a gang of thirty men armed with lead-loaded sticks fell upon a man and beat him down. The Know-Nothings went looking for an ax to chop off his head, but failing to find one, they settled for a pitchfork, instead. They prodded him to his feet and jabbed him down the street to the jail where he was apparently locked up by Know-Nothing cops.

In the Irish section, the mob set fire to no fewer than twenty buildings. Eleven of them were a long row of homes and businesses called Quinn's Row. They were owned by Francis Quinn who, until this day, had prospered in Louisville. He begged the mob to spare his property. He offered them all the money he had to go away, but they took both his money and his life, and set his buildings on fire. An old woman named Long made it outside, but her three sons were trapped in one of Quinn's buildings. Two of them burned to death while their mother watched. The third son was shot thirteen times before he fell and the mob dragged him to jail, as they had done the pitchfork victim.

Mayor Barbee, who had come from saving a second church, the Cathedral of the Assumption, was on the scene. He beseeched the Board of Aldermen for fifty additional police officers, but the board voted the request down. Fire companies tried to leave their stations to fight the many fires, but the mob prevented it and the fires raged through the night.

At midnight, the arson-minded mob made a move against the offices of the anti–Know-Nothing newspapers in town and, in their blind anger, even against the pro–Know-Nothing *Daily Journal*, but editor George Prentice somehow turned them away.

Bloody Monday was the name they gave to this terrible August 6. No one has ever known how many lives were lost; estimates range anywhere between twenty-two and one hundred. Two-thirds to three-fourths of those killed were German or Irish born.

Likewise, the total of the property damage has never been calculated with any certainty. Quinn's Row alone represented a loss of over $34,000. It is known that the shamed city council authorized Mayor Barbee to distribute the anemic sum of $500 in increments of $5 to $20 to the homeless.

In the August 8 story of the riot, the *Daily Courier* editorialized, "However we may regret and shudder to hear of such outrages, they are the sure results of Know Nothism, wherever its proscriptive and unhallowed principles have been urged."[7]

During the several days following the riots, Prentice's *Daily Journal* maintained that foreigners were responsible for the bloodshed and accused those papers who tried to blame the August 6 riots on the Know-Nothings of being anti–American. The *Daily Courier*, though, was having none of it. The editor, Walter N. Haldeman, wrote on August 9, "We fully agree with the *Journal* that there is a terrible responsibility somewhere and that no language is too strong for its condemnation. And the *Journal* knows full well where the responsibility belongs."[8]

Lovell H. Rousseau had been in the middle of it, doing what he could with boldness and military bearing, at the request of a mayor with whom he did not agree politically, to restore order and to protect both lives and property. It was repeatedly said in biographical sketches in later years that Rousseau was shot through the abdomen during the Know-Nothing riot while defending the right of a citizen to vote. Some writers add that the wound was so serious that it required two months for Rousseau to recover. This tale, though possibly true, is not well-supported by contemporary evidence. Rousseau's friend Thomas Speed wrote of Rousseau saving a German citizen in his letter to Thompson, but did not say anything about him being shot. Neither was such an incident mentioned in the contemporary newspaper accounts, though the names of many obscure wounded were given. And, Rousseau himself made no mention of it in his 1866 biographical sketch.

Some have claimed that the shooting occurred not in 1855, but in the 1856 elections. Once again, the newspapers fail to mention any such attempt to murder Rousseau in their election coverage. Indeed, the 1855 riots seem to have been so extreme as to shock the city into good behavior. Of the August 1856 election, the *Daily Courier* reported that there was no trouble out of the Know-Nothings, nor was there any sort of disturbance in the November 5 elections: "The polls closed yesterday, throughout Louisville, without the stigma and strain of blood upon the elective franchise."[9]

Rousseau behaved with honor and exemplary courage during the Know-Nothing troubles, but there seems to be no first-hand evidence that he was shot during the elections of 1855 or 1856.

Know-Nothism faded quickly in Louisville. On January 3, 1857, the *Daily Journal* reported that the Know-Nothing Headquarters had become, of all things, a German theater. In 1865, Louisville elected a mayor whose native tongue was German.

Through the remainder of the 1850s, Rousseau concentrated on his legal career. He continued to cement his reputation as a defense attorney, and to add to his bank account by his fees.

Excitement was never far from Rousseau, however, and some of his work was more controversial than lucrative. In an 1857 case, Rousseau defended four black men who were accused of murdering a family by the name of Joyce. Rousseau won an acquittal, which caused a near riot in the courtroom. The gallery rushed toward the defendants. Rousseau grabbed up a chair and shouted, "I'll brain the first of you who moves a step forward!" While Rousseau held the mob at bay, the four blacks were spirited out of the courtroom by way of a tunnel that connected to the jail.[10]

Rousseau's presentation to the jury must have been inspired and his defense of the black men's lives against the outraged courtroom mob was certainly physically courageous, but the satisfaction was short-lived. Later that same afternoon, a crowd stormed the jail where the four acquitted men still waited for their safe release. The jailer and his deputies, plus Mayor William S. Pilcher and twenty policemen, were not enough to hold the mob back and agreed to turn the blacks over. One Negro had a razor and cut his own throat before the lynchers could get into his cell. The other three were taken out and hanged. Not yet sated, the bloodthirsty whites kindled fires beneath the bodies while they still dangled from stout limbs.

* * *

Aside from the occasional courtroom riot, the last few years of the 1850s passed uneventfully for Rousseau. It was a rare period of domesticity in Rousseau's life, a time to enjoy his family, which now included a fourth child, George Russell, the last of the Rousseau children, who was born in 1852.

Of course, it could not last. There was a disruption coming that would throw memories of the Know-Nothing years into deep shadow. Unexpected alliances would be made among some of those who had fought one another on Bloody Monday, even as the nation divided. And, once again, Rousseau would find himself at war.

5

Kentucky's Secession Crisis of 1861

In 1860, although he did not seek and did not want the office, Lovell H. Rousseau was elected to represent the 24th District, Louisville, in the Kentucky Senate. So great was his popularity, he was the candidate of both the Democratic and the Republican parties. Rousseau had always identified himself as a Henry Clay Whig, but for all practical purposes, there had been no Whig Party since Clay's death in 1852. Rousseau was really a man without a party. That being the case, a voter of either party affiliation could feel comfortable in voting for Rousseau in the secret conviction that he really leaned toward *us*, not that other bunch. He was sworn into office in the domed capitol building in Frankfort on Friday, January 18, 1861.

Many of his fellow senators were getting their first glimpse of Rousseau. When he walked into the senate chamber, they saw before them a man 6 foot 2 inches in height, with a head of dark hair (slightly receding), a full moustache, and sideburns that extended down to the angle of his jaw. Though powerfully built ("Herculean"), he was graceful and lithe. There was often a gleam in his eye, a hint of the vigorous sense of humor that could be either biting or self-deprecating. He had an appreciation of the ironic. As the legislators conversed with him and grew to know him, they would learn that humor was only one component of his personality. His mind was alert and logical and his manners were described as "elegant." He believed passionately in the causes he adopted, but his speaking style was not reckless or heated. Rousseau was a sociable man who liked music and bourbon, but he had a deeply ingrained sense of honor and he was not a man to be slighted.[1]

In the General Assembly, he was attentive to those matters that fell within the sphere of his committee assignments, the Joint Committee on Public Offices and the Judiciary Committee. For example, he introduced a bill to amend the law relating to the competency of witnesses.

This, however, was not an ordinary session of the General Assembly (Rousseau described it as "stormy"), and whatever bills were introduced and debated, there was really only one issue on every legislator's mind: secession.

The states that had withdrawn from the Union when Abraham Lincoln was elected the previous November, and those that had joined them after the president called for volunteers to put down the rebellion that began when Fort Sumter was fired upon, were making ardent overtures to Kentucky, and for a reason that was obvious to anyone who could read a map. The northern boundary of Kentucky was the Ohio River; the addition of Kentucky as the twelfth state of the Confederacy would give the South an easily defended boundary between the Appalachians and the Mississippi. In addition, Kentucky had badly needed agricultural resources, essential minerals like coal and iron, a desirable number of men of fighting age, and was one of the predominant producers of mules in the nation. Mules are a ridiculous-looking, easily mocked animal in the modern world, but in the nineteenth century, they were the muscle — the engines — behind many of the machines of both peace and war.[2]

Secession was on the mind of the constituents at home, too. There were many petitions presented to the Senate from the ladies of the various counties, as well as from religious groups, to prevail upon the legislators to prevent war upon Kentucky's soil. Rousseau presented one such petition from the ladies of Louisville.

Rousseau voted in favor of a senate resolution saying that Kentucky would not end her connection with the United States government. However, just as she would not be part of the secession movement, neither would she arm herself for a campaign of aggression against the South. The resolution ended with the idealistic offer to serve as mediator between the belligerent parties.

As desirable as a peaceful outcome to the crisis was, Rousseau and others saw that Kentucky's efforts at neutrality were doomed to fail and there was an immediate need to prepare for war. Rousseau favored efforts to neutralize Governor Beriah Magoffin, who was an avowed Southern sympathizer, by such measures as the one that passed on May 24, which created a five-man board to be in charge of Kentucky's military establishment. Rousseau also voted in favor of a measure allowing Governor Magoffin *and* the five-man board to borrow $1 million to buy arms. This bill failed to pass.

In another measure which did pass, a force called the Home Guards was created to be a counterbalance to the pro–Confederate State Guards. The State Guards were four thousand men strong and they had access to the state arsenal. The Home Guards would not be under the authority of the governor, but of the five-man board of commissioners. To arm the Home Guards, the Lincoln administration quietly began shipping rifles to Kentucky.

The General Assembly adjourned on May 24, 1861. The following month, Rousseau resigned his seat. Already, he had been working for the Union cause, speaking in Louisville and other towns where he denounced neutrality as "a mask of the secessionists on the one hand and a disgraceful subterfuge of the Unionists on the other."[3]

On April 20, 1861, he took his efforts a step further when this notice appeared in the Louisville papers:

> To the Public
>
> We propose to organize four companies of good law-abiding citizens for the protection of the property, persons, and houses of our people and for the maintenance of the laws of our land.
>
> To this end we propose that all those favorable to the project meet at the east room of the courthouse on Monday night, the 22nd inst. At 7:30 o'clock.
>
> Lovell H. Rousseau
> W. B. Woodruff
> Charles L. Thomasson

The *Daily Journal* and the *Democrat* reported in the next day's editions that the courthouse was filled "by the most respectable and patriotic men of the city to form themselves into a body of military.... It was an enthusiastic meeting and showed a noble response to the call."[4]

By emphasizing that the purpose of the companies was the protection of persons and property and by carefully avoiding any reference to Southerners or Northerners, of secession or Unionism, there was no technical violation of Kentucky's fragile neutrality. This was simply a Home Guard unit, allowed by the new state law.

At the next meeting at the courthouse, on May 2, Rousseau addressed an even larger crowd, as did Walter C. Whitaker, another prominent attorney in the city, and James Guthrie, the president of the newly completed Louisville & Nashville Railroad. The papers said that it was a "rare assemblage of talent, eloquence, and patriotism." Enthusiasm for the project was growing and at the May 24 assembly Rousseau was elected colonel of the four companies, William P. Boone was chosen for his lieutenant colonel and James Speed for major.[5]

In the June 20 congressional elections, Unionists won nine of Kentucky's ten seats. The sentiment of the state had plainly shifted in favor of the Union and it was time for Rousseau to make his next move. He went to Washington to obtain a commission as colonel and for authority to enlist Union troops on Kentucky soil. He carried with him a letter of introduction to the president from Joshua F. Speed. Speed called him "an esteemed friend," and continued, "You will find him a very intelligent gentleman, thoroughly posted as to the feelings of the Union party here and a fair and faithful exponent of their sentiments."[6]

Speed was an important ally, but Rousseau underestimated the influence of those other men who still hoped to keep Kentucky neutral. On his way to Washington, he stopped to see General George B. McClellan, commander of the Department of Ohio, at his headquarters in Cincinnati. No one yet knew how timorous a commander McClellan was. Raising troops for U.S. service inside the boundaries of Kentucky seemed "rash and ill-advised" to him, too aggressive. He opposed Rousseau's plan and actually sent his aide, Major John J. Key, to Washington to filibuster against the tall Kentuckian's reckless idea.[7]

Rousseau met with President Lincoln on June 15. Initially, the powers of persuasion he had polished before juries in Indiana and Kentucky did not fail him. William Sumner Dodge in his *History of the Old Second Division* (1864) gave the gist of Rousseau's presentation. He told the president "that to save the State only one course could be pursued — to discard the neutrality scheme, give the Kentuckians to understand they must be either *for* or *against* the National Government ... that to secure her to the Union the loyalists must be strengthened in their devotion, and the rebels in arms and their sympathizer intimidated by the presence of an adequate military force, armed and equipped and well supplied with the munitions of war; *that Kentucky would furnish with alacrity such a force.*"[8]

Rousseau got his commission and with it the authority to raise twenty companies. Back in Kentucky, Colonel Rousseau began to recruit immediately. However, in the background, his opponents — those who agreed with McClellan — men like Jeremiah Boyle, Garrett Davis, and even James Guthrie (who had been his ally when the goal was simply local defense) were raising a fuss and they persuaded the Lincoln administration to rescind permission for Rousseau to raise troops in Kentucky. An order arrived from the capital city ordering Rousseau to move those men he had already enlisted to a camp on the north side of the Ohio River. Rousseau obeyed, reluctantly. On July 2, he crossed to near the mouth of Silver Creek, about one mile up from New Albany on the Indiana side and established Camp Joe Holt. It was well-known ground to the Colonel; during the Mexican War the 2nd Indiana had bivouacked in the same spot.

Rousseau had 334 men in six companies with him when they crossed from Louisville. Captain Harvey M. Buckley was appointed to be Rousseau's lieutenant colonel and Captain William W. Berry was his major. A familiar face was David Quincy Rousseau, the Colonel's younger brother, who was a first lieutenant in Company G. Before long, they had upwards of 1,500 Union-minded men in camp.

Rousseau later spoke about how poorly supplied his soldiers were while at Camp Joe Holt. He spent his own funds to buy for them such necessities as blankets and tents, and there were donations of supplies from loyal Louisvillians, but that "what we most needed was transportation. I called on my old friend, that tried and true patriot, Captain Zack Sherley, for help. He promptly said ... whether he was ever paid for it or not ... he would cheerfully bring to my camp all the soldiers I could get, and he did so." With Captain Sherley's help, the volunteers at Silver Creek soon numbered 2,200.[9]

Things were progressing on the Kentucky front, but too slowly to suit Rousseau. Out in Missouri, General John C. Frémont was planning a southern offensive and calling for reinforcements, so Rousseau asked for permission to lead his men to Frémont and permission was granted. His men were going to see some action against the Rebels, at last. However, Rousseau was determined to march his men into Kentucky at least once. In the early morning hours of August 24, openly defying those who opposed him, Rousseau ordered his men to prepare to march. Ammunition was distributed and then, according to an account written many years after the event, Rousseau "declared to his soldiers that he proposed to make a march through Louisville and make a display. In earnest words he warned them that there must be no violence, no shot fired, unless by orders of the officers. Taunts, jibes, and jeers were to be utterly disregarded and the soldiers who would notice them or depart from orders would be severely punished."[10]

Rousseau and his junior officers had trained their men well, evidently, for the display was performed without incident on the part of the soldiers. Likewise, the secessionists, the "damned scoundrels" whom Rousseau was challenging by his demonstration, decided that this was not the time for an incident. They stayed quiet and out of sight. The fresh-minted soldiers of the 5th Kentucky Infantry returned to Camp Joe Holt. Soon, perhaps in only a day or two, the troops from Silver Creek would be on their way to Missouri.[11]

Or so Rousseau thought. Once again, persons behind the scenes were working to undercut his plans. This time, it was his own supporters; they sent a petition to Washington demanding that Rousseau's force be kept near Louisville. Washington agreed. Catching wind of this, Rousseau — who was in a defiant mood these days — decided to head downriver before the order arrived that would pin him in place on the north bank of the Ohio. He was too slow. According to an 1895 *Courier-Journal* article, the Louisville Legion was actually in line and ready to march when a buggy came careening into camp. A man, not the driver, was standing up and frantically waving a letter in his hand. It was Richard Rousseau. The buggy came to a halt in front of the Colonel, and his brother handed him the letter. It was an order for the troops of Camp Joe Holt to remain in camp, practically in sight of the Rebels, but forbidden to go after them.

About the 1st of September, the recruits began to be organized for official service to the U.S. government. What became known as the 2nd Kentucky Cavalry was organized under Colonel Buckner Board and ten companies of foot soldiers were designated to be the 3rd Kentucky Infantry, the Louisville Legion, under Colonel Rousseau. (The 3rd Kentucky Infantry is better remembered by its later designation, the 5th Kentucky Infantry. It is by that name that the regiment will be called in the pages that follow.) They were mustered in by Major W. H. Sidell on Monday, September 9, 1861. There were too many men at Camp Joe Holt for this one regiment, so the extra companies remained unassigned for the present. (They continued to act in cooperation with the Louisville Legion until they were finally transferred to the 6th Kentucky Infantry.)

Six days earlier, on September 3, 1861, Rebel general Leonidas Polk had overtly violated Kentucky neutrality and occupied Columbus, on the Mississippi River. The Federal higher authorities used Polk's advance as an excuse to move their headquarters to Louisville on September 7. Even as southern boys began marching south out of the city to enlist in the Confederate cause, General Robert Anderson, the hero of Fort Sumter, arrived to command the Department of the Cumberland from his new headquarters on 4th Street.

Things were moving quickly now. On September 17, 1861, word arrived at Federal headquarters that a Confederate force ordered north by General Simon Bolivar Buckner had passed through or around Elizabethtown to Lebanon Junction where they burned the Louisville & Nashville Railroad bridge over the Rolling Fork River. A panic seized Louisville. Lebanon Junction was only about thirty miles away.

From his headquarters in Louisville, General Anderson dispatched his subordinate, William Tecumseh Sherman, to Camp Joe Holt with an order for Rousseau to move south. The 5th Kentucky Infantry ("very reliable troops," Anderson called them) were ferried across the Ohio River and joined the one thousand Home Guards under Sherman at the L&N Railroad Depot.[12]

The train left at 2:00 A.M. on September 18 and arrived at Lebanon Junction at daylight of an unusually cold day. The Home Guard got off the train at the town, while Rousseau and his men went forward to find that the bridge was still smoldering. Sherman ordered Rousseau forward across the river with four hundred men. Rousseau is said to have risen in his saddle and shouted, "Follow me, boys! I expect no soldier to undergo any hardship that I will not share!" He leaped down from his horse and waded to the far bank, with four hundred men behind him. Another four hundred soon followed. But there was no enemy awaiting them. The Rebels who had done the mischief to the bridge were gone. Rousseau and his men returned to Lebanon Junction and the Federal bivouac. Other troops arrived the next day, including the one mounted regiment available to them, the 2nd Kentucky Cavalry.[13]

The men camped at Lebanon Junction until Sunday, September 22, when Sherman ordered Rousseau to move up the Clear Creek Valley to Muldraugh Hill. According to a soldier whose letter appeared in the *Louisville Daily Journal*, Rousseau's men forded the Rolling Fork and made a rapid march up Muldraugh Hill, advancing on Elizabethtown in silence "till we reached the outskirts of that town, when the band struck up a fine national air, and after marching and countermarching, through the town, we encamped in a beautiful grove near it.... The day after this we changed our encampment and marched to a forest within almost gunshot of Elizabethtown." General Sherman explained the importance of Muldraugh Hill, saying, "Had it fallen into the hands of our enemies, the cause would have been lost."[14]

Sherman arrived at Muldraugh Hill shortly after Rousseau made camp. Not yet uniformed, he made a strange sight in his stovepipe hat and civilian coat. At his headquarters, a reporter wrote a sketch of Sherman: "A tall spare man, not wiry nor bent. His form, though slight, has a commanding appearance. He is quick spoken, rather gruff in his manners and answers ... his mind is visibly absorbed in his duties, and his time is devoted to performing them.... He is a busy man ... seen everywhere, and seeing everything. Nothing escapes him, and nothing goes unnoticed."[15]

He might have added a sentence about Sherman's incessant pacing, fidgeting, and cigar smoking. He did not seem to enjoy his cigars; indeed, he destroyed them by his vigorous puffing, as if disposing of the cigar in the shortest time was an order from General Anderson. Altogether, Sherman created a strong but strange impression on all who saw him. One officer later wrote that Sherman was like a "splendid piece of machinery with all of the screws a little loose."[16]

By October 1, Sherman had two brigades at Camp Muldraugh, enough manpower to meet any immediate emergency, but there was another worry. Sherman wrote in his *Memoirs*, "The daily correspondence between General Anderson and myself satisfied me that the worry and harassment at Louisville were exhausting his strength and health, and that he would soon leave." Sherman was right. On October 8, the odd, brilliant Sherman succeeded Robert Anderson as commander of the Department of the Cumberland, and returned to Louisville.[17]

The next day, in Special Orders No. 38, Sherman ordered Rousseau (now promoted to brigadier general) to "move his camp as soon as practicable forward to the vicinity of Nolin, selecting with the advice of Captain [Frederick E.] Prime, a position for a large force. He will cause scouts to be sent forward towards Green River."[18]

Scouting the area south of Elizabethtown with Captain Prime, Rousseau saw that the farm of the secessionist David Nevin was the most likely campground for his command. Nevin, until a year ago, had owned a marble shop in the 7th Ward of Louisville, but in 1860 he had paid $40 an acre for a six hundred acre farm near the village of Nolin in Hardin County. It was a prosperous little community on a bluff above the Nolin River. The western branch of the Louisville and Nashville Turnpike ran nearby and the newly completed L&N Railroad passed through the village. Captain Phillip Lee, CSA, had paid a visit to Nolin on September 18 and burned the railroad bridge over the Nolin. The Rebels, having pointed out the strategic importance of the railroad at Nolin, and the broad, open acres of Nevin's farm being available within sight of the downed bridge, Rousseau and Prime agreed that this was the place for their camp. One can only imagine the outrage of Mr. Nevin to see all these Federals marching onto his land. He was described as a "violent secessionist." While Nevin fumed, it appealed to General Rousseau's wry sense of humor to name the new installation in honor of his host. Rousseau named it Camp Nevin, just to rub it in.[19]

Though it is hard to determine perfectly, it appears that arriving at arriving at Nolin with General Rousseau on October 9 were the 5th Kentucky Infantry, Co. C of the 6th Kentucky Infantry, the 2nd Kentucky Cavalry, Battery A of the 1st Kentucky Artillery (Stone's Battery), the 6th Indiana Infantry, the 38th Indiana Infantry, and a battalion each of the 15th and 16th U.S. Infantry. The 30th Indiana Infantry was close behind and arrived before the end of the day.

The rattle and clatter of soldiers setting up camp announced that the first contingent of the Army of the Cumberland had arrived. Rousseau did not dispossess the Nevin family from their home; instead, he set up his headquarters in the 1793 cabin of Hardin County pioneer Adam Monin. From there, he could supervise not only the building of the new L&N Railroad bridge, but also a stockade complete with two-story blockhouses to protect the bridge against future outrages.

With thousands of troops massing at Camp Nevin, Lebanon, and Paducah, it was plain that the Federals were positioning themselves to do some real harm to the Confederacy in the West come the new year.

6

Camp Nevin and the Federal Advance in Kentucky

If President Lincoln read Sherman's dispatches, and he always showed an insatiable interest in the news from his commanders in the field, these early reports from Kentucky must have been especially interesting. Nolin, Muldraugh Hill, Rolling Fork — these were names from his childhood. He had been born on the South Fork of Nolin River and had lived as a boy in the craggy shadow of Muldraugh Hill beside Knob Creek, a tributary of the Rolling Fork. Each wire bearing these familiar names must have conjured a picture in the president's mind.

Certainly, he must have been pleased that the Kentuckian Rousseau, who had paid him a recent visit, was genuine in his devotion to the Union and that he was applying pressure on the Confederates from his advance position with the Army of the Cumberland. Some of Lincoln's generals were not showing the same aggressiveness in late 1861.

The day after Rousseau arrived at Camp Nevin, three more infantry regiments arrived: the 39th Indiana, the 15th Ohio, and the 49th Ohio. And any doubts about the nearness of the enemy were quickly dispelled. That very night the 49th Ohio captured twelve secessionists and one Indiana trooper on picket duty was killed by a man wearing civilian clothes who approached him peacefully and then pulled a gun and shot him.

The threat of sudden violence was at odds with the calm, autumn landscape that surrounded these young soldiers. Many of the letters of the Northern boys gathering at Camp Nevin mentioned the beauty of Hardin County. The hill country between Louisville and Elizabethtown surprised them — boys who were raised on the flatland farms of the Midwest thought they were seeing mountains — but below Elizabethtown the land flattened out to create a gently rolling landscape as lovely as any in Kentucky. J. W. Leonard of the 49th Ohio mentioned the vivid October colors in one of his letters and wrote home, "We are now encamped in a very beautiful country."[1]

After the 34th Illinois Infantry arrived on October 11, Sgt. William C.

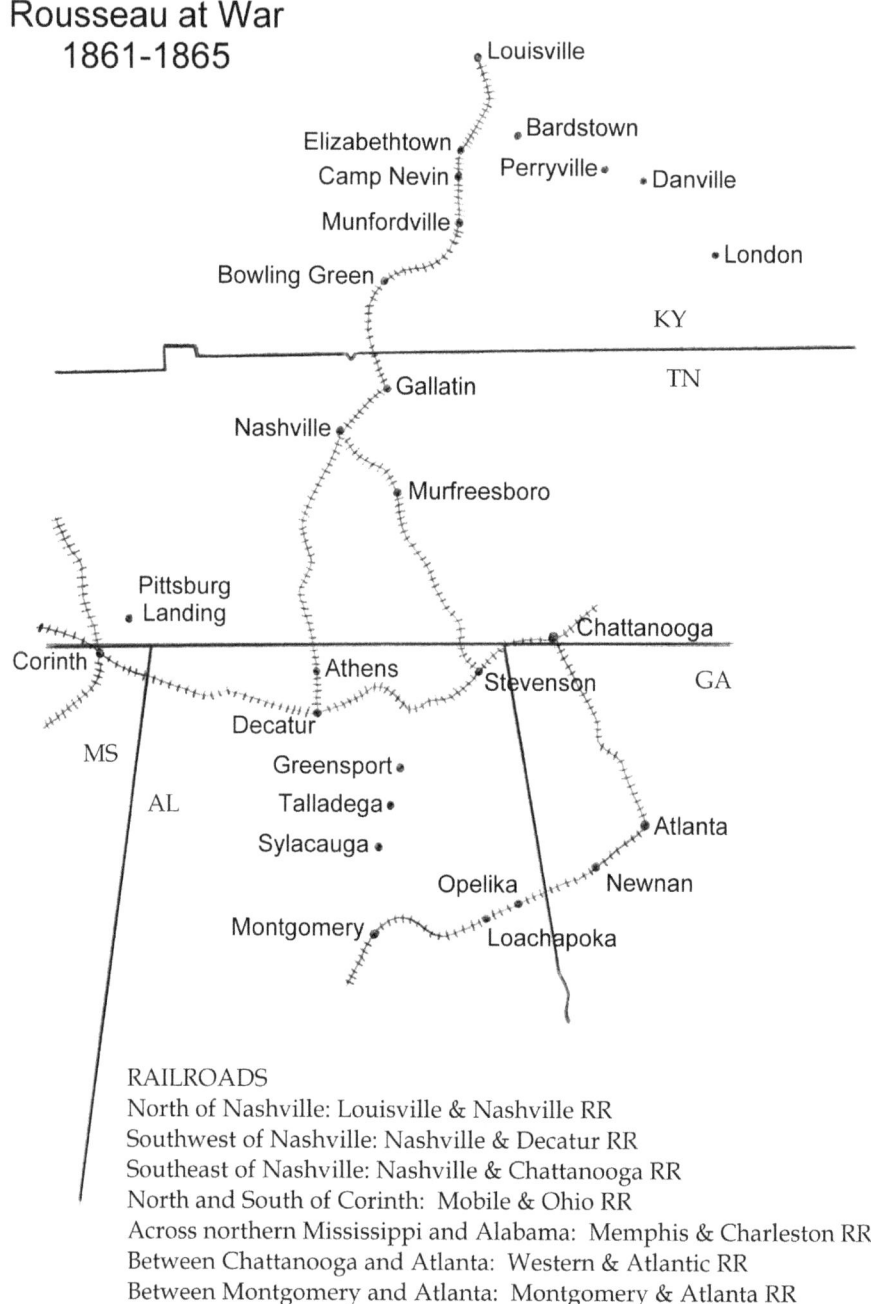

Rousseau at War, 1861–1865 (map by the author).

Robinson found that he shared Leonard's opinion. He wrote, "Our camp is located in a splendid place, a very swift and beautiful stream running near."[2]

The 29th Indiana reported on October 12, and more regiments were on their way. As each unit arrived, it made its own campground until Camp Nevin was eventually six miles long, resulting in "very little communication" between the regiments, according to Sgt. Robinson. The camp was so large that different areas were called by different names, all military annexes of the main camp. In the end some of the names included Camp Hoosier, Camp Negley, and Camp Sixth Ward. This last name was bestowed on November 28 when a group of Louisvillians from the Sixth Ward came down with James Guthrie on the L&N Railroad, bringing with them a Thanksgiving feast and a singing group. Brigadier General Rousseau was among those officers attending, as well as Colonel Thomas T. Crittenden, who accepted a flag on behalf of his regiment, the 6th Indiana, and gave a stem-winder of a speech.[3]

There was an established pattern followed by the army in arranging a camp of long duration. Bell I. Wiley, in his classic *The Life of Billy Yank*, described the layout: the cabins or tents of the privates "were grouped by company with a street running between.... Perpendicular to the company streets at the front of the camp ... [were] the quarters of the noncoms, then those of the company officers and finally those of the regimental commander and staff. Back of the officers' quarters were the baggage trains."[4]

By mid–October, there were ten thousand men at Nolin, divided into three brigades. They were:

1st Brigade — Brigadier General Lovell Harrison Rousseau
    5th Kentucky — Colonel Harvey M. Buckley
    6th Kentucky — Colonel Walter C. Whitaker
    6th Indiana Infantry — Colonel Thomas T. Crittenden
    Battery A, Kentucky Light Artillery — Captain David C. Stone
    2nd Kentucky Cavalry — Colonel Buckner Board
    15th U.S. Infantry (battalion) — Captain _____ Gilman
    19th U.S. Infantry (battalion) — Captain _____ Gilman
2nd Brigade — Brigadier General Thomas J. Wood
    29th Indiana Infantry — Colonel John F. Miller
    30th Indiana Infantry — Colonel Sion S. Bass
    38th Indiana Infantry — Colonel Benjamin F. Scribner
    39th Indiana Infantry — Colonel Thomas J. Harrison
3rd Brigade — Brigadier General Richard W. Johnson
    15th Ohio Infantry — Colonel Moses R. Dickey

49th Ohio Infantry — Colonel William H. Gibson
32nd Indiana Infantry — Colonel August Willich
34th Illinois Infantry — Colonel Edward N. Kirk

General Rousseau's was the only brigade at Camp Nevin to contain both volunteer and regular units. Rousseau relied on the regular army officers for advice and used the regular soldiers as an example for his volunteers to follow.

Rousseau knew some of the volunteer officers very well. He had worked with Colonel Walter C. Whitaker in the creation of the Louisville Home Guard in 1861 and knew Colonel Benjamin F. Scribner from the Mexican War, when they both served in the 2nd Indiana Volunteers. He certainly knew August Willich, the noted German communist from Louisville. There were others that he did not know at all before 1861, but no matter; he would come to know them all, eventually.

But not just yet, for Rousseau had become dangerously ill and, at some point earlier in the month, had gone home to Louisville. A *Louisville Daily Journal* item dated October 15, 1861, said, "The health of the army continues excellent. General Rousseau, however, has just come out of a most violent attack of quinsy — so violent, indeed, that at one time his life was in imminent peril. He is now almost well again. May he be spared to the army and the country." Once before in a moment of intense effort directed toward an uncertain outcome — while he was reading law in Louisville — Rousseau had driven himself into a severe illness. The pattern had now repeated itself at Camp Nevin and would again before Rousseau was through.[5]

It is possible that it was Rousseau's absence from camp that cost him command of Camp Nevin and the 1st Division, Army of the Cumberland. On October 12, while Rousseau was back in Louisville, General Sherman had issued Special Orders No. 51, naming Brigadier General Alexander McDowell McCook to command.

McCook was a native of Ohio and an 1842 graduate of West Point. There, his classmates had called him "Guts," a reference not to his grit but to his girth. He had seen action against the Apaches in New Mexico before returning to the academy to teach tactics. At the start of the Civil War, he had led the 1st Ohio Infantry into Virginia and handled them well enough in the Battle of First Bull Run that he was promoted to brigadier general. Wearing his new stars, he had come to the Western Theater, where Sherman gave him his appointment. Upon their arrival on the Nolin on October 14, General McCook and his muddy-booted staff requisitioned the brick home of Mr. David Nevin for use as camp headquarters.

Perhaps Rousseau would not have received the appointment in any case. He was not regular army, had not attended West Point, and was not a fellow Buckeye with Sherman. Still, it is hard to believe that Rousseau would not have been the better choice to command the 1st Division. Almost none of McCook's fellow officers had anything good to say about "Guts." He had a silly grin that led one to believe that he was "deficient in the upper story." Other comments made about him (over a period of time) included the description of him as nothing more than "an overgrown schoolboy," and "a blockhead." Sherman called him "a juvenile." He had an irritating sense of humor and had a knack for blurting the inappropriate comment. Yet, he was arrogant. Even the soldiers came to see McCook as a posturing peacock of a general. One later observed that General McCook was awfully proud of being General McCook.[6]

The one soldier who thought highly of McCook, without reservation, was McCook himself. In a letter he wrote from Camp Nevin to Governor William Dennison of Ohio on November 15, 1861, McCook unveiled much of his nature. He bragged about a visit from Governor Oliver Morton of Indiana and said that the governor was "so delighted" with his visit to Camp Nevin that he sent McCook "a mounted body guard of 100 picked men." This was Co. I, part of a detachment of the 3rd Indiana Cavalry, which was never brigaded at Camp Nevin and whose only duties seem to have been to cluster around headquarters and accompany McCook when he ventured out.[7]

On the subject of military matters, McCook boasted, "I am now in command of the most important army in the field." Though opposed by what he believed to be a superior Rebel force, he was "ready to meet and whip him at our ... convenience." And in a postscript, "I can break the Back of this rebellion in three moves, and thank God I have the confidence in myself to do it."[8]

It was McCook who assigned the regiments to their respective brigades. After October 23, he had a fourth brigade in camp, a Pennsylvania unit that steamed down the Ohio River from Pittsburgh. Here was the new brigade:

4th Brigade — Brigadier General James Negley
    77th Pennsylvania Infantry — Colonel Frederick S. Stumbaugh
    78th Pennsylvania Infantry — Colonel William Sirwell
    79th Pennsylvania Infantry — Colonel Henry A. Hambright
    Battery B, Pennsylvania Lieutenant Artillery — Capt. Michael Mueller
    Battery A, Ohio Light Artillery — Captain Charles S. Cotter

Battery A, Ohio Light Artillery had not come to Kentucky with the Pennsylvanians, but joined them at Louisville, had traveled with them to

Camp Nevin, and was assigned to the 4th Brigade there. With the addition of this fourth brigade, General McCook now had 13,995 men in his command, exclusive of runaway slaves, sutlers, and officers' wives who were also in the camp.

Such numbers did not intimidate the Rebels, who were no more than ten or fifteen miles away. The men could see their signal flares at night and Samuel O. Thomas (49th Ohio Infantry) and others mentioned seeing an enemy observation balloon — a surprising fact about Camp Nevin, if it was true.

The Indiana man killed by the Rebels on the night of October 10 was only the first of several to die while on picket duty. Additionally, there were encounters with the Rebels when the various units were out on maneuvers. On October 14, a citizen came to camp to beg for protection against the Rebels who were swarming close to his home, and the men of the 39th Indiana went out. A few miles south, they found a bunch of Rebels (whose numbers were estimated to be anywhere from fifty-eight to two hundred), at the log house of a man named Murrell. The Confederates were caught off guard eating their midday meal in Murrell's yard when the Hoosiers flew into them. The surprised Rebels fought back but finally retreated, leaving behind some horses and five men killed and three wounded. The accounts differ, but two Federals may have been wounded.

Understandably, the horse soldiers of the 2nd Kentucky Cavalry, Rousseau's brigade, ranged the farthest and they had frequent clashes with the enemy. They traded lead with the Rebels on October 14, and again on the night of October 15, when Captain Augustus C. Vandyke's men of Co. I were scouting against the enemy cavalry. These mounted graybacks were not a mere nuisance but something far more serious to the Yankees and their sympathizers. The reporter for the *New York Times* wrote on October 21 about the enemy cavalry "scouring the country below our pickets, plundering, robbing, and destroying everything they can lay their hands on." And, again, on October 24, "Such plundering, devastation and marauding as the rebels are now practicing in the neighborhood below would disgrace barbarians.... They steal horses, cattle, sheep, hogs, bed-clothing, wearing apparel, in short, everything."[9]

Most feared were the lurking raiders of John Hunt Morgan, the "Thunderbolt of the Confederacy." Morgan was a man genuinely to be feared, even in these earliest days of the rebellion. He made his bloody mark quickly. No Confederate leader was more active than Morgan during the fall of 1861. Even before he and his men were officially entered in the Confederate service, they were pushing north from the Green River camps toward Camp Nevin. His second in command, Basil Duke, wrote that Morgan's nature required excitement so, with a dozen or so mounted volunteers, he would slip through the Union lines after nightfall, gathering intelligence and trying to catch inattentive pickets whom they would stalk like game, locating them in the dark and then waiting until just before sunrise to gun them down with shotguns. After the war, Duke remembered Morgan's Raiders' talent for shotgun killing: "Every flash was followed by a groan."[10]

It was a nerve-racking business, performing this picket duty at such remote places as White Mills, Millerstown, or Buffalo, when Morgan was out there roaming around, maybe even disguised in a captured Federal uniform so that he could circulate easily among the bluecoats, chatting with them and sharing the warmth of the campfire, until the shotgun came up and the Federal pickets fell dead.

* * *

When the Federals under Lovell Harrison Rousseau first advanced to the Nolin River in early October 1861, the Confederates recoiled and burned the L&N Railroad bridge over Bacon Creek, near the town of the same name (present-day Bonnieville). After establishing Camp Nevin, Rousseau's next task was to rebuild the small but important Bacon Creek Bridge and so he moved south with the 5th Kentucky Infantry, the 2nd Kentucky Cavalry, and a reporter from the *New York Times* on the afternoon of Saturday, October 20. The reporter became whimsical as they left Nolin and thought of all the sights the "clattering old, red, moss-grown mill" had seen in its long years and decided that "in all its quiet, grey, old life [it] never saw such a spectacle before."[11]

At Upton, only about five miles down the Louisville and Nashville Turnpike from Camp Nevin, Colonel Harvey M. Buckley stopped the infantry column for a rest while Rousseau and the cavalry scouted ahead. From 8:00 P.M. until 2:00 A.M. they waited. Then, summoned forward by Rousseau, they moved out under the light of a full moon, past the Murrell cabin where the 39th Indiana had tangled with the Rebels a few days before and on toward Bacon Creek, five miles beyond. The Federals could see, perhaps, the backs of the forty Rebels who fled when they drew near.

The records are incomplete and it is unclear exactly when the construction crew went to work on the new bridge or how permanent of a presence Rousseau's men were at the work site. It seems that they traveled back and forth on the railroad and on the turnpike between Nolin and Bacon Creek, and it also seems that different units rotated through guard duty at the bridge. Rebel spies reported that as many as three thousand men were there under Rousseau, at one time.

It is known that the bridge job was almost finished by quitting time on the afternoon of December 5. The workers and the guards boarded a train that took them back to Camp Nevin. They would return in the morning to spike down the last rail and trains could begin to cross the new Bacon Creek Bridge.

The complacent Federals had left no sentries, so John Hunt Morgan and his raiders were confident of success when, after dark, they emerged from the woods where they had been watching. They made a pile of flammables on the bridge and set it on fire. The resulting blaze destroyed not only the floor of the bridge but also four of the five uprights. Then the Rebels disappeared into the breaking dawn.

This was an outrageous and insufferable challenge to the Federal authorities. McCook was ordered to throw a brigade and a battery forward to Munfordville and to move his division to Bacon Creek, "leaving a small guard over the bridge at Nevin."[12]

All was activity now at the camp. On December 9, the 15th and 49th Ohio infantry regiments moved out, taking five days' rations in their haversacks. Captain Amos Glover wrote in his diary, "After loading our wagon which [was] a borrowed one we bid farewell to our 'Cabin Camp' and our baggage for a time and started through the mud."[13]

So it went over the next few days until, according to Dyer's *Compendium*, only the 30th Indiana, the 38th Indiana, and Battery B of the Pennsylvania Light Artillery were left behind to garrison Camp Nevin. These regiments were the effectives; in addition there was a large contingent of men who were too sick to move. During November and December, every nearby home, church, school, and barn had been requisitioned by the army for use as hospitals and they were all filled to capacity and beyond their capacity to *comfortably* accommodate so many sick.

Most of the fourteen thousand men who had trained to become the hard core of what history would remember as the Army of the Cumberland were gone. William Sumner Dodge, writing in 1864, summed up what Camp Nevin had meant to the men: "Camp Nevin is a name never to be forgotten by the troops who occupied it, and it will be equally remembered by the friends of many a poor soldier who there rendered up his last account."[14]

The camp had been well chosen, both for its qualities as a camp and for its strategic importance, and the men who trained there were now ready to go out and meet the enemy on something like equal terms. That was due in large part to the intelligent leadership of Lovell Harrison Rousseau. Those in Louisville who had dismissed his calls for action, as well as those who, though loyal to the U.S., had *opposed* his calls to prepare for war, now recognized that he had been right all along. The *Daily Journal* had spoken for all of them back on October 4 when the paper paid him a compliment (which the *New York Times* reprinted and called "most deserved"): "Louisville and Kentucky are under deep and lasting obligations to Gen. Rousseau and they know it. He saw further into the future than the rest of our fellow-citizens and, fortunately for us all, he acted vigorously upon his foresight. The chivalry of our State has never bore a nobler flower than Gen Rousseau. A thousand cheers for Brig.-Gen. Rousseau!"[15]

7
The Battle of Shiloh

William T. Sherman's personality was not calibrated to meet the demands of a departmental commander. In his autobiography, Sherman remembered uncomfortably "the everlasting worry of citizens complaining of every petty delinquency of a soldier, and forcing themselves forward to discuss politics." As bad or worse were the commanders who hounded him for guns, mules, wagons, and camp equipage.[1]

Sherman's aggravations grew and, with them, a bad case of nerves. He was in a fine state when, in mid–October, Secretary of War Simon Cameron and Adjutant General Lorenzo Thomas dropped in to see him at the Galt House in Louisville. As Sherman recited his long litany of problems and worries, he must have made a poor impression. No doubt the fidgety Ohioan was running his fingers through his unkempt hair, pulling at his rumpled clothes, jumping up to pace the floor, and puffing his cigar furiously as he chattered away in his staccato way of speaking. Then, the General made a big mistake — he blurted out that it would take sixty thousand men to clear the Rebels from Kentucky. If he noticed the look of shock on his visitors' faces, he did not admit it in his *Memoirs*, but they were shocked, and they came away from the meeting convinced that Sherman was insane. Assistant Secretary of War Thomas Scott summed up the feeling of them all when he bluntly wrote, "Sherman's gone in the head, he's luny."[2]

The consequence of Sherman's nervous outburst was that he lost his command. On November 9, 1861, General Don Carlos Buell replaced Sherman as commander of what was now called the Department of the Ohio. The two men made an inspection tour of the camps, including Camp Nevin, and then returned to Louisville. Buell, suffering from a cold he contracted from sleeping on the ground, settled into his new job and Sherman temporarily went off to Missouri, where things were quieter, to get control of himself.

General Buell was a good organizer and a man who paid meticulous attention to detail. One thing he did right away was issue General Orders No. 32, which re-organized the Army of the Ohio into five divisions.

McCook's division at Camp Nevin became the 2nd and contained the same four brigades as before, but they were renumbered: 4th (Rousseau), 5th (Wood), 6th (Johnson), and 7th (Negley).

* * *

Responding to Buell's orders, McCook moved most of three brigades from Camp Nevin to Bacon Creek, while General Richard W. Johnson's 6th went ahead to Munfordville, taking along David Stone's battery of Kentucky artillery. When General Ormsby Mitchel's division was shuffled forward from Elizabethtown, McCook moved his own down to join Johnson at Munfordville.

The first job was to rebuild the L&N Railroad bridge over Green River, which had been destroyed by order of Simon Bolivar Buckner in October. The bridge had been an engineering masterpiece. It was four hundred feet long and the railroad tracks rested upon a deck which was supported by six graceful pillars of stone masonry. The center pillar soared 115 feet from the waterline to the tracks above. The bridge cost $165,000 to build and it was not yet three years old when the Rebels brought two spans of it (about one hundred feet) tumbling down to the Green River below.

When work began to rebuild the bridge, pickets were placed three miles out to protect the construction crew and McCook's men began erecting substantial defensive works south of the river. The bridge started to rise again.

Sergeant Major Lyman S. Widney of the 34th Illinois Infantry came to Munfordville on December 11 in Wood's 5th Brigade of McCook's division. The brigade stopped there out of necessity. Without an intact railroad, provisions could not keep up with the advancing men. In his wartime diary, Widney described watching from the riverbank as an L&N work locomotive "darts back and forth on the frail, temporary track, as busy as an ant moving its household goods…. Thee locomotive is being used to draw, with a heavy line, the timbers from the river."[3]

The Rebels' vandalism was widespread, so McCook's men had more work to do besides just rebuilding the bridge. Miles of track had been torn up, the railroad tunnel at Horse Cave had been caved in, and the Louisville and Nashville Turnpike had been blocked with felled trees and the culverts collapsed. For the time being, McCook's soldiers were used as construction gangs.

In the midst of all this axe and shovel work, an order arrived for McCook to march his division north through Hardin County to the mouth of Salt River, where steam transports would be waiting to carry the men down the Ohio to the mouth of the Cumberland River and from there upstream to U.S. Grant, who was fighting his Fort Donelson campaign. Accordingly, on a snowy February 14, the 2nd Division moved north on a road that was in such dreadful shape that General Rousseau had his men abandon it in favor of the heavily graveled bed of the L&N Railroad. They outdistanced the wagons, which had no choice but to use the old turnpike and there sank to their hubs in the cold, sticky mud. The wagons were caught so thoroughly in the muck that, in trying to force them forward, the teamsters broke the wheels and snapped off the wagon tongues. The march quickly became a misery for the infantrymen, whose blankets were in the wagons, stranded far behind.

The foot soldiers had nearly reached Upton when they received the order to halt. Buell had changed his mind about using river transports; he decided that McCook's men could move overland and still reach Grant quickly enough. The tired, muddy men were ordered to do an about-face and march to Bowling Green. The mud was unrelenting. One day the men made only one mile. Nevertheless, the men crossed the swollen Barren River into southern Kentucky's largest city on or about February 24, eight days after Grant captured Fort Donelson.

So far, the marching of 1862 had been largely pointless. But beyond Bowling Green, there was a definite purpose to the forward movement. The Army of the Ohio was going to Pittsburg Landing, there to combine with Grants's Army of the Tennessee (fresh from its victories at Fort Henry and Fort Donelson) for another short march and the capture of Corinth, Mississippi. Corinth was a railroad center whose capture would not only disrupt Rebel supply lines, but would also be a step toward the permanent crippling of the Confederacy's transportation in the West. It was easy to see how, Corinth gone, other cities like Memphis might be isolated and forced into surrender. At last, the troopers of the 2nd Division were going to earn their soldier's pay of $13 a month. They left Bowling Green on February 26.

The march to Tennessee was easier thanks to better weather and the drying roads, which helped them to make good time, though there were occasional encounters with the enemy. On February 27, McCook's division crossed the Kentucky-Tennessee line and on March 2 came to Edgefield, opposite Nashville across the Cumberland River. As usual, the Rebels had burned the bridge. General Buell was already there; he had preceded the infantry, leaving Bowling Green by rail, and arriving at Edgefield on February 24. The day after, February 25, Mayor R. B. Cheatham had crossed the Cumberland to Edgefield and surrendered the city to General Buell.

More Federal soldiers continued to arrive over the next few days, both by transports on the Cumberland and overland, on the road from Kentucky. McCook's men waited at Edgefield until March 5, when they crossed the pontoon bridge into the city and marched out the Franklin Pike, where they bivouacked.

The soldiers from the North found Nashville to be a strange City. In the decade of the 1850s the city had thrived and boasted a population of more than seventeen thousand. It had six hotels and five newspapers, two theaters and sometimes an opera company came up the Cumberland River by steamboat. It was a young American city, but it was a comfortable one and was, by fits and starts, becoming a cultured one. All of that had been swept away by war. Civil authority had given over to a military government, headed by former U.S. senator Andrew Johnson. The stores were closed and the streets were empty. The city's seventy-three manufactories were quiet. Students were not on their way to any of the city's three institutions of higher learning; their schools (as well as many of the city's churches) had been taken over by the Federals for use as hospitals and warehouses. The damp air stank with the smell of charred wood, and the stumps of the burned Cumberland River bridge stuck up over the waterline like black tombstones in a flooded graveyard. Heavy rains had caused the river to rise and some lower wards of the city were inundated, so Nashville had suffered the double curse of both fire and flood. The people who were seen on the street were worried; the outlying farms had been requisitioned to death and could supply very little in the way of vegetables, grain, or fresh meat. And, the Yankees faced a populace which was almost unrelentingly hostile and did not mind to show it, especially the women, whose bitterness was unmistakable and undisguised. Passing by two belles on the street, a soldier heard one turn to the other and say, "Lordy, I do wish we had the eyeballs of the Yankees to play marbles with."[4]

Yet, there were islands of grace in this bitter city. Shortly after setting up his headquarters at the St. Cloud Hotel, General Buell paid a courtesy visit on Mrs. Sarah Polk, the widow of President James K. Polk. Though Southern in her sympathies, she received the general and his party with hospitality and, according to Walter Durham, the excellent historian of wartime Nashville, Buell's visit helped "set a precedent that was followed, without exception, by succeeding Federal commanders in the Nashville area."[5]

Even ordinary soldiers were made welcome by the gracious lady, right up until the end of the war. N.G. Markham, a soldier in the 18th Michigan, visited the president's widow as late as March 26, 1864, and wrote to his wife the next day, "I had an invite the other day to go over and take a peep at the inside of Mrs. James K. Polk's house so yesterday I accepted the invitation and went over and was showed through the house and saw the curiosities that he received while he was President. Mrs. Polk is a very sociable old lady and a very good looking woman too. She has got a very nice residence and seemed to enjoy herself very well."[6]

When the Federals were approaching, perhaps as many as one thousand civilians had left the city. Now, they were slowly making their way back to take the loyalty oath and be paroled. One of them was George C. Harris, the rector of the Church of the Holy Trinity. Walter Durham recounted that Harris was arrested as he approached McCook's camp on Franklin Pike. Brought to the general's headquarters, Harris had to listen to a little lecture sprinkled with threats. McCook told him to "pray for the President of the United States or be hung," and warned the rector that the Federals "were trying to handle rebels with 'white gloves' but that, if that method failed, they would not hesitate 'to use rope.' The general then paroled him."[7]

The Army of the Ohio could not have been sorry to leave the haunted, hostile city when they stepped off on March 15, McCook's division in the lead. They made the fourteen miles to Franklin with no difficulty. As was their custom, they marched through the town with flags flying and music playing, and went ten miles beyond before they camped. The next day, they marched twenty-one miles to Spring Hill.

Columbia was the next destination, but the security of the bridges there was a worry to the Federals. The cavalry raced ahead to prevent the Confederates from burning the bridge over Rutherford Creek and the bridges over Duck River, but they were too late. The Rebels had downed them all. Nature added insult to injury; rain and snow were causing the creeks and rivers to rise. Fording was impossible. There was no choice but to rebuild the bridges.

The army was finally able to cross on March 31. The days that followed were rainy, and the roads were mush, but the army kept moving. McCook's division followed Rousseau's lead brigade toward Savannah, Grant's headquarters. They were drawing near on the morning of April 6 when they were surprised to hear the distant heavy guns of the battle that had already begun near Pittsburg Landing and a little Methodist meeting house called Shiloh. The men arriving were not the only ones surprised. General Grant had repeatedly said that there would be no fighting here; the enemy was in Corinth. General William T. Sherman (who had calmed down and returned to duty east of the Mississippi) was also fooled. Only moments before the shooting started, he ridiculed an officer of the 59th Ohio who warned that the enemy was close by. "Take your damned regiment back to Ohio," Sherman said. "There is no enemy nearer than Corinth."[8]

Now, that undetected enemy had appeared in force and was driving the Yankees back to the Tennessee River. McCook and his men were needed. They hurried forward to Savannah, ready for action with forty rounds of ammunition in their cartridge boxes, but they found when they arrived that there were no transports to carry them down to Pittsburg Landing and marching was out of the question. The ground between Savannah and Pittsburg

Landing was all swamp. McCook hurried around and finally got some boats together and, leaving his cavalry behind to guard the wagon train, moved his men downstream to join in the fight, Rousseau's brigade still leading the way. It was dark before they arrived.

The bank of the Tennessee River at Pittsburg Landing was a nightmare. It was raining hard again, lightning crackled above, and two Federal gunboats, the *Lexington* and the *Tyler*, were firing at intervals, adding their noise to the confusion. Thousands of panicked men, some of them walking wounded and some of them sick with fear, cowered at the water's edge, dazed by the day's fighting. They had been driven back three and a half to four and a half miles and were unnerved at the enormity of their defeat.

Rousseau's men forced their way through the frightened mob at daylight and made their way to the front. They stacked their knapsacks and lined up to move forward, across acres of dead men and horses. Before they stepped off, Rousseau stood up in the stirrups of his fine sorrel mount and addressed the men. He is reported to have said, "They had a little ballgame yesterday and we'll have another today, but we'll fix them. Shoot low, don't hurt them much. Shoot them in the shins!" Cheered up, the men advanced. They arrived in position to receive the enemy about 6:00 A.M.[9]

McCook, after conferring with Buell, had deployed his division on Buell's right flank, which put it near the center of the combined Federal army. Rousseau's brigade consisted of the 6th Indiana; 5th Kentucky; 1st Ohio; the 1st Battalion, 15th U.S.; 1st Battalion, 16th U.S.; and the 1st Battalion, 19th U.S. Skirmishers from each regiment of Rousseau's brigade edged forward and came under immediate hostile fire. They were driven back on Rousseau's main line, which then came under general attack in a heavy fight that lasted not quite a half hour before the Rebels fell back. They rallied, but were forced back a second time by a well-directed fire of the Regulars and the 1st Ohio. General McCook, who witnessed the fight, wrote, "The enemy attack ... was continuous and severe, but the steady valor of General Rousseau's brigade repulsed him."[10]

Every student of the Rebellion knows, however, that there was valor on both sides of this war, and it was not long before the enemy rallied around two artillery pieces. Rousseau's men advanced with a yell to within two hundred yards of this point before they came under the heaviest rifle fire that Rousseau ever remembered hearing. Across the way was Colonel Robert P. Trabue's brigade of Brigadier General John C. Breckinridge's corps, Alabamians and Kentuckians. They knew how to fight and they were bringing all of their knowledge to bear on the largely untested 4th Brigade. Rousseau's men were steady, though. The General reported, "My line when fired on halted of itself and went to work." The Rebel artillery here occupied a critical position on the road to Pittsburg Landing; a Federal repulse would create an open road to the river, an unacceptable risk, and Rousseau knew it. He ordered Colonel Harvey Buckley forward with the 5th Kentucky, the old Louisville Legion.[11]

The 5th slammed into the Rebel flank and peeled them away from the two guns, which the Federals captured and four others, besides, plus three flags and a couple of prisoners. One of them, an officer said, "You have killed all my men and horses, left only myself and a boy of seventeen, who are wounded, now you can take the guns and be damned!" It had taken forty minutes to drive the Rebels back, and now they were forming up again across Woolf Field on the edge of some woods.[12]

Rousseau pushed his men across the clearing. His advance created a gap on his left, which McCook plugged with Colonel August Willich's reserve regiment. Near the edge of the woods, the enemy opened up on Rousseau's line with a "most withering fire of shell, canister, and musketry." The Yankees were staggered, partly because of the ferocity of the enemy fire and partly because their ammunition was exhausted.[13]

While they fell back to refill their cartridge boxes, the 5th Brigade (now commanded by Colonel Edward Kirk), came through Rousseau's line to take their place in front. Rousseau admired the neatness of the maneuver and mentioned it in his report. It was Kirk's brigade, joined on the left by the 6th brigade (Colonel William H. Gibson), who dislodged the Rebels while Rousseau's men got their cartridges.

Once they had re-supplied themselves with ammunition, Rousseau's men prepared to move forward again. There was a moment of confusion when, without any apparent orders to do so, two regiments unexpectedly began to advance at the double-quick. One of them was Rousseau's own 1st Ohio. Rousseau galloped over to halt them, but was told that General Grant himself had ordered the advance. Rousseau saw Grant and his staff behind the lines, so he knew it was true and knew, too, what Grant wanted. This was the moment. Rousseau threw his whole brigade forward. A heavy fire came from the enemy, but when Rousseau's men returned fire, the Rebels fell back, pursued by Federal cavalry, and the fight sputtered to an end.

Rousseau waved his broad-brimmed hat in the air and cried out in his most ringing politician's voice, "The Rebels are flying! The Rebels are flying! The victory is ours!" The men of the 4th Brigade cheered and threw their hats in the air and shook hands all around, congratulating one another for winning the fight and for surviving it.[14]

The battle had cost General Rousseau an aggregate of 311 men killed, wounded, or missing. Rousseau had led his men into battle rain-soaked and sleep-deprived and yet, as Rousseau later wrote, "During the whole of the long and terrific battle neither officer nor man wavered for one moment."[15]

In his report, General McCook wrote, "General Rousseau led his brigade into action and opened the conflict in this division in a most handsome and gallant style. He was ever to be seen watching the contest with a soldierly care and interest, which made him the admiration of the entire command."[16]

8

The Corinth Campaign

After the Battle of Shiloh, the weather continued to be dreadful. There were over 1,700 dead Federals to bury, along with wagonloads of amputated arms and legs. It was a big job and one that was made harder because heavy rains kept washing the bodies out of their graves. Long trenches were dug to receive as many as two hundred bodies at once. Piles of dead horses, set afire but extinguished by the drizzle, smoldered here and there across the field like altars to some vengeful, horse-hating god.

There were large numbers of wounded, too, and soon civilian relatives of the soldiers began arriving to either help treat the wounded or to retrieve the dead. Souvenir hunters—some of these same relatives, no doubt—wandered over the battlefield, getting in the way of the burial parties.

The soldiers were suffering. Officers like General McCook who were anxious to get their divisions into the battle on the afternoon and evening of April 6 had left their supply wagons on the north bank of the Tennessee River near Savannah, and they were not being brought up with any haste. In addition, soldiers going into battle had piled up their knapsacks, and came back later to find that they were gone. No tents, no rubberized blankets, no change of socks—the men were miserable. General Buell, in his report of operations between April 8 and June 10, 1862, spoke of the great discomfort his men suffered at Pittsburg Landing. He wrote, "Rains and use rendered the roads almost impassable, so that the wagons and baggage that had been left behind ... arrived very slowly. The troops, therefore, had not only to live in the open in miry camps and frequent cold, drenching rains, but to carry their provisions some two miles from the river." Luckily, the charitable organizations and governments of the northern states were generous with their donations and steamboats were arriving daily at Pittsburg Landing, bringing supplies and equipment that helped to make the men more comfortable.[1]

The weather continued wet and the blood-soaked ground stank after each rain. The water supply was tainted with the gore of battle and the filth of thousands of encamped men. Naturally, under such conditions, illness quickly spread through the camps, especially dysentery "of a very threatening type," according to General Buell.[2]

The only good thing about the three-week encampment after the battle was that the enemy was mostly quiet. They had their own troubles.

On April 12, General Henry W. Halleck arrived. Rising from his military collar was a peculiarly shaped head with a great, round top and a face as slick and as lumpy as a pile of potatoes. He was balding, slightly cross-eyed, and had a deeply dimpled chin. When lost in thought, which he often was, he would absent-mindedly cross his arms and scratch his elbows. His appearance and awkward carriage notwithstanding, Halleck had a formidable intellect and, more than that, he was the superior officer of any general at the Shiloh encampment. As the man responsible for coordinating the movement of the Western armies, he had come to take command of the campaign against Corinth. This had, after all, been the original aim of the concentration of armies at and near Savannah. The battle was an unexpected and bloody interruption in the plan, but the plan had not changed.

A third army, the Army of the Mississippi under Major General John Pope, arrived to join the campaign. Pope would advance on the left flank. Major General Buell's Army of the Ohio would be the center column, and Grant's Army of the Tennessee would be on the right, but Grant would not be leading it. The Hero of Fort Donelson was out of favor just now for having been caught off guard at Shiloh and was given the meaningless job of second in command to Halleck. Leading Grant's former army on the march to Corinth would be the loyal Virginian Major General George H. Thomas.

The march commenced on April 29, and the men were not sorry to go. Pittsburg Landing had not been a pleasant interlude, even with its abundant diversions of prostitutes, gamblers, and sutlers peddling their dollar-a-pint whiskey. The gagging, damp stench of unburied (or rain-disinterred) bodies and burning horses, the bad water, and the camp diarrhea had been nearly all that the men could bear. Corinth would certainly be better than Pittsburg Landing and they could not get there quickly enough.

Unfortunately, quickness was not one of General Halleck's virtues. The long blue columns advanced an average of only 1,200 yards a day, unbelievably slow for an uncontested march. The Confederate cavalry was often seen, but continually fell back as the Yankees crept forward. The mosquitoes and ticks were more of a bother than the Rebels.

The slow progress of Halleck's armies encouraged the men to drop out of the march and slip away for a little looting. Even loaded down with plunder, the foragers had no problem catching up again to the main column crawling along the muddy road. And, they were *very* good at finding plunder. One planter along the route moaned that the bluecoats had robbed from him "everything except my hope of eternal salvation."³

* * *

Unfortunately, Lovell Harrison Rousseau left no report of the Corinth Campaign. One can only infer his actions during the advance within the context of what was going on in General McCook's division.

The campaign was largely an exercise in engineering. Bridges had to be built and the bottomland approaches to them had to be corduroyed. The Hamburg-Corinth Road had never been better than it was after the Federals passed by, and McCook's men did their share of the axe and spade work, but it was not why the boys enlisted. Yet, the enemy would rarely give them any opportunity to fight, except for some inconsequential skirmishing at the river crossings. McCook's three brigades, the 4th under Lovell H. Rousseau, the 6th under Richard W. Johnson, and the 5th under Frederick S. Stumbaugh (temporarily commanding in place of Edward N. Kirk, who had been wounded at Shiloh), traded fire with the enemy on May 3, May 8, and May 14, actions which cost a total of five casualties, all from the 29th Indiana of the 5th Brigade.

There was a more serious skirmish of thirty minutes' duration on May 27 as Buell's three columns were approaching Corinth. General Halleck wanted Buell to set artillery batteries on Serratt's Hill. McCook's division, which had been marching in reserve, was brought forward and given the assignment. McCook chose Rousseau and Brigadier General Richard W. Johnson to lead the action. Having learned a lesson, perhaps, from the episode of the stolen knapsacks at Shiloh, Rousseau's men went into action with two days' rations in their haversacks. General Johnson, advancing on the left, soon ran into some stiff resistance. At the same time Rousseau, on the right, also faced an enemy so stubborn that Stumbaugh was ordered to his support. Both flanks were able, after about a half-hour, to shove the enemy beyond the Bridge Creek and over Serratt's Hill to the very edge of Corinth's outer defenses. The skirmishers were ordered to halt, but to hold their position. Rousseau had lost thirteen men.

Avenues of fire were cleared on heavily forested Serratt's Hill on the night of May 27 and 28 and men with picks and shovels dug entrenchments four hundred yards long. Artillery was rolled forward and muscled into place behind the battlements. McCook wrote, "Every preparation was made to give the enemy a warm reception should he show a disposition to attack."⁴

The enemy did attack on the morning of May 28. A brigade of graybacks hit Johnson on McCook's left flank and were not driven back until Captain Charles Cotter's artillery sprayed them with grape and canister. The

Federals had only seven men wounded, but the Rebels lost forty-one killed and seventy-three wounded. Meanwhile, the enemy slammed into Stumbaugh in the center, but they had no better luck than they did with Johnson. Rousseau, alone, was not pestered by the Rebels this day.

There was more skirmishing on the 29th, but late that night — actually, early on the morning of the 30th — General William Nelson reported that the enemy were evacuating Corinth. He advanced his division and found that the enemy was, indeed, gone except for one hundred men who were sick and had been left behind.

The Confederate commander, General P.G.T. Beauregard, knew that Corinth was lost when the Federals gained Serratt's Hill. Rather than risk the investment and certain capture of his 84,000 men, Beauregard began to evacuate Corinth. The skirmishes of May 28 and 29 were simply demonstrations to fool the Yankees. His soldiers slipped away toward Tupelo, taking with them most of the supplies from the town. Everything that could not be moved was destroyed.

The supplies did not matter to the Federals. Far more important was the capture of the junction of the Memphis & Charleston Railroad and the Mobile & Ohio Railroad. James Lee McDonough, in his book *War in Kentucky: From Shiloh to Perryville*, called Corinth "the greatest railroad prize in the Western Theater of the war." From Corinth, the Northern armies could launch deeper incursions into the South.[5]

Halleck informed his men in his congratulatory message that their victory was "as brilliant and important as any recorded in history." Plainly, that was an exaggeration, but there was no denying that Corinth was, truly, an important acquisition for the Federals. The proof was in the immediate aftermath: Fort Pillow on the Mississippi surrendered shortly afterward, as did Memphis. Their overland supply route was lost, and so were they.[6]

The Northern newspapers were critical of Halleck's Corinth victory, pointing out that Beauregard had been allowed to escape unbloodied. Halleck did finally order a pursuit on June 4, but after three days and twenty miles the enemy still had not turned to make a stand, so the chase was called off. The Federals returned to Corinth. During the chase, they had slept in an abandoned CSA camp and woke up in the morning with lice; the rest of their time in Corinth was a campaign against the rapidly multiplying cooties in their clothes. General McCook was placed in charge of Corinth and his itching division garrisoned the town.

P.G.T. Beauregard came under criticism, too, for his performance at Corinth. The charge that he had abandoned Corinth without a fight stung him and he tried to defend himself, saying, "The retreat was conducted with great order and precision, doing much credit to the officers and men under my orders and must be looked upon, in every respect, by the country as equivalent to a brilliant victory." The country did not look upon the loss of Corinth as a brilliant victory. Neither did the government in Richmond. Beauregard had only been in command since the death of Albert Sidney Johnston on the first day at Shiloh; but now, after a brief tenure of only a few weeks, he was relieved. The new Confederate commander in the West was General Braxton Bragg.[7]

9

Following General Bragg to Kentucky

After Corinth, General Halleck scattered his armies. The Army of the Ohio was given a mission in which General Buell did not believe: to move eastward along the Memphis and Charleston Railroad, across the top of Mississippi and Alabama, then slip over the state line into Tennessee and capture Chattanooga. The dreaded order arrived on June 9.

Not that the goal was unimportant. Though Chattanooga was a relatively small town of fewer than five thousand, its location gave it importance. Chattanooga guarded the mountain gap that led into northern Georgia. In addition, its capture would extend Federal control far up the Tennessee River toward the mountains of East Tennessee, which was a region of special interest to President Lincoln. Finally, Chattanooga was at or near the junction of four railroads: the East Tennessee Railroad, the Nashville & Chattanooga Railroad, the Western & Atlantic Railroad, and the Memphis & Charleston Railroad.

Buell did not quibble about the importance of Chattanooga as a prize, nor did he have any complaint about the size of his army. He would leave Corinth with four divisions, a total of about 35,000 men. Another eighteen thousand men would join him en route and, if that weren't enough, another two divisions were near enough that they could be ordered to join him, if necessary.

However, an army of this size presented supply problems, and here was the rub. Buell would need three and one-half pounds of food per man per day, twenty-three pounds of forage per mule per day, and twenty-six pounds of forage per horse per day. The army could not carry enough food along and would not be able to live off the land since this was cotton country and few food crops were grown. Supplies would have to be delivered to the Army of the Ohio.

The Tennessee River might have been a supply line for Buell, but after a miserably wet spring, the weather had turned dry. This was, in fact, the beginning of one of the worst droughts in U.S. history. The river was dropping and supply boats were not going to be able to reach Buell's army as it moved upstream.

This meant that the army was going to have to get supplies via the Memphis & Charleston Railroad, a particularly vulnerable railroad. Buell could see this even if Halleck could not. Buell tried to explain that the railroad ran just north of, and parallel to, the enemy's lines and that the graybacks could attack isolated stretches of the track anywhere along an eighty mile length, as they pleased. A broken track would mean supply shortages for the Army of the Ohio, and supply shortages would mean a halt to the advance.

Not only was the Memphis & Charleston Railroad itself a fragile link to the supply bases, but the railroads that joined it from the North were vulnerable, as well. They, too, would have to be guarded, especially the Louisville & Nashville Railroad, with its many tunnels and bridges, all of them tempting targets for the enemy. They would not even have to attack Buell's marching column. All they had to do was tear up the railroads to the North and the country itself would defeat Buell.

Buell was a careful planner. He fretted over the problems that Halleck ignored, but Halleck was the commanding general. So, in the second week in June, Buell stepped off toward Chattanooga.

McCook's division left Corinth on June 11 and arrived at Tuscumbia on June 15. On June 21, while the army was still in that vicinity, Halleck began to complain by telegraph about Buell's lack of progress. It was a cheeky attitude from a man who moved his army less than a mile a day on the Corinth Campaign in May, and Buell ignored him at first. He had other concerns.

By now, the Confederates had seen what was up and had begun a delaying campaign. Just as Buell had predicted, Rebel raiders were breaking up the railroads. Wagons had to deliver supplies over bad roads from the railroad breaks, but there weren't enough wagons. And the army marched farther and farther away from the breaks, so what few wagons there were could not keep up. Buell's men went on half rations. The country could not feed them. Rousseau later said, "Supplies were very scarce on the whole line of march; in fact I think the inhabitants had not enough for their own purpose." On June 29, the columns of the expedition came to a complete halt for lack of food, forage, and munitions. McCook's division stopped at Huntsville.[1]

At some point along the dusty road toward Huntsville, Rousseau left on a furlough and returned home to Louisville. There, on June 16, he was given a banquet at the Galt House. Mayor John M. Delph was the master of ceremonies and offered a toast that said, in part, "Our guest and friend, General Rousseau: When treason reared its hideous head he was among the foremost to meet it; he rallied his countrymen to repel it from the soil of our State, and on the field of Shiloh his valor has made him still more distinguished. Kentucky views with pride the conduct of her son, and we will cherish his fame as one of the jewels of the State."[2]

James Guthrie rose next. This man, president of the L&N Railroad, who was sometimes a friend and sometimes a foe of the guest of honor, was all compliments tonight. He praised Rousseau's leadership in defeating the secessionists in Kentucky as spoke in praise of his "decisive action" in raising troops to defend the city and the state.[3]

Then it was Rousseau's turn to speak. In what might have been a jibe at Guthrie, he spoke of his disappointment when he was not allowed to raise troops in his native state in 1861. He reviewed the difficulties he faced in supplying his troops with the equipment and commissary stores they needed at Camp Joe Holt. He recalled how his friend Captain Zack Sherley had ferried men to the camp, with no guarantee of ever being recompensed by the government for his efforts.

"I raised my troops and equipped them," Rousseau said. "The traitors hated us intensely — called them 'Rousseau's Silver Creek Ruffians,' 'Lincoln Hirelings,' and 'Abolitionists.' They were drilled and disciplined and on the field of Shiloh they repaid me — and their enemies, too ... I am proud to say that a braver or more gallant brigade never entered a field of battle."[4]

The banquet did not break up until 2:00 A.M. It was a glittering occasion, a gratifying night for Rousseau. To be fêted by one's fellow citizens like this would have been the career climax for many men. But, though they could not have known it in the Galt House banquet room that night, the war had barely begun and there was still work for Rousseau to do. In a few days, he rejoined his brigade at Huntsville.

The supply situation had become critical for General Buell and, in order to maintain his supply lines, he had to disperse his troops to repair railroads, build stockades, and to guard the trestles along with the miles of remote track in between. On July 4, McCook was ordered to Battle Creek, Tennessee, to help protect the railroad there. But, Rousseau did not go with his brigade; he had been appointed to command the eight thousand officers and men of the 3rd Division of the Army of the Ohio, with headquarters at Huntsville. The appointment was made official by Special Orders No. 99 on July 11, 1862.

Huntsville, a small city of five thousand citizens, was one of the most pleasant and attractive towns in the South. Lieutenant Alfred Pirtle, a Louisvillian serving in the 10th Ohio Infantry, saw Huntsville during this period and said that the city "is situated in a valley termed, I am told, the Happy Valley, which I should judge is very appropriate, for the scenery is beautiful, climate healthy, the people wealthy and prosperous, or rather were before the war.

The supply of water for the city is furnished by a magnificent spring.... The public buildings except the courthouse are handsome, some of the churches decidedly ornamental and would be deemed so in any city. The private residences are however the chief beauty of the place ... a display of good taste, combined with cultivation." The city's smooth, shady streets were gaslit and kept free of excessive dust by watering. Huntsville was also the home of a population of people whose enthusiasm for the Confederacy had been cool during the secession movement, but whose attitude toward the North had hardened because of the ham-handed policies of the commanding officer of the occupying forces, General Ormsby Mitchel. Pirtle and his friends lamented a lost chance to win over the citizenry and said, "If things had been better managed we might now have many friends and by no means so many enemies."[5]

Rousseau also admitted that, between the military and the civilian population of Huntsville, "very bitter feelings existed." He continued, "It was partly induced by the shooting of the soldiers by bushwhackers and they in turn handled the people very roughly. I believe that many of the soldiers had been very much in the habit of taking everything they wanted and many things they did not, such as men and women's and children's clothing.... The complaint was soldier and officers entered private residences and took out of them whatever they wanted — silver plate, money, and anything else — and [destroyed wantonly] the furniture of the houses."[6]

Across the entire front there was a controversy breaking about Buell's policy toward Southern civilians. He understood (correctly, at the time) that the policy of the government was that property of inoffensive Southerners was to be protected. This included slaves, but more upsetting to hungry soldiers, it also applied to sustenance for both men and beasts. Buell did what he could to prevent individual foraging and when he learned that Colonel John B. Turchin had allowed his men to run wild in Athens, Alabama, he had the offending officer arrested. Turchin, by indulging his riotous troops, had violated the government's policy of respectful military behavior toward civilians, a policy Buell had earlier explained to his troops in General Orders No. 13. Buell said, "We are in arms, but not for the purpose of invading the rights of our fellow countrymen anywhere, but to maintain the integrity of the Union and protect the Constitution." Buell was not the only general who tried to enforce the unpopular policy. William T. Sherman, who is remembered in history for his fiery march through Georgia in 1864, shared with Buell a disdain for unauthorized foraging in 1862. He ordered that soldiers who molested civilians or who stole would be confined and restricted to a diet of bread and water.[7]

Men who were living on half rations found no comfort in a policy of such generosity toward the civilians on their line of march and there was more than grumbling about it. There was a good deal of disobedience, which went unpunished by junior officers who agreed more with their troopers in the ranks than with their president and their General. It was an ugly disregard of orders and breakdown of discipline that was developing in the army.

Rousseau, however, agreed with Buell. He said, "I had many conversations with General Buell as to the proper course to be pursued. His policy was one I cordially approved myself and that was that whatever the Government needed its officials should take peaceably and peacefully and that all private marauding, stealing, and robbing, which tended to the destruction of discipline and the efficiency of the army shout be repressed." In cases where supplies were requisitioned, payment should be made on the spot or a receipt given — a competent officer must be assigned to see to it. Individual plunderers should be punished. At Huntsville, Rousseau followed the policy and enhanced his reputation as a fair but insistent disciplinarian.[8]

Many of the newspapers were critical of the course of action that Buell and Rousseau believed in and tried to enforce. The *Nashville Daily Union* of August 3, 1862, bitterly criticized "Generals Buell and Rousseau, sitting snugly in their tents like squires in the office, listening to the complaints of rebels about chickens stolen, negroes sloped, peach orchards plundered, when all around the guerrillas were growing bolder and making rail lines to Huntsville more unsafe than before."[9]

As the post commander at Huntsville, Rousseau found many of the citizens were in as tight straits as the soldiers. Rich and poor alike were "in want of the necessaries of life," and they came to Rousseau for relief. There was little that he could do. The railroads suffered continual attacks by raiders like John Hunt Morgan and Nathan Bedford Forrest, slowing to a trickle the flow of supplies coming down from Louisville and Nashville. What few supplies did get through were barely sufficient for his own troops, much less to divide with destitute citizens. Rousseau sent patrols out in a six to ten mile radius to requisition cattle (in return for receipts, presumably), but they were scrawny and starved. He had somewhat better luck in finding corn, but it was still green at this season.[10]

In addition to the ever-lasting problem of supplies, there were the local guerrillas who swarmed Northern Alabama. Rousseau had regiments posted at Stevenson, one regiment with a field battery at Decherd, another regiment with a battery at Battle Creek, and a regiment to guard railroad bridges between Huntsville and Stevenson. He had the cavalry wearing out horses trying to prevent depredations. And yet, the guerrillas, who were fluid and dangerous, could not be entirely contained — often all that the conventional forces could do was respond, not prevent. Rousseau found a creative way to discourage guerrillas who persisted in firing into the windows of troop trains leaving Huntsville — he boarded prominent citizens on the cars and let them ride along with his soldiers. The guerrillas were reluctant to risk accidentally killing their fellow Confederates.

* * *

General Don Carlos Buell's problems were the same as Rousseau's, but on a vastly larger scale.

On July 12, it appeared that the campaign against Chattanooga would be able to continue. News came that the railroad repairs had all been completed. The hungry soldiers must have eagerly waited for boxcars of supplies to arrive, but they never did. On July 13, the "Wizard of the Saddle," Nathan Bedford Forrest, attacked Murfreesboro, Tennessee, and destroyed the railroad bridge over Stones River. He also captured 1,400 men and 200,000 rations. About a week later, Forrest destroyed two more bridges closer to Nashville. News also came that the Memphis & Charleston Railroad was broken again.

The construction crews went back to work. Buell kept prodding his men forward and had reached Stevenson, Alabama, when word came that the trains would again be running. On July 29, a trainload of 210,000 rations arrived and a similar amount arrived the next day. There was a renewed hope that the campaign against Chattanooga could continue.

Then, on August 12, John Hunt Morgan swooped down on Gallatin, Tennessee. He captured the town and the garrison of 375 men and more than one hundred horses. He torched 40 railroad cars, tore up 600 feet of track, and collapsed one of the two L&N tunnels by burning rail cars inside, effectively closing its nearby twin, also. Morgan had sliced Buell's main supply artery once and for all. The Chattanooga Campaign jerked to a halt. The most advanced units of Buell's army never got to within thirty miles of Chattanooga, "with the rest of the command still strung out across Alabama and parts of Tennessee," as Kenneth Noe wrote. He added that some veterans "considered it to have been the hardest march of the war."[11]

* * *

While Buell's army was still staggering toward Chattanooga, Braxton Bragg, the new Confederate commander, had gotten there by using a more southern route. With the Army of the Ohio in a weakened state and apparently stalled in Alabama, Bragg saw an opportunity. He could make a quick move north through Tennessee and into Kentucky and win back the ground that the Confederacy had lost since the war began. John Hunt Morgan reported that he had discovered strong Southern sentiment during his first raid into Kentucky and there, too, was another incentive for Bragg to strike north. If he could bring the manpower and resources of Kentucky into the Confederacy, the South's chance of winning the war would be enhanced immeasurably.

The idea behind the late summer campaign was unassailable, but the plan to accomplish it was clumsy: a two-pronged invasion with Bragg on the western flank and Edmund Kirby Smith a hundred miles away on the eastern. The generals did not make a good team. Neither had a talent for cooperation and the gains of a promising start would not result, ultimately, in the Confederates' hoped-for conclusion.

But, that was in the future. It was with high hopes and faith in their commander that Bragg's 28,000 Confederates prepared to move north from Chattanooga.

On August 9, Buell learned through some captured documents that the Rebels intended to soon make their move, and he developed his plans accordingly. General Alexander McDowell McCook was ordered to keep watch for Rebel movement in the Sequatchie Valley, northwest of Chattanooga. If the enemy advanced, McCook was to move forward to try and stop them. If he could not, he was to fall back, summon General Thomas L. Crittenden's 5th Division for a rendezvous and together they would stall or stop Bragg's men as they climbed up the face of the Cumberland Plateau.

On August 19, there were signs of Confederate movement. McCook advanced as planned. The next day, his skirmishers unexpectedly ran into some Rebel cavalry and McCook did not try to develop the situation or gain a clearer idea of where the main Rebel force was located. He fell back to Jasper, Tennessee, with the news that thirty-six Confederate regiments were on the move. He gathered up Crittenden and together they returned to Battle Creek.

General Buell was livid that McCook had merely side-stepped after his slight brush with the enemy; now he must hurry to obstruct Bragg. Buell moved to Decherd to direct the placement of his troops

From Decherd, the orders began to fly. On August 22 he wired General Rousseau at Huntsville: "Your regiments must make forced marches and reach here in forty-eight hours. Keep your whole command in readiness to march, but without exciting suspicion; I may call it here or elsewhere."[12]

Only a day later, Buell changed his mind regarding the placement of Rousseau's troops. He decided that they must gather in Nashville. He sent a wire to J.B. Anderson at Nashville saying, "Two trains must at once be sent on Decatur road to take troops to Nashville. The trains must run together.

One of them will go to Huntsville and report to General Rousseau and take up all the bridge guards between that place and Athens and one train take on 21st Ohio as soon as the other train approaches from Huntsville. Both will then proceed up the road and take all the bridge guards and infantry on the line up to Columbia. As soon as these trains have passed Columbia, the troops will march for Nashville. This must be done with the greatest secrecy. General Rousseau will accompany the trains up and be in command." At the same time, Buell sent Rousseau the order to take command in Nashville "and defend the place to the last and try to open our communications with the north." And then, still worried, Buell sent another wire to Rousseau that said, "You will have to leave [at Huntsville] the sick and medical attendants with rations for twenty days.... If you can't get your trains through you must leave them and march through."[13]

Rousseau was still at Huntsville three days later. Buell, sounding considerably more confident now, wired him, "No fight. Bragg is very slow. If he wants one he can have it. We are all ready." Bragg's lollygagging was a gift to the Federals; it gave Rousseau the time to do a more complete job of gathering supplies to take north. All the military supplies from Athens and Pulaski were brought to Huntsville, as well as all the bales of cotton stored at Athens and Decatur. General Ormsby Mitchel and General E. A. Paine were ordered to drive to Huntsville "all the beef cattle they can get on the march, giving receipts." Rousseau did a more than adequate job, according to Lieutenant Colonel Francis Darr, Buell's chief commissary officer, who later testified that, when he was evacuating Huntsville, his troops took to the railway station "all they could possible haul away" in their wagons. He continued, "I do not think over 10,000 rations were destroyed." Ten thousand rations sounds like a lot to destroy, but Darr thought that no troops he had ever known "managed better or made better use of their rations."[14]

The next day, the 26th, Buell wired Rousseau, "You must go to Nashville in person at once." But Rousseau was already at Columbia, having left the final details of moving men and materiel to Colonel William H. Lytle. Rousseau reached Nashville later that night or sometime on the 27th.[15]

The Nashville to which Rousseau returned after five months was a city transformed. The recent depredations of Forrest and Morgan had frightened the army into ringing the city with wooden stockades at bridges and other vulnerable points. More formidable were the fortifications crowning St. Cloud Hill and Capitol Hill. These earthen-wooden-stone defensive works were each manned by sixty men and protected by four artillery pieces. Two more of these behemoths were under construction by slave gangs.

Since John Hunt Morgan had closed the L&N tunnels at Gallatin, there were no trains arriving from the north. To serve passengers who had business in Kentucky, two stagecoach lines had been started. Aside from this, private business had continued to suffer in occupied Nashville. The army sutlers, however, thrived, as did a vigorous black market which included prostitution.

The closing of the Gallatin tunnels had another consequence besides inconveniencing travelers. It deprived the city of one of its main supply routes. The other was the Cumberland River, which was too low in this summer of drought to allow steam transports to reach Nashville. With no efficient way to bring food in from the North, Nashville suffered. Walter Durham wrote in *Nashville: The Occupied City*, "When Rousseau arrived, troops in and around the city were on half rations and military authorities in some instances had found it necessary to confiscate 'flour and other supplies in the hands of individuals.'"[16]

There was a shortage of news in Nashville, as well as of food. Rebel cavalry kept the telegraph lines to Kentucky cut down. In such a vacuum, rumors rushed in to satisfy the need of the people to know what was happening and, in the case of the Nashville citizenry, the rumors often had a decidedly pro–Confederate thrust. In that way, Nashville had not changed—the people were Rebels—and every little victory of Morgan, Forrest, or the "War Child," Joseph Wheeler, filled their hearts with hope. The most optimistic sign was the retrograde movement of the Federals who, by increments, were on their way back to Kentucky. Bragg was rolling back all of the Union advances of 1862 and the people were glad.

Of that retrograde, General Don Carlos Buell felt the need to inform Military Governor Andrew Johnson. In an August 30 message sent from his headquarters at Decherd, Buell detailed the manifold difficulties of his march across Northern Alabama: "At first it was necessary to rebuild the bridges over a long line of railroad, and in some cases it has had to be repeated several times. So constant has been the interruption of our communications that it has been with the greatest difficulty the troops could be sustained at all, and even then some 15,000 men were required to occupy positions and guard our communications which, starting necessarily from Louisville, extended in all over some 400 miles of railroad." This, Buell explained, reduced his number of effectives to between 25,000 and 30,000 men with which to fight Bragg, who had twice as many men. Therefore, the Federals had to return to Nashville and to the large garrison there. "By falling back to Nashville my force will increase to 40,000 of the Army of the Ohio proper," Buell said, "and including troops that are coming from Corinth it will be about 50,000."[17]

The general concluded, "These facts make it plain that I should fall back on Nashville, and I am preparing to do so. I have resisted the reasons which lead to this necessity until it would be criminal to delay any longer. That we shall triumph in the effort to preserve Tennessee I do not for a moment doubt."[18]

This communiqué was sent to General Rousseau to deliver to Governor Johnson. If Rousseau took it to the governor in person, it was probably his first meeting with the loyal Tennessean whose post-war career would be so important to his own.

The message to Governor Johnson shows that Buell had made a mathematical and a strategic error. He had badly overestimated the number of soldiers in Bragg's command, which was only about 36,000. By this miscalculation, he felt the need to curve his line of march to Nashville to absorb the garrison there, a detour that took him far west of the most direct route to Kentucky. Thus, Buell would be moving north along the arc while Bragg moved along the chord, as Abraham Lincoln would have phrased it, and these added miles threw Buell behind Bragg, and forced him, over the next several weeks, to exhaust his foot soldiers by playing the frustrating game of catch-up.

While the Army of the Ohio was on its way to Nashville, Rousseau received bad news from the North. Edmund Kirby Smith had crossed into Kentucky far to the east on August 13. At London on August 17, Smith's little army put 138 Federals in the hospital or in the grave and captured forty-five supply wagons. The next day, the graybacks headed for Lexington. At Big Hill on August 23, Smith brushed aside a Union force and pushed on. At Richmond on August 30, Smith met the largest force gathered against him yet, but the men were badly trained and poorly led and Smith's hardened veterans made short work of them. The entire Bluegrass region lay before them now, all the way to the Ohio River and the gates of Cincinnati. It was the news of this last defeat that Rousseau had to share with Buell. "It has been a terrible battle," the August 31 message from Kentucky read. "We have lost many valuable officers and men.... The enemy is in the heart of the State in force."[19]

Buell's army rendezvoused in Nashville between the 2nd and the 7th of September. Some of the men received new uniforms and equipment there, but there was no mail and no pay and the Rebel women hissed at them when they passed by and the disgruntled Army of the Ohio grew more disgusted at their commander. The move into Nashville was equally unpopular with the Northern press. A reporter for the *Cincinnati Enquirer* wrote, "It seems incredible that Bragg has succeeded in scaring so powerful a body as the Army of the Ohio into seeking refuge behind the works around Nashville."[20]

In spite of the recent fortifications, General Alexander McD. McCook advised Buell to burn the city and leave it behind him. "I told him that I did not consider it a very defensible place," McCook later remembered. "I believe it to be the most treasonous place in the Southern country, except the little place of Murfreesboro."[21]

Buell did not take McCook's advice to put Nashville to the torch. Instead, he left General George H. Thomas with five thousand men to guard the city and, on September 8, ordered the rest of his army toward the Kentucky line. Generals Rousseau and Thomas J. Wood led the way. Three days later they were in Bowling Green and three days after that, Buell arrived. Rousseau took command of the post and, while he repaired the dilapidated fortifications on College Hill, he also kept Buell aware of enemy movements. A few miles east, Bragg was quickly moving toward Louisville. Buell was trying, but he could not get ahead to cut him off. Buell said, "I moved my army sixty-five miles, while he [Bragg] was moving fifty and I was still thirty miles in rear of him."[22]

The news only got worse. On September 14, General Rousseau received a message carried by Munfordville native A. G. Craddock. The dispatch was from Colonel John T. Wilder at Munfordville. Wilder had been attacked by Brigadier General James R. Chalmers and a small army of Mississippians, a detachment from Bragg's Army of the Mississippi. Wilder was requesting reinforcements. About a half hour later, General Buell came and Rousseau showed him Wilder's message. Buell sent for Craddock for a verbal explanation of what was happening at Munfordville and when Craddock explained the situation, Buell commented that Wilder had better evacuate the fort. With no reinforcements from Bowling Green, Wilder could not hold out. Bragg soon brought his whole army up and invested the fort. The result was inevitable. Wilder surrendered the fort and the Federal garrison at Munfordville on September 17. It was a good fort there; McCook's men had built part of it only last February and the new commander, Colonel Wilder, had added to it and added immensely to its strength in both size and artillery, but his force was small and he could not hold against Bragg's army. The Rebels captured the fort, as well as the important L&N Railroad bridge over the Green River, and paroled the garrison and sent them packing. Reportedly, Bragg was dug in on the south bank of the Green River and was waiting there to do battle.

Some of Buell's subordinate officers expected him to accept the challenge and move quickly to Munfordville, but he did not. His men were in terrible shape. Many of them were carrying wounds from the almost daily skirmishes with Wheeler's cavalry, but even greater was the number of men who were suffering from sickness and exhaustion. An estimated ten thousand had fallen out of the march from Nashville. The men were weather-beaten and half-starved. They had left their tents in Tennessee and, as usual, were on short rations. When their hardtack ran out, the men were reduced to wrapping wheat flour dough around their ramrods and roasting it over hastily built campfires. They cramped from eating green apples and unripened corn foraged along their line of march. Water was scarce in this drought summer. Marching thirty miles a day, the men had worn out their shoes and many were barefoot. Buell knew the condition of his army and he knew that he could not reach Munfordville quickly, knew that he would kill these men with marching if he tried and, even if he got to the Green River before Bragg left, he would arrive with men too wasted to fight. Saving Louisville had to remain his main concern.

To that end, Buell decided on a risky move. He would sever his heavy, slow supply wagons from the rest of his army. The wagons would move toward Louisville in a separate column with a cavalry escort, rolling north through Brownsville and Leitchfield toward West Point and on to Louisville, while the infantry (soon to be joined by the bulk of General Thomas' men from Nashville), would march up the Louisville and Nashville Turnpike. Buell wired General William Nelson, who was commanding in Louisville, that he expected the Confederate generals Bragg and Kirby Smith to link up in Elizabethtown and that the big fight for the Commonwealth would occur there. On September 16, Buell's foot soldiers moved out of Bowling Green, each man carrying three days' cooked rations in his haversack.

For the Army of the Ohio, it seemed that each succeeding march was worse than the last. The march from Bowling Green was a nightmare. The drought that had descended on them after Corinth had never released its grip on the land and the turnpike was as dry as powder. The road was hot on the feet of the barefoot men and choking clouds of fine red dust rose up to smother them. They drank out of scummy barnyard ponds and fell out of the march to vomit in the rank ditches along the road. And at each bivouac, the men called Buell a traitor and cursed him in language that chilled some listeners' hearts.

Everywhere were the signs of destruction that proved the enemy had preceded Buell up the turnpike. Carcasses of hogs rotted on the roadside and miles of telegraph wire were ripped down from the poles and either cut up or festooned over the weeds and bushes. North of Munfordville, the Rebels had derailed a locomotive and nine railroad cars.

And there was daily skirmishing. A reporter for the *New York Times* who was traveling with the army wrote in an article that appeared on October 2, "Since camping at Cave City, we have taken, by skirmishing and surprising the enemy's outposts near 700 prisoners."[23]

The men marched on, past familiar locations for those who had been in McCook's command since the winter of '61. They marched by Bacon Creek, Upton, Nolin, and the small stockade at Camp Nevin. Then, on or about September 21, Bragg made a surprising move. He veered off the Louisville and Nashville Turnpike and headed toward Hodgenville and Bardstown. For his own reasons, which historians still debate, Bragg had forfeited the race to Louisville. The way to the City at the Falls was clear and Buell hurried on toward Elizabethtown.

A reporter for the *Louisville Daily Journal* saw the General there and wrote of his appearance and demeanor, "He wore a shabby straw hat, dusty coat, and had neither belt, sash or sword about him ... Buell is certainly the most reserved, distant and unsociable of all the Generals in the army. He never has a word of cheer for his men or his officers, and, in turn, his subordinates care little for him save to obey his orders, as machinery works in response to the bidding of the mechanic."[24]

The Army of the Ohio continued past Elizabethtown to West Point on the Salt River and from there to Louisville. The lead units under General Thomas L. Crittenden began entering the city on September 25. The soldiers had covered 120 miles in a week. By September 27, Buell's entire army had arrived (except for the wagons, which rolled in a few days later). Dirty and ragged though they might be, Buell's men were "greeted with joy and delight," according to Robert McDowell's excellent *City of Conflict*. The people of Louisville gave the thirsty men water and fed them. Some of the soldiers who were not fed resented it and returned to their old Huntsville habits; they assumed the right to forage liberally inside the abandoned homes of those who had refugeed across the river to Indiana.[25]

No one was happier to see the arrival of the Army of the Ohio than General William "Bull" Nelson. He had nineteen thousand infantry and artillery plus two thousand cavalry, but they were green troops, many of them Home Guards, and would have been no match for the veterans of either Braxton Bragg in Bardstown or Edmund Kirby Smith, who was still in the vicinity of Lexington and Frankfort. Just by being in Louisville, Buell's divisions had bought Nelson some security; by their mere presence there, they would discourage an attack.

It would be good to know the details of Rousseau's reunion with his wife, his children, and his brothers and their families after his return to

Louisville. Surely there was one. But, as is so often the case with Rousseau, there are no known letters, diaries, or journals to pull back the curtain for a glimpse of the all-too-brief homecoming on 6th Street.

* * *

Buell had expected Bragg to turn and fight at Elizabethtown, but then the Rebels had sheared off toward Hodgenville. Now, in Louisville, Buell figured that it must be Danville, further east, where the great fight for Kentucky's future would take place.

Before moving out of Louisville to challenge Bragg, Buell took the time to reorganize his army into corps. The order came down from Buell's Galt House headquarters: the First Corps would be commanded by General Alexander McD. McCook; the Second Corps by General Thomas Crittenden; the Third Corps by General William "Bull" Nelson. General Lovell Harrison Rousseau's 3rd Division would be in McCook's First Corps and would contain the 9th Brigade (Colonel Leonard A. Harris), the 17th Brigade (Colonel William H. Lytle), the 28th Brigade (Colonel John C. Starkweather), six companies of the 2nd Kentucky Cavalry (Colonel Buckner Board), and three companies of the 1st Michigan Engineers and Mechanics (Major Enos Hawkins).

But, before the newly organized army could begin its march against Bragg, General Buell's plans were upset by one of the most notorious crimes of the war.

Back before Buell arrived, when "Bull" Nelson had summoned all available Home Guards to help defend the city, he had turned to a professional soldier to organize them. The man was a Hoosier, a brigadier general with the ironic name of Jefferson C. Davis. It could scarcely have been a worse partnership. Nelson hated people from Indiana, whom he considered to be the second and third generation descendants of Kentucky's poor whites, and he blamed them for the Union defeat at Richmond, Kentucky, on August 30. Jefferson C. Davis was a son of Indiana. Also, Nelson was a navy man by training and inclination who had been brought into army service only at the start of the war. Jefferson C. Davis was a career army man; he had been in the Mexican War and had been inside Fort Sumter when the opening guns of the war were fired. Davis felt that he deserved a job where he did not have to take orders from an old sailor, a job that was more in keeping with his rank and his experience than organizing amateurs, these pitiful Home Guards. General Davis went about his assignment with an ill-disguised lack of interest.

Later, when Nelson questioned him about the progress he was making with the green troops, Davis was sulky and unresponsive. He answered every question in sullen monosyllables: "I don't know." Nelson asked him how many troops he had. Davis answered, "I don't know."[26]

Nelson was a man with a violent temper and he exploded at Davis' insolence. In a dressing down that must have turned the air blue with oaths, he relieved Davis of his duties and ordered him from the city. If he refused to leave, he would be arrested.

Davis did leave, but not for long. Early on the morning of September 29, he returned to Louisville with a group that included the Indiana governor, Oliver Morton, and went stalking after Nelson. He found him about 7:30 in the lobby of the Galt House, just coming from breakfast. Davis rushed up to Nelson, demanding to know the reason that he had been dismissed. Nelson rebuffed Davis, called him a "damned puppy," and ordered him from his sight. Davis threw a balled up calling card at Nelson and Nelson slapped Davis across the face.[27]

Davis rushed over to one of his friends and was handed a pistol. He turned back toward Nelson, who had continued across the lobby to the staircase. Davis pointed the pistol and shot Nelson in the chest. The general weighed three hundred pounds and was a hard man to kill. Even with a chest wound, Nelson made it up the stairs before collapsing in the second floor corridor. He asked for a minister. "I wish to be baptized," he said. "I have been basely murdered."[28]

General Thomas L. Crittenden, one of Nelson's closest friends, was finishing up his own breakfast when he heard the pandemonium in the Galt House lobby. He rushed upstairs to his dying friend's side and asked, "Nelson, are you seriously hurt?"

"Tom, I am murdered," Nelson answered. And so he was. Nelson was dead in an hour.[29]

General Crittenden and others of Nelson's friends demanded the arrest of Davis for murder and at least two officers reportedly planned to call Davis to answer on the dueling ground for his crime. Some regiments that had served under Nelson at Shiloh and Corinth were so outraged that they were placed under guard as a precaution against vigilante justice. It is claimed that there was some rioting, nevertheless.

General Davis was arrested by the military authorities, but was released from custody on October 13. He was restored to duty on October 21, almost certainly because of the influence of Governor Morton. Since the military courts had faltered, the civilian courts took up the case. The Jefferson County Circuit Court indicted Davis for manslaughter on October 27. He was released on $5,000 bail. The hearing of the case was continually delayed until May 24, 1864, when it was dismissed.

The murder of William Nelson left the commanding general with a vacancy to fill and little time to do it and few choices to pick from. General Buell offered Nelson's corps to first one general and then another, finding no takers. If he offered the command to General Rousseau, there is no record of it. Finally, he offered it to Charles C. Gilbert. Gilbert's rank was murky. He was an acting, but as yet unconfirmed, major general. Before that, for a short time, he had been a brigadier general, but that promotion had never been confirmed, either. Gilbert was actually a captain. Now, suddenly, he was assigned to command a corps. It was a remarkable turn and an unfortunate one, as events would soon prove.

On October 1, the army moved out of Louisville to meet Braxton Bragg.

10

The Battle of Perryville

The Army of the Ohio left Louisville by different routes. Joshua Sill's division of McCook's corps was sent off toward Frankfort, but that was just a diversion. The rest of McCook's First Corps followed the Taylorsville Road, Crittenden's Second Corps moved along the Bardstown Road, and Gilbert's Third Corps, with whom General Buell rode, left Louisville by the Shepherdsville Road.

The men looked nice in fresh uniforms, but they were in poor condition to meet opposition. Many were hung over, and the new recruits were unaccustomed to marching in the heat, wearing wool uniforms and stiff shoes, carrying a knapsack and a rifle. They dropped out of the line of march by the score and the veterans mocked them as "troopees." However, no one was laughing at the end of that first day's march when the men discovered that General Buell had ordered all heavy baggage and staff wagons to be left behind at Louisville, an order that did not come down until the march had begun. The men had left Louisville with wagons, but then, unknown to them, the wagon train was stopped and sent back. Each regiment was allowed only one ambulance and ammunition wagon. Now, the men were at their first bivouac of the Perryville Campaign with few blankets and no rations. The men went to bed hungry, cursing Buell.

On October 2, one day out of Louisville, McCook wrote, "There is no water in Plum or Elm Creek for man or beast." A stray rain shower did not relieve the suffering of the troopers. When a water hole was found and the men rushed down to drink, an officer foolishly rode his horse into the pool. The men drove him away, pelting him with rocks and dirt clods. There was some light skirmishing with the Rebel cavalry approaching Taylorsville, but McCook's men were able to nudge them aside and move on down to the Salt River where they spent that night and also the day of October 3.[1]

On October 4, McCook's corps moved on to Bloomfield and, if water was scarce, at least the money flowed, for the paymaster set up his table and the men lined up for their wages. And in the Army of the Ohio when money flowed, a freshet of whiskey inevitably followed.

The next day was Sunday and the men did not march. The combination of nervous anticipation, hours of free time, and abundant liquor was guaranteed to have a bad effect on discipline among the soldiers, even those with stripes and shoulder-boards. Major David McKee Claggett (17th Kentucky Infantry, Starkweather's brigade) recalled that "about half the officers got drunk." There was a disturbance when two runaway slaves entered the camp, hotly pursued by two whip-wielding planters. The 21st Wisconsin quickly surrounded the slavers, treating them to a pelting such as the officer at the water hole had received. Rousseau rode into the melee and ordered his Wisconsin soldiers to fall back. He placed a few better-regulated troops around the hot-headed Badgers as a guard and tempers began to cool. That night, though, the offending planters' homes were burned and the two blacks were sneaked out of camp. Somewhere down the road, they came back and stayed with the regiment as servants.[2]

General Buell by this time had decided that Bragg was not going to turn and fight at Danville, but rather at Perryville, a small town of three hundred citizens in Boyle County. His three corps were ordered to converge there. On October 6, McCook's corps camped at the Chaplin River and the next day moved into Mackville. Late that night (or, more likely, early on the morning of the 8th), Major Claggett wrote of the town, "More pretty ladies and Union people here than I have ever seen since I have been in the army." Then, he added ominously, "We hear some firing ahead a great battle is expected."[3]

The artillery fire the men heard was coming from Perryville, where General Philip Sheridan of Gilbert's corps had advanced some men down to Doctor's Creek to secure control of the water there. Those whom Sheridan sent forward were in the brigade of Colonel Dan McCook (brother of the First Corps commander). At 2:00 A.M. on October 8, they advanced to claim the water before the Rebels could, "but after we crossed the bank," Sheridan wrote in his memoirs, "I found that we could not hold the ground unless we carried and occupied a range of hills called Chaplin Heights." A Rebel regiment was on the heights, but Sheridan's men shoved them off and began to entrench.[4]

Sheridan was using the editorial "we." Three hours passed before he, himself, arrived on the field to see two enemy regiments and an artillery battery positioning themselves beyond Bull Run Creek, to the east. An artillery duel broke out and the Confederates charged Sheridan's position, but they had no luck. The weight against Sheridan was growing, though; at 6:00 A.M. clouds of dust in the distance showed that Bragg's whole army was on the move.

Hours were passing. No corps except Gilbert's was on the field and no division except Sheridan's was yet engaged, but at 10:30, Sheridan saw six companies of the 2nd Kentucky Cavalry approaching on the Mackville Road, followed by Rousseau's advance division of McCook's corps. McCook had gotten his divisions on the move at 5:00 A.M., with Rousseau in the lead. McCook said in his report, "The Tenth Division (General [James S.] Jackson's) was entitled to the advance, but it being composed entirely of new troops, I ordered General Rousseau's division to take the lead." Rousseau had gotten two of his brigades, Harris' and Lytles', in motion while Starkweather's was drawing supplies. Jackson impatiently moved his division out, cutting off Starkweather, whose brigade would arrive on the field later than Rousseau's other two.[5]

Rousseau began filing into place four to five hundred yards to the left (north) of Gilbert, placing Harris and Lytle along a steep ridge, facing east, dressing off of the Russell family farm house which stood near the angle where the Mackville Road and the Dixville-Benton Road came together. These farm boys forming up on the ridge top would have noticed that the dark soil was thin and in places white stone showed through, lying flat like the bones of an extinct race of giant men who once walked these hills.

The 10th Ohio and the 42nd Indiana were sent forward, the 10th as skirmishers and the 42nd in support of Captain Ebenezer Gay's cavalry and Captain William Hotchkiss' section of artillery, both of Sheridan's division, Gilbert's corps. Rousseau also edged two Parrot guns of Captain Cyrus Loomis' artillery battery a little closer to Doctor's Creek to lay down some long-range fire on the distant Rebels.

Satisfied with the deployment of Rousseau's two on-scene brigades, McCook rode off to find General Buell. Buell had suffered an injury two days earlier. Riding with General Gilbert's Third Corps, Buell had noticed some men pillaging a farmhouse. He rode over to admonish the soldiers, who jumped up, spooking the general's horse and causing it to rear. Buell was thrown and the horse fell back on him. His injuries prevented Buell from sitting up for the next several days, much less riding, and he traveled by ambulance to the farmhouse of John Dorsey, which he made his headquarters and where he listened now to McCook's report.

Back on Rousseau's front, things had grown quiet. An hour passed. General Rousseau rode down to see Loomis. They observed some dust on the Harrodsburg Pike and concluded that Bragg's army was now in retreat. Rousseau ordered Loomis to "give them a small sized hell," and the captain lobbed a few shells in their direction.[6]

The morning was hot and the men were parched from their long march, so during this lull, Rousseau began to send regiments down to get a drink and fill their canteens at Doctor's Creek in the shadow of the cedars and the sycamores, beginning with the 42nd Indiana of Lytle's brigade. Suddenly, the Rebels' big guns began to speak and Rousseau's batteries under Loomis and Captain Peter Simonson returned fire.

Six miles to the south, General Thomas L. Crittenden's corps was now deployed along the Lebanon Road, facing east. Crittenden was the far right of the Union line. The men and officers alike believed that they would soon be engaged. They could see Joseph Wheeler's cavalry in the shadows ahead and a little after 10:00 the Confederates came out to fight. The skirmish that followed was the first of the cavalry clashes that would sporadically erupt through the day. The fighting was indecisive; it was not to Wheeler's advantage to make a stand-up fight out of it and when the pressure became too great, he sidled away. After a while, the sound of gunfire from the north began to reach Crittenden's Federals. Something was going on, but no orders arrived for the Second Corps to move toward the sound of the guns, and when Crittenden sent a query about the situation of Gilbert to his north and of McCook further still in that direction, Gilbert's reassuring reply was that "his children were all quiet and by sunset he would have them all in bed." So, Crittenden concluded that the noise was no more than a skirmish and held his men where they were. Through the long afternoon, the Second Corps would have no role in the battle that was coming.[7]

Back on the left flank, Rousseau had been busy adjusting his lines, but worried that Starkweather still had not arrived, he rode back to search for him. While he was gone, Brigadier General Jackson's men began to arrive and Major General McCook, who had returned from his conference with Buell at the Dorsey house, directed them to get in line to the left of Harris.

Shortly before Jackson's men deployed, the 2nd Kentucky cavalry had a little dust-up with Colonel John Wharton's Rebel cavalry. Wharton was probing, looking for the Union left. His skirmish with the cavalry and the cannon fire he encountered convinced Wharton that he had found the left, and he rode back to the Confederate line to make his report. Thus, the Rebels did not observe Jackson's final disposition and the arrival and deployment of Colonel John Starkweather's brigade. Colonel Starkweather had grown more and more frustrated with the slow progress his men were making jammed up behind Jackson, so they abandoned the road and struck off through the fields and woods. When they emerged from the timber onto the ridge, Jackson's men had already begun to form their line. Since there was no place for Starkweather's men next to their own division, they took up position in the middle of Jackson's line, between Brigadier General William R. Terrill to the left and Colonel George P. Webster to the right. The arrival of these later units extended the Federal line and pushed the left flank farther north than where the Rebel Wharton had originally supposed it to be. Rousseau now reappeared, riding down the line on his thoroughbred, waving his hat in the air, while the men cheered him. He readjusted Starkweather's line, somewhat, in order to create a cross-fire on the Rebels, when they attacked.

The Federals did not have to wait long. About 2:00 P.M. a long line of Rebels charged out of the east and slammed into what they believed was the left flank of the Federal line. What they mistakenly hit instead was the junction of Harris' brigade of Rousseau's division and Webster's brigade of Jackson's. The Confederate attack surprised the Union soldiers by its ferocity and the Rebels were, in turn, surprised to find that they were not attacking the extreme Union left. Both sides fought with a spirit, but the Rebel momentum was unstoppable for the moment. They pushed the Federals back about a mile before their attack stalled near the cabin of a widow named Mary Jane Gibson. Widow Gibson was at home with her children as the bullets and canister began to chew up her cabin walls and chip away at her chimney. To save her little family from the storm raging outside, the widow chopped a hole in her floor and she and her children hunkered there between the joists through the long afternoon.

Stalled the graybacks might be, but they were far from finished. Terrill and Starkweather were next. The Rebels rammed forward once more, into the Union left, and, almost simultaneously, began to move against Lytle's brigade on the right.

Brigadier General Philip Sheridan of Gilbert's Corps observed from his advanced position on Chaplin Heights that the Rebels were about to crash into Rousseau's southernmost brigades on McCook's right flank. He tried to send a warning by signal flag, but, somehow, the message was not noticed and before they knew it, the Yankees at the creek and on Henry Bottoms' farm found themselves in a desperate fight against fresh Confederate troops. They were pushed back up the hill from the creek, back up the pike toward the Benton Road and the Russell House. Some of the Yankee wounded crawled into Mr. Bottoms' barn and when a Rebel shell hit it and set it on fire, they burned alive.

Sheridan, seeing the Rebels coming at Lytle's brigade, had turned his big guns toward them and began ripping the enemy flank with artillery rounds. The Rebels were hurt by it, but they kept advancing up the steep hill, pushing the Federals back and increasing the pressure on Harris in the center. These Midwest boys were "repeatedly assailed" by the enemy, but continually repulsed them. They exhausted their forty rounds and had to replenish their supply of ammunition by taking cartridges from the dead.[8]

Rousseau was in the center with Colonel Harris when he received the message that the left was giving way. The left was the critical sector, so before the conclusion of Harris' and Lytle's fight, Rousseau galloped back to Colonel Starkweather and ordered him to open on the enemy with artillery fire from Captain David Stone's and Captain Asahel K. Bush's batteries. It seems like an order that Starkweather scarcely needed to be given, considering that the enemy was advancing *en masse*, but that is how Rousseau reported it, adding that "the order was promptly and effectually executed." The placement of the guns had been Rousseau's doing, and now it was paying off. Rousseau remembered, "The artillery repulsed the enemy again and again, and held him in check for several hours, until finally a fresh and overwhelming force moved straight forward toward the guns." The line fell back toward the Russell House, but Stone and Bush saved their guns and set them up for more action later on.[9]

While the fight between Starkweather and the Rebels continued, Rousseau learned that Lytle's brigade on the right had been outflanked. Lytle had held stubbornly through the afternoon, but the fresh Rebel troops that were brought against him pushed him back toward the Russell House. Rousseau hurried over to them. The correspondent W.F.G. Shanks commented on this habit of Rousseau's to try and be present on all parts of the battlefield: "Rousseau made very little use of his aides. If he had an order to give he galloped across the field and gave it himself. If he had an advance to order it was done by leading the troops in person." Rousseau later reported, "During the day I was so hard pressed on the left and center by the continuous and persistent attacks of the enemy, and knowing if our left was turned our position was lost and a total rout of the army corps would follow, I felt the importance of my presence there and could not look after the interests of the Seventeenth (Lytle's) Brigade; but the whole division fought under the eye of Major-General McCook ... but late in the afternoon an immense force of fresh troops of the enemy ... turned his [Lytle's] right flank.... Hearing of this condition of things I galloped over toward the right." By the time he arrived, Lytle's brigade was reforming on the ridge near the Russell House, joining there the survivors of the Jackson-Starkweather fight on the left flank.[10]

When Rousseau appeared, the tired, powder-grimed men of the 15th Kentucky stood and cheered until the General told them to lie back down. From the top of the hill, Rousseau could see the enemy approaching. As Rousseau rode among the men, cobbling together the defense, he noticed the men flinching from the minié balls that were beginning to plink around them. Kenneth Noe wrote that the General cried out to encourage his men, "Oh, never mind those little things." He was in mid-sentence when a shell came by and nearly decapitated him. He concluded, "But damn the big ones!"[11]

It was now that Rousseau noticed that his own artillery, Cyrus Loomis' battery, was standing idle. He rode over and ordered that the big guns open fire. Loomis resisted, he said that McCook had ordered him to "reserve what ammunition he had for close work." Rousseau pointed at the approaching enemy and shouted that they were "close enough and would be closer in a moment." Loomis was persuaded and opened fire "with alacrity and fearful effect," Rousseau said. Still, the enemy was determined and kept advancing. Soon, the roar of the cannons was joined by the flat crack of musketry.[12]

Rousseau, still on horseback, rode along the firing line and shouted, "My brave boys, I know you will never desert me in the day and hour of danger." The great Civil War writer Bruce Catton believed that these battlefield declarations were often improved upon after the fact, and that might be the case with Rousseau's "My brave boys" speech, but this is how it was remembered. Whatever his words might have been, George Landrum of the 2nd Ohio noticed the inspiration of Rousseau's physical presence at this moment. He remembered the General as "perfectly fearless, his countenance all aglow." He also thought that the Rebels were making a special target of Rousseau and were trying to shoot him off his horse "but he escaped without a scratch." Correspondent Shanks also commented about Rousseau's conspicuous presence on the battlefield. He wrote, "It was alluded to by rebel officers who had witnessed it, and who stated to our prisoners taken during the day that they frequently saw and recognized Rousseau riding up and down the line during the battle."[13]

Four hundred yards away, General Charles Gilbert held his Third Corps men in position. Some of his division commanders saw that Rousseau was being roughly handled and begged to be allowed to march into the fight, but Gilbert was reluctant to commit. Finally, a little after 5:00 P.M., Gilbert sent some help — a brigade and one artillery unit — to reinforce Rousseau, who certainly had need of them. Rousseau later wrote, "The brigade moved directly into the fight like true soldiers, opened a terrific fire, and drove back the enemy. It was a gallant body of men." He regretted that he did not know who commanded the brigade — but history knows. It was Colonel Michael Gooding, who was wounded in the late day fighting.[14]

Gooding's 30th Brigade were men from Illinois and Indiana, except for the artillery gunners, who were from Wisconsin. With these reinforcements coming on line, Rousseau's infantrymen began to retire. The attacking Rebels must have noticed the change in the defenders, but these were tough Mississippi and Alabama men and even though they, too, had had a long and exhausting afternoon, they kept trying to dislodge the Yankees around the Russell House. In the end, the Southerners did not have the muscle to drive

Gooding's men away, but it was a close thing. The Rebels were only yards away when the Yankees stopped them and drove them back down the ridge. The sun was on the western horizon, and the fight was winding down. The rising moon was so bright that some fighting continued even after night fell, but aside from that, the Battle of Perryville was done.

Regarding the night of October 8, Rousseau later testified, "The right of my line had fallen back some distance; the line, in fact, was turned, pressed back; the left fell back perhaps two hundred or three hundred yards, the center more, to about the original line of battle selected that morning. The enemy, it is true, were near us; their cavalry were within two hundred or three hundred yards of our pickets, but we had a front to the enemy, and were ready to renew the fight had there been any effort to drive us from our position. The artillery on the left fired guns, under my immediate orders, till after dark, and the infantry was there to support the guns."[15]

It had been a strange day. Buell, lying injured at the Dorsey House, had no idea until about 4:00 P.M. that a battle was going on. The unfortunate Jackson's and Rousseau's divisions of McCook's corps were practically fighting Bragg's whole Rebel army alone, while Gilbert's corps, except for Philip Sheridan's division, sat unengaged within sight of the contest. Over on the Lebanon Pike, on the far right of the Federal line, General Crittenden's corps remained in position all day, skirmishing a little with Joseph Wheeler's Rebel horsemen, but otherwise nearly as unengaged as Gilbert's corps. Now, in the moonlight, the Rebel and Yankee pickets, men who had tried with primordial fury to kill each other all day, sat only forty yards apart from each other, talking as if they were friends from adjoining farms chatting across the boundary fence. Of course, some friends were absent from the scene and would never chat with anyone again. Harris' brigade of Rousseau's division had lost 591 men that day; Lytle had lost 822 men, and Starkweather's losses totaled 756 — an aggregate of 2,169 men out of McCook's total loss of 3,400. Until now, Shiloh had been the benchmark against which all battles were compared, but Rousseau later remarked that the battle at Pittsburg Landing did not compare to the fury of the fighting at Perryville. General McCook agreed. He called Perryville "the bloodiest battle of modern times for the number of troops engaged on our side." General Buell alone could not seem to grasp how hard a fight his First Corps had gone through at Perryville. Rousseau recalled, "I thought it had been an exceedingly hard [battle], but the general was pretty cool about it.... It was very clear to my mind, from all that occurred between General Buell and myself, that he did not fully appreciate the fight we had had, though as the news came in from various persons he learned the true state of affairs."[16]

His mind awake at last to what had happened that day, Buell began planning an attack for 6:00 the next morning.

* * *

That night, around the campfires, the soldiers reviewed the day. As had become habitual, they ripped Buell for his performance, or, more accurately, his lack of performance. They condemned him for not throwing Gilbert's and Crittenden's corps into the battle. The old talk of Buell as traitor was revived.

In some regiments, the men did not spend their time remonstrating their absent general. They organized prayer services, while others formed burial parties. They went back out on the killing ground to locate and bury their dead comrades. A good many wounded were still on the field where they had fallen and their cries were so pitiful that both blue and gray commented on how unnerving it was to hear them. The burial parties had to be careful because Rebel soldiers were also roaming the battlefield, stripping the Union dead and taking their superior weapons.

Locating their day's position on the field, some survivors would go to work with their shovels and picks and dig a trench while others collected the bodies to be interred. The burial trench of the 79th Pennsylvania, one of the old Camp Nevin regiments, was three hundred feet long. Digging graves was hard work for tired men, but they could feel proud of themselves for doing it, especially the next morning when they saw that free-ranging hogs had been on the battlefield overnight, feasting on the unburied. That was only one vignette in a whole festival of grisly scenes.

Inching forward across the battlefield on the morning of October 9, the men were shocked at the appearance of the dead men and, worse, the parts of dead men. In life, these now unrecognizable boys had loved and hated, some had prayed and some had cursed, educated and ignorant, crude and refined; it made no difference now — they were all the same.

The scenes at the hospitals around Perryville were unlike anything most of the men had ever seen before. Every barn and dwelling house became a surgical theater, but the numbers were overwhelming and the doctors could not begin to keep pace. The wounded lay in neat rows in the yards outside, moaning and crying, or lying still with unnatural serenity. The men who lived to be taken inside came back out lesser men, physically, than they had been. Rather than treat the ragged bullet wound in an arm or a leg, the surgeon would amputate, an operation that took only fifteen minutes. Time was essential; men were dying outside. The amputated extremities were gathered up and stacked along the fences bordering the yard like a load of carelessly dumped firewood.

(Rousseau's surgeons had chosen the Wilkerson House northwest of the crossroads as their hospital. They believed they were safe so far back, but during the late-day fight around the Russell House, shells began to scream overhead. The surgeons worked on during the battle and through the night, determined, though distraught at the increasing volume of work piling up outside.)

One thing the men did not see on the morning of October 9 was Braxton Bragg and his grayback army. Bragg had used up 20 percent of his army and realized now that he had fought only one Federal corps — there were two fresh ones nearby. Small wonder that he began pulling out during the night.

Buell's Federals did not travel far on the 9th. They probed ahead only far enough to confirm that the Rebels were gone. The chase after Bragg did not really begin until October 10. This was the same day, incidentally, that Braxton Bragg and Edmund Kirby Smith finally effected their junction at Harrodsburg. Crittenden's Second Corps led the chase, and over the next few days, they fought several sharp skirmishes with the retreating Confederates. Joseph Wheeler's cavalry did a masterful job of delaying the Yankees while the Southern infantry and rolling stock got further and further out of reach. At London, General Buell called off the chase.

Gilbert's corps and that of McCook did not leave the vicinity of Perryville until October 12. For McCook, the chase after the fleeing Rebels ended in Lincoln County. One would like to know what thoughts were in Lovell Harrison Rousseau's mind as he saw once more Stanford, Crab Orchard, and even, perhaps, the old Rousseau farm that had been lost to the family so many years ago. He had a couple of days to look Lincoln County over. Then the corps was ordered to return to Danville.

Braxton Bragg escaped through Cumberland Gap and proceeded to East Tennessee. The War Department wanted Buell to follow Bragg into the mountains, to Knoxville, or even to Chattanooga, but Buell refused, explaining why it was impractical to continue. The Kentucky Campaign was finished.

As it happened, so was General Buell.

11

The Battle of Stones River

After the Battle of Perryville, General Buell recommended Brigadier General Rousseau's promotion "for distinguished gallantry and good service." Rousseau received his second star and was now Major General Rousseau; his promotion dated from October 8, the day of the battle. It was a final act of grace and gratitude from Buell toward Rousseau, for as Rousseau's fortunes rose, those of General Buell fell, never to rise again.[1]

Once before and not too long ago, the Lincoln administration had wanted to replace Buell. In September, while the Army of the Ohio was still in Louisville, orders came to General George H. Thomas to assume command. Thomas was as ambitious as any other general, but he also had a large portion of patriotism and he realized that this was not the time for a change of generals, not on the eve of the move against Bragg. He explained to Washington his reasons for declining the opportunity to lead the Army of the Ohio and Buell was reprieved, given a final chance to prove himself a leader. His poor, nearly non-existent, leadership at Perryville did nothing to endear him to the War Department and his refusal to continue after Bragg into Tennessee was a convincing reason to remove him from command, at last.

The natural choice to succeed him was George H. Thomas, considering that he had been offered the job only weeks before, but Thomas' earlier refusal, no matter how well-intentioned, had insulted the administration a little and he was passed over. "Let the Virginian wait," Lincoln is said to have remarked. Instead, command of the army went to General William Starke Rosecrans.[2]

Don Carlos Buell was not allowed to exit quietly, however. The government felt that the general's 1862 performance was so marginal as to warrant an investigation. The Buell Commission, as it was called, took the testimony of no fewer than seventy-two witnesses between November 1862 and May 1863. The commission found that there was no merit to the most serious accusations (including disloyalty) and preferred no charges, but did find that: (1) Buell delayed too long in pursuing Bragg north. He should have attacked before the Rebels crossed the Cumberland River, where, the commission believed, Bragg could have been defeated. (2) Buell could not be held responsible for the Confederate capture of Munfordville, except that he should have attacked south of the Cumberland, which would have prevented it. (3) Buell failed to order support for McCook's corps while it was under attack at Perryville and Crittenden should have been ordered to attack Bragg's line of retreat. (4) Buell was too slow in pursuing Bragg, which allowed him to escape. The commission did admit, though, that the Rebels had not escaped "without loss." Many had been killed, many more were wounded, and the Rebels had been compelled to destroy quantities of stores rather than haul them along on the retreat.[3]

One of the most important findings of the commission blunted the commonly held and widely shouted criticism of General Buell's policy toward the Southern civilians in the areas where the Army of the Ohio operated. The commission stated, "This we find to have been what is familiarly known as the conciliatory policy. Whether good or bad in its effects, General Buell deserves neither blame nor applause for it, because it was at that time *understood to be the policy of the Government*" [italics author's].[4]

Lovell Harrison Rousseau testified before the commission for three days beginning on January 20, 1863. Before that, there was yet another battle to fight.

* * *

Major General William S. Rosecrans liked to go around with an unlit cigar in his teeth, wearing an ordinary blue overcoat and a misshapen old hat. He was forty-three years old, an energetic and often impatient perfectionist, ate his meals on horseback, and cursed like an infidel, though he was a convert to Catholicism and was often seen with a rosary twined in his fingers. He had a reputation for intellect, and his mind, though restless, was analytical.

Rosecrans knew that he must quickly make his mark. All traces of the discredited General Buell had to be sponged out, even including the name of the army. Now, it was known as the 14th Army Corps, the Army of the Cumberland.

He moved the army to Bowling Green and began reorganizing his army into three wings. On November 5, 1862, General Orders No. 8 announced the new configuration: The Right Wing was under Major General Alexander McDowell McCook. The Center Wing was under stoic and reliable Major General George H. Thomas. The Left Wing was under Major General Thomas L. Crittenden, a thin, goateed man who looked more like he belonged around Arthur's Round Table than in the modern service. A separate order created a new Cavalry Corps and Brigadier General David S. Stanley was assigned to command it.

Rousseau was assigned to command the 1st Division in George Thomas' Center Wing, an aggregate of 6,160 men. In his division were the 1st Brigade, commanded by his old Mexican War friend, Colonel Benjamin F. Scribner; the 2nd Brigade, commanded by Colonel John Beatty; the 3rd Brigade, commanded by Colonel John C. Starkweather, who had performed so well at Perryville; and the 4th Brigade, a unit of U.S. Regulars led by Lieutenant Colonel Oliver L. Shepherd. There were also Battery A, Kentucky Artillery; Battery H, U.S. Artillery; and Battery A, 1st Michigan Artillery. Finally, there were six companies of the 2nd Kentucky Cavalry.

Rousseau was ordered to advance his division to Edgefield, Tennessee, on November 13. At about this time, it appears that Rousseau considered giving up his field command in the newly organized army and seems to have spoken to Rosecrans about a different sort of assignment. Rosecrans thought that Rousseau's reasons for wanting rear-echelon duty were legitimate. The commanding general wrote to his superiors on November 20, "I will give you [Rousseau] for Louisville, if you will send [Jeremiah] Boyle to Bowling Green. Reason: Rousseau has a predisposition to that species of croup of which Washington died and fears a winter camp. I would give him Nashville, but think he will suit Louisville better."[5]

Whether it was Rosecrans or Rousseau who changed his mind, the Kentuckian remained in the field and in command of the 1st Division and there was no more talk of assigning him to Louisville. On November 22, he was ordered to proceed into Nashville with two of his brigades. The remainder were to guard the Mitchellsville Depot and patrol the railroad between there and Edgefield.

One of Rosecrans' innovations as the new general of the Army of the Cumberland was meant to be a corrective to Buell's crippling failure to adequately guard his railroad supply lines. Rosecrans developed the idea of an expanded system of blockhouses at all the vital points along his main supply line—the L&N Railroad—and posting garrisons to man them. It would necessitate leaving a lot of men in the rear areas, but the Union *had* a lot of men, and their presence behind the lines would help guarantee that the soldiers at the front were well-supplied and able to campaign against the enemy. The Cumberland River was still too low from the drought to allow steam transports to reach Nashville, so the railroad from the North took on an even greater importance. Until the recent damage to the L&N was repaired and a build up of the supply depot at Nashville was achieved, an advance south was out of the question.

In addition to reorganizing the army and overseeing the restoration of rail service, Rosecrans modernized the artillery and worked to achieve a uniformity of weapons. The man's energy was inexhaustible. Between the long stints of tedious office work, Rosecrans liked to get out among the men. He endeared himself to the soldiers by his genuine concern for their well-being. Often, they would see Rosecrans riding through their camps, smiling and speaking with encouragement to those who came forward to get a look at the new general. He saw to it that they were fed, clothed, armed, and paid. Many of the men had not seen a cent of pay in nine months. It would take a million dollars to pay them for their service through August 31, but Rosecrans got it for them, along with extra paymasters to help distribute it more quickly. How could the men not love such a general?

It all took time; too much time for an impatient Washington. Neither the civilian nor the military authorities shared the soldiers' admiration for Rosecrans' rehabilitation of the army. On December 4, a telegram arrived from the War Department: "The President is very impatient at your long stay in Nashville." If he did not move within the week, the telegram warned, he might be replaced.[6]

Rosecrans refused to be bullied and he did not move. In his reply to the War Department he said, "If my superiors have lost confidence in me, they had better at once put someone in my place.... To threats of removal or the like I must be permitted to say that I am insensible." Having put the white-tower men in Washington back in their place, Rosecrans went back to the job at hand. There was more work to be done before the army was fit for a campaign.[7]

* * *

While the commanding general attended to a thousand pressing details and deflected criticism from the War Department, his men were kept busy. Bragg's cavalrymen were slashing at Rosecrans from every direction. Nathan Bedford Forrest was raiding in West Tennessee, "Fighting Joe" Wheeler was attacking supply trains outside of Nashville, and John Hunt Morgan captured the entire 2,100 man garrison at Hartsville, Tennessee. Morgan was a particular headache, because he chose as his special target the L&N Railroad. In late November the twin tunnels at Gallatin reopened and trains were again able to reach Nashville, but the situation was quickly reversed. Morgan went on his celebrated Christmas Raid in central Kentucky and destroyed the L&N bridges at Bacon Creek and Nolin and, later, both of the great trestles at Muldraugh Hill.

During this period, Rousseau's men were frequently ordered out to do reconnaissance and also to support the patrols of other units. They seem to have spent a considerable amount of time guarding shipments of flour to Nashville from Spring Hill, a mundane duty in ordinary times, but not so mundane when Wheeler, Forrest, and Morgan might spring out of ambush anywhere along the route.

With Confederate cavalry swirling all around him, Rosecrans could have been excused at feeling a sense of hopelessness. Instead, he perceived an opportunity. Now was the time to take the offensive, while the enemy horsemen were away from the main Rebel camp at Murfreesboro, leaving Bragg blind by their absence. Rosecrans called a council of war on Christmas night and excitedly told his generals, "We move tomorrow, gentlemen.... Strike hard and fast! Give them no rest! Fight, I say!"[8]

* * *

The move to Murfreesboro commenced in the rain. General Thomas, though leading the Center Wing, was not in the center of the Federal advance. Instead, he was situated on the far right (west), moving south along the Franklin Pike. McCook's Wing, on the Nolensville Pike, was in the center, and Crittenden's was on the left (east) flank moving down the Murfreesboro Pike. The roads looked like a chicken's foot pointing down, each road representing a toe, spreading farther apart as they moved south. Nearing the end, Thomas and McCook would have to veer sharply east to get to their proper positions at Murfreesboro.

Rousseau's division of Thomas' Wing moved out about 7:00 A.M. on December 26 and marched unopposed to Owen's Store, where the men bivouacked. Next morning, they headed for Nolensville, shifting over to the Wilson Pike near Brentwood. The roads were dreadful and Peter Cozzens, in his excellent study of the Stones River Campaign, *No Better Place to Die*, wrote that Rousseau struggled along "with cannon and limbers frequently mired up to the hubs." Lieutenant Alfred Pirtle, now serving as Rousseau's chief of ordnance, wrote to his mother, "Well you can imagine what a sweet condition the road was in after fifteen regiments, four batteries, and a great many wagons had passed over it, during a tremendous rain that fell this morning, making every pool a mud hole." The march was long in time, if not especially so in miles, and it was dark before the 1st Division could set up camp.[9]

Rousseau was suffering his usual winter ailment during the march, for Pirtle also said in his December 27 letter, "General Rousseau caught a severe cold this week before we left Nashville and the wetting he got today has made him quite hoarse, but he is not complaining much."[10]

The next day, December 28, was Sunday and Rosecran's religious scruples prevented much forward movement during the day. The general was almost as fanatical about the sanctity of Sunday as Stonewall Jackson. General Bragg at Murfreesboro was thus given precious time to prepare and many boys in blue would die on account of Rosecrans' righteousness. But, for now, the tired and muddy men in the ranks enjoyed the chance to rest.

That night, however, the general received intelligence that Hardee's powerful corps had joined Bragg at Murfreesboro. The Rebels were gathering for a fight and Rosecrans could not afford to let them grow too strong before he arrived to give them one. The order came down to break camp. Rousseau's division took to the road about dusk, heading east on the Old Liberty Road to support Crittenden's Wing. The night was foggy and wet and the muddy road was bottomless. The various units became intermingled and men started to straggle. At midnight, when the sky began to clear, the temperature dropped and increased the suffering of the cold, tired men. They reached Stewart's Creek about dawn on the 29th and rested in camp all day before moving out again the next morning.

About 4:00 P.M., on December 30, the 1st Division arrived at Murfreesboro. Most of the other regiments and divisions of all the wings had already arrived and Rousseau was told to make his camp in some woods about a mile behind the front line, near General Rosecrans' headquarters.

Rousseau had only three of his brigades with him: Scribner's 1st, Beatty's 2nd, and Shepherd's 4th. Colonel John C. Starkweather's 3rd brigade had been farther back with its wagon train when it was attacked by Joseph Wheeler. Starkweather, with the help of the 2nd Kentucky Cavalry, drove the Rebels back after a fight of several hours' duration, losing twenty wagons. Starkweather went into camp about six miles from Murfreesboro, near Jefferson, and was isolated there when the enemy burned the only bridge. Starkweather reported the day's events and estimated that a force numbering three hundred opposed him — consequently, General Thomas ordered him to join his division when relieved, "but on no account to leave unless relieved." So, Starkweather stayed put and missed the fight that began the next morning.[11]

If Rousseau could have seen the Federal line in panorama, he would have seen that General McCook's Wing was on the Union right. His extreme flank was anchored on the Franklin Pike, where Brigadier General Richard W. Johnson's division was placed. Proceeding toward the northeast, McCook's other divisions were Jefferson C. Davis, the murderer of William Nelson, and Philip Sheridan. Next to McCook's Wing was General Thomas' in the center. Thomas' divisions were scattered on detached duty and he had only two at Murfreesboro, James Negley, who was next in line to Sheridan, and Rousseau, who was behind, held in reserve. The Union left flank was held by Thomas L. Crittenden's Wing. His divisions, in order, were John Palmer, Thomas J. Wood, and Horatio Van Cleve. Crittenden's sector of the line was bisected by the Nashville Turnpike, the Nashville & Chattanooga Railroad, and Stones River.

11. The Battle of Stones River

The whole line was oriented southwest to northeast and was facing southeast.

Rosecrans, thinking about the Rebel army that stood across the river, with Murfreesboro at its back, developed a simple plan. Crittenden, on the left, would cross Stones River with his entire wing and envelope the Confederate right flank. As the Rebel line began to fold up, Thomas' men would move into action — a great wheel to the right, pivoting on McCook's Wing on the south. McCook would pin down the CSA left until Crittenden completed his arc. The Rebels would be swept away by the Army of the Cumberland attacking in echelon, then the Yankee divisions would march into Murfreesboro together and occupy the comfortable town for the winter. Simple as that. It would all begin at sunrise on the last day of 1862.

The night before the shooting battle was to begin, there was a musical battle of the bands, with those in blue playing their favorites, alternating with those in gray playing theirs. The finale was both bands joining for a poignant rendition of "Home, Sweet Home." Tomorrow, for many of these boys, the hope of home would be lost forever.

Late that night, there was a sound other than the fading notes of sentimental songs that worried Philip Sheridan. The faint clatter and rattle coming from across the way convinced him that the Rebels were on the move. He tried to warn General McCook, who did not share Sheridan's concerns. It was a strangely nonchalant attitude from the man whose corps had been chewed up so badly at Perryville. Sheridan, though, was sure of what he was hearing. Still, if McCook would not take defensive action, there was little that Sheridan the subordinate could do for the other commanders in the Right Wing. But, he could do something about his own division. He ordered his men up — the infantry regiments in line, the artillery crews gathered around their pieces, and his one company of the 2nd Kentucky Cavalry ready to mount up — at 4:00 A.M. Then, Sheridan walked along the line to make sure that everyone was just where he wanted them. Sheridan was ready.

And Sheridan was right. At dawn, the Rebels crashed into the army's right flank and Johnson's division evaporated. In the opening minutes of the fight, the Louisville communist Brigadier General August Willich was wounded and captured and his brigade scattered. Another officer from the Camp Nevin days, Brigadier General Edward N. Kirk, was mortally wounded. His brigade, too, was hurled toward the rear. The Rebels moved en echelon to Davis' division. Bragg had developed the same plan of attack as Rosecrans, to attack the enemy right. The only difference was that Bragg had struck first and now the Army of the Cumberland was not attacking en echelon, but rather *collapsing* en echelon.

While the fight was raging on McCook's front, John Wharton's brigade of Confederate cavalry rode around the flank to gain a position behind the Federals. Wharton did some damage back there. He threatened McCook's ammunition train and forced it to withdraw and he captured an artillery battery and a field hospital. Surgeon A. J. Phelps remembered that the Rebel cavalrymen "even despoiled some of our medical officers of their personal property." The Confederates also tried to swing around the Union left flank where they could cross Stones River and get in the Federal rear from that direction, as well. But, in this attempt, they failed. When the fight began, Rousseau advanced a half-mile from his camp and, though in reserve, had taken the initiative to send his companies of the 2nd Kentucky Cavalry back to the left and rear of the Federal line to guard the fords on Stones River. The Confederates made some attempts to gain a crossing of the river, but they never achieved their goal. The 2nd Kentucky Cavalry prevented it.[12]

Back on the front line, Jefferson C. Davis' collapse was nearly as quick as Richard W. Johnson's had been. That left only Sheridan of McCook's Wing. Within thirty minutes of the opening guns, Little Phil was in a desperate fight, but *his* men were ready to absorb the shock.

The Rebels hammered at Sheridan for three hours, trying to flank him. To counter them, the young brigadier repeatedly refused his line, bending it back until it was at right angles to its original position. Sheridan was on the flank now; the survivors of McCook's two other divisions were far in the rear. General George H. Thomas was among them, coolly trying to establish a new line along the Nashville Turnpike and the Nashville & Chattanooga Railroad. This position must be held or the army would lose its connections to Nashville. While he organized the defense, Thomas took a moment to order General Rousseau to move forward across a cotton field and take position alongside Sheridan. Rousseau rode in front of his men and shouted, "Old Rousseau is here and he intends to stay!" as they moved forward.[13]

Privately, Rousseau did not feel so confident. He later said, "I knew it was hell in there before I got in, but I was convinced of it when I saw Phil Sheridan with hat in one hand and sword in the other, fighting as if he were the devil incarnate."[14]

As Rousseau's men formed a ragged line in a cedar thicket, Jefferson C. Davis' defeated men streamed through them, heading for the rear. Rousseau deployed his infantry lines as well as he could in this tiny scrubland of rock slabs and cedar trees, but his field pieces could not find a place in this boulder-studded thicket. Rousseau rode back accompanied by a single sergeant to begin placing his artillery (with the help of his chief of ordnance, Lieutenant Pirtle) and, at the same time, to search for a spot to which he could retreat, for he believed that his men would not be able to hold the vulnerable position they had been assigned. By the time he rejoined his men in the cedar brake, the fight was on. His men repulsed the first enemy assault, but the Confederates reformed and tried again and the fighting raged. It wasn't long before they were all alone — Sheridan's men were running out of ammunition. They were calling for more, but there was no more — Wharton had forced back McCook's supply train. When they were down to three cartridges apiece, about 11:00 A.M., Sheridan had to withdraw. Sheridan's retrograde movement left a gap between Rousseau's left flank and the right flank of the next adjoining division, that of James Negley. The Rebels charged toward this gap and Rousseau had to fall back, but he did so in good order: Colonel Shepherd, who had lost a third of his men retreated first, and then Colonel Scribner, falling back out of the woods and across the cotton field to where the big guns were. The openness of the cotton field made the retreating men an easy target. A Regular said of the Rebels, "On they came pouring voley after voley into our ranks," but the men remained scrappy. Whole companies stopped to turn and return small arms fire at the enemy; others helped the musicians who had come out to carry off the wounded.[15]

Meanwhile, Beatty's 2nd Brigade was still in the thicket, partly because they could not see any distance at all in the smoke-filled cedars and partly because Beatty did not receive the order to retire. After a while, Beatty noticed that there was no firing on either of his flanks. He sent men out to see what was going on and they came back to report that the 2nd Brigade was fighting the Confederates single-handedly. Beatty began to withdraw and this encouraged the Rebels who hit him hard. The 2nd Brigade men broke out of the woods into the field. Beatty's horse was killed. He could not rally his men, so he joined them as they hurried toward the others, who had gathered near the artillery at the turnpike.

In a bit, the Confederates began emerging from the woods, a patchwork line of gray, butternut, and captured blue uniforms led by a sword-wielding officer. They were running and yelling as they came across the cotton field, but there was almost no shooting. When the charging Confederates were close enough, the artillery pieces that Rousseau and Lieutenant Pirtle had placed between the turnpike and the railroad opened up on them and some Union regiments on the edge of the field added their musket fire. Major Cyrus Loomis ordered his gunners to "give them double-shotted canister as hot as hell will let you!" Lieutenant Pirtle later said, "I never saw guns served on trial drill as fast as those were now." And the Rebels were sent reeling back into the cedar trees.[16]

Like Rousseau, Brigadier General James S. Negley, commander of General Thomas' 2nd Division, had also been put in a hard position when Sheridan pulled back. He found himself fighting on his front, left, and right and had to withdraw. He joined Rousseau in the fall-back position south of the Nashville Turnpike. The Regulars advanced again into the cedars to buy time for the new defensive line to form. Rousseau, temporarily leading two of Negley's regiments, came up to join them, but the Rebels were too strong and soon they all had to retreat.

When Negley withdrew, the focus of the main Rebel attack fell on Brigadier General John Palmer's division, and more particularly, the brigade of Colonel William B. Hazen, whose brilliant last stand defense at the Round Forest on this day would become a Civil War legend. The Union line now resembled a huge letter C with the opening to the northeast. Hazen's Round Forest was nestled in the lower curve of the C and Bragg kept trying to break him. Hazen repulsed two attacks. Bragg called over fresh troops from the Rebel right and threw them at Hazen, but the Yankee colonel had some fight left and he repulsed them, too, not once, but twice. Hazen had a horse shot from beneath him and his shoulder was nicked by a nearly spent rifle ball, but he held on and kept his men fighting. The loss of life was grievous, but worse for the Rebels.

Twilight, which came about 4:30 P.M. on this short winter's day, finally brought the fighting to an end.

The evidence of the day's slaughter was all around. One eyewitness was affected by the sight of so many dead horses and noticed that three had been killed by a single shell, their bodies shredded and intermingled in one gruesome pile. Dead men were everywhere on the battlefield and wounded men who tried to get up found that they were frozen to the ground by their own blood in this frigid night.

It was not just enlisted men. Sheridan had lost all three of his brigade commanders. Even General Rosecrans' aide, Colonel Julius P. Garesché, was killed. A solid shot smashed into his head and then he had no head from the jaw up. His atomized brains and blood showered all over Rosecrans, giving the commanding general the appearance of having suffered a devastating wound. "Oh, no," Rosecrans explained, "that is just the blood of poor Garesché."[17]

Rosecrans had been on the field all day. Early in the morning, he was with Crittenden, whose attack from the left flank would soon begin, surprising the Confederates at their breakfast. When the sound of firing came from the right, Rosecrans misinterpreted it and believed that McCook had begun his assignment of holding down the Confederate left. It was soon obvious that the increasing sounds of battle from McCook's front were something more serious. Rosecrans rode over, and found himself in a maelstrom. He spent the rest of the day barking out orders, throwing fresh troops into the weak spots in his lines, troubleshooting wherever reports of impending doom reached him. All the while, he chomped down on the cold stub of a cigar stuck in his teeth. Those who stayed near him heard the general repeatedly muttering, "This battle must be won."[18]

That night, Rosecrans called in his generals for a council of war. There were not enough chairs, so the generals in their overcoats and capes sat on the floor of the cabin, except for Rosecrans, who sat on a stool. McCook began by complaining about the death of two of his horses — a remarkably inappropriate gripe to make in the midst of such human carnage.

Everyone knew it had been a hard day; ten thousand casualties, nearly thirty artillery pieces lost, 150 wagons lost, and all those horses. After a day of such shocking loss, the question was a simple one — should the army stay or withdraw? There was a division of opinion among the generals. McCook and Stanley the cavalry commander advised retreat. Thomas and Crittenden spoke up for remaining. Bragg had not retreated; they should continue the fight. Sheridan agreed. More importantly, the commanding general agreed and so it was decided. The Battle of Stones River was not over.

Rosecrans had ordered that no fires be built, but that night, as the generals sat inside drinking whiskey to fight off the cold, cavalrymen rode over the battlefield with torches to light campfires for the shivering infantrymen. They had with them nothing more than corn and probably hardtack to eat, but General Rousseau related that "some of them ate horsesteaks, cut and broiled, from the horses upon the battlefield."[19]

Behind the scenes, the surgeons were once again working as fast as they could. Rousseau's division was lucky to have Dr. Charles S. Muscroft in charge. Of him, Rousseau said, "The wounded were kindly and tenderly cared for by the Third Division medical director, Surgeon Muscroft, and the other surgeons of the command." Ebenezer Swift, Medical Director for the Army of the Cumberland, was a more objective judge, but he agreed with Rousseau's evaluation, saying that Muscroft "established a hospital in the rear and accommodated completely a large number of wounded. Many of the serious cases are in an advanced state of recovery. His zeal, skill, and industry are commendable."[20]

New Year's Day 1863 was a cold, cloudy day. There was an occasional infantry foray and some artillery fire, but the cavalry had a good watch over the flanks, so there were no surprises. Bragg was nonplussed that the Federals had not pulled back, but he would not make an assault. Rosecrans was content to tighten his lines and strengthen them with the few reinforcements that arrived and to wait and see what Bragg would do.

What Bragg decided to do was launch a late-day attack on January 2, so late that the Yankees would not have time to respond before the intended gains were made. General John C. Breckinridge, a Kentuckian who had grown up in Lexington's elite, was to chase the bluecoats off of a hill on the east side of Stones River because from there the Federal guns could rake the Rebel right flank. Breckinridge observed that, while making the attack, his own men would suffer enfilading fire from the batteries under Captain John Mendenhall across Stones River on the West. But, Bragg insisted.

Breckinridge was so infuriated at the order to make this suicidal charge that he wanted to kill Bragg. Talked out of that, the former U.S. vice president decided to join his men in the attack he was sure would fail.

At 4:00 P.M., with less than an hour of daylight left, Breckinridge's five brigades plunged forward. The general was behind the center of his second line. Mounted on horseback, he made the most conspicuous target of all. Breckinridge may have come from a different social class than Rousseau, but the two men shared some characteristics, courage foremost among them.

The Confederates surged on. They chased the Yankee defenders off of and over the crest of the hill and down the backside where they ran straight into the range of Mendenhall's batteries. The Federal field pieces were tightly arrayed and loaded with double canister. They pumped one hundred rounds a minute into the Confederate lines and continued to fire as the CSA survivors turned to flee. This may have been the most concentrated and deadly artillery barrage of the entire war in the Western Theater. Certainly, the effects support that point of view. The outcome of the fight on January 2 was just as Breckinridge had expected. The field across which his men had charged looked as if it was studded with bloody gray boulders; 1,700 dead Confederates, one-third of Breckinridge's men, lay dead. Only forty-five minutes had passed.

Rousseau's division had played no role in the fight against Breckinridge, but a portion of his men were in another little fight on the evening of January 3. Some CSA sharpshooters were making a nuisance of themselves from their position in a patch of woods near one of the fords on Stones River. General Rousseau and General Thomas asked Rosecrans for permission to attack them. General Rosecrans agreed and assigned two of Rousseau's regiments to go in with the 85th Illinois under Daniel McCook and a brigade of Tennesseans under Brigadier General James G. Spears. As Rousseau reported it:

> Just before night I directed the batteries of Guenther and Loomis to shell the woods with six rounds per gun, fired as rapidly as possible. This was very handsomely done, and ended just at dusk, when the Third Ohio Regiment, Lieut. Col. O. A. Lawson, and the Eighty-eighth Indiana, Col.

George Humphrey, both under command of the brigade commander, Col. John Beatty, moved promptly up the woods. When near the woods they received a heavy fire from the enemy, but returned it vigorously, and gallantly pressed forward. On reaching the woods a fresh body of the enemy, attracted by the fire, moved up on their left to support them. On that body of the enemy Loomis' battery opened up with shell. The fusillade was very rapid, and continued for, perhaps, three-quarters of an hour, when Beatty's command drove the enemy at the point of the bayonet and held the woods. It turned out that the enemy was posted behind a stone breast-work in the woods, and when ousted, about 30 men were taken prisoners behind the works. This ended the battle of Murfreesborough.[21]

The next morning, General David Stanley's cavalry reconnoitered and discovered that Bragg was gone from the Federal front. The grizzled old North Carolinian *could* sneak away — he had done it at Perryville and now he had slipped the noose again. Gathering his horsemen, Stanley moved down to the fords across Stones River and waited for orders to cross. On January 5, General Thomas's Center Wing, the Army of the Cumberland, marched into Murfreesboro.

12

The Tullahoma Campaign

The Battle of Stones River had cost the Federals 8,778 in killed and wounded, plus another 2,800 captured, according to General Rosecrans' report. But the Confederates had suffered worse. The Yankees had killed 1,279 of Braxton Bragg's soldiers and wounded 7,969. The retreating Southerners had left three thousand of this latter group in Murfreesboro. The town was crowded with them, so the Army of the Cumberland passed on through and made their camp south of town.

Rousseau's reputation among his men was only enhanced by his performance during the battle. Pirtle wrote enthusiastically (and possibly with some exaggeration) to his father on January 3, "General Rousseau has covered himself with glory again, for all agree that the 3rd Division [sic] turned the fortunes of the day on the 31st when all seemed to be lost. At that time I was riding by the General's side and he was as cool as if on Review and inspired his men with the same feeling, rallied the Regulars for a desperate charge, which was successful and threw the enemy into confusion, producing a lull in the engagement which gave General Rosecrans time to reconstruct his line and form a new line of battle."[1]

On January 7, Rousseau had the officers of Shepherd's brigade at his headquarters for a small soirée. He was grateful to them for their performance at the battle of December 31. Lieutenant Arthur B. Carpenter, 1st Battalion, 19th U.S. Infantry, wrote, "He shook hands with us all and chatted as familiar as could be. He is a splendid man." It was a bravura performance on the part of the host, for he was not well. He still had not recovered from the winter cold he contracted before the army left Nashville and, in fact, left camp the next day for home where he hoped to recover before appearing at the Buell Commission. The General's testimony was scheduled to begin in Louisville on January 20. Pirtle was afraid that he would never return.[2]

As Rousseau departed for Louisville, he may have crossed paths with Brigadier General James A. Garfield from Ohio, who was one of many officers who were coming to Murfreesboro to take the place of those who were killed.

Garfield came to take command of a brigade, but ended up with a more conspicuous position as Rosecrans' chief of staff, replacing the unfortunate, decapitated Garesché.

* * *

The Buell Commission questioned Rousseau on a wide range of subjects over the three days he was on the witness stand. There was nothing very explosive in what he said about General Buell. His most critical observation was that Buell did not seem to understand on the night of October 8 how severe the Battle of Perryville had been. "I told the general about the fight. I thought it had been an exceedingly hard one, but the general was pretty cool about it. I told him that I thought he did not appreciate the fight we had had, and that it was the hardest fight I have ever seen." In some accounts, Buell flared at the accusation that he did not comprehend what McCook and Rousseau had been through. Rousseau did not mention that Buell was angry, just that Buell insisted that he did, indeed, understand the intensity of the fight.[3]

Rousseau spoke of his estimate, at the time of the Kentucky Campaign, of the strength of Bragg's army—a pretty accurate tabulation of between 35,000 and 40,000. He spoke, too, of the good discipline in the Confederate army and the quality of the fighting men that Bragg led, "the best army for its numbers that I ever saw." He thought that the Rebels were "generally less intelligent than our own soldiers," but that their hatred of the Yankees gave them power.[4]

He said, "In attacking it seems almost impossible to repel the rebels; their dash is very hard to resist and I have rarely seen it resisted when their troops were fresh.... Individually, I think the rebel soldiers are generally superior to our own."[5]

Rousseau spoke in praise of Colonel John T. Wilder, the defender of Munfordville during Bragg's invasion. While at Bowling Green, when the news of the Munfordville fight arrived, Rousseau remembered "feeling a good deal of exultation and pride in Wilder for his spunk and confidence." Rousseau's memory was not clear about whether any of the people who brought news of the contest at Munfordville were actually sent by Wilder and testified that he had believed at the time that Wilder would not be attacked again after he repulsed Chalmers' attack. This is not in agreement with others' recollections of the news that came to Bowling Green from Wilder, but one can hardly fault Rousseau for not remembering every detail of the last six months; a great deal had happened in the meantime.[6]

Rousseau talked about the hard march across barren North Alabama and about the relations between the Federal soldiers and Southern civilians. The subject naturally came around to slaves. What Rousseau had to say on the subject was of special interest, for the Emancipation Proclamation had gone into effect on New Year's Day, only about three weeks before. It may also be that Rousseau's views on this subject had personal consequences later in the year.

Rousseau testified, in so many words, that his views agreed with General Buell's: as of 1862, slaves were still legal property under the Constitution; therefore, like other property of loyal Southerners, they should be left alone. If they ran away, they must be returned (under the same legal theory which held that a runaway horse should be returned to its rightful owner). Slaves might be temporarily conscripted to work on fortifications and as teamsters, but it was not proper to use them as servants in camp. It was not desirable to have slaves in camp at all, in fact, for they "consumed the supplies intended for the army." This same protection of slave property did not extend to secessionists, who had renounced their U.S. citizenship, who no longer benefited by its laws, and whose slaves, like Rebel property of any description, were subject to be taken.[7]

Rousseau also testified that he considered the military information provided by slaves as being of no value, "not of the least." It was either flatly untrue or so exaggerated as to be useless.[8]

His testimony concluded, Rousseau was excused. Presumably, he visited his wife and children, as well as his brothers and their families, a final time before leaving the city. Then, he rejoined his division at Murfreesboro.

* * *

The Federal encampment near Murfreesboro lasted six months. Before a new offensive could be considered, there was much work to do to repair the damages of Stones River on the Army of the Cumberland, and Rosecrans went about it deliberately.

Stones River had so decimated the number of officers serving under Rosecrans that the army had to be reorganized. The wing designation was discarded and corps used in its stead. As of May, Major General Thomas' Center Wing was called the XIV Corps. Rousseau commanded the 1st Division, which included the 1st Brigade, Colonel Benjamin F. Scribner; the 2nd Brigade, Colonel Henry A. Hambright; the 3rd Brigade, Brigadier General John H. King (these were the U.S. Regulars); and three batteries of artillery under Colonel Cyrus O. Loomis.

Earl J. Hess, in *Banners to the Breeze*, observed that the ordeal at Stones River had an effect on Rosecrans' personality, that he lost much of his optimism and self-confidence, that the battle "produced a more cautious and carping commander." Certainly, the general's behavior in the spring of 1863 could lead one to this conclusion. He bullyragged the Washington authorities constantly for more rifles and Colt's revolvers, more swords, more horses with "equipage," and more officers until he was finally admonished that he was burning up much of the goodwill that he had earned by defeating Bragg. Still, he fretted and continued to pester the War Department.[9]

The demand for more firearms was not purely a matter of numbers, but also of uniformity. There was a distressing variety of firearms within the same regiment. The 33rd Ohio, of Scribner's 1st Brigade in Rousseau's division, was armed with four different types of rifles, some of them so antiquated that they were smooth-bore conversions. The 1st Wisconsin in Hambright's 2nd Brigade was not much better, with three different types of rifles to use. The complications of such a system are obvious.

A project that seemed more eccentric than the attempt to make the firearms more consistent was the construction of Fortress Rosecrans, the largest earthen fort of the Civil War. The fortress was two hundred cleared acres surrounded by dirt walls and prickly with fifty cannon. The men labored in the mud all through the rainy winter and spring to build this behemoth, along with its two smaller brothers at Franklin and Triune.

Rosecrans was always forward thinking, and one of his innovations at the winter camp was to mount a brigade of infantrymen and to arm them with Spencer rifles, those wonderful repeaters with a bullet for each day of the week. This 1st Brigade of Major General Joseph J. Reynolds' 4th Division in the XIV Corps is known to history as the Lightning Brigade. It was led by Colonel John T. Wilder, whose stubborn defense of Munfordville in September 1862 so impressed Rousseau. In the campaign to come, the Lightning Brigade would prove its worth.

Wilder was paroled after his surrender at Munfordville and, properly exchanged, he had now rejoined the army. Other popular officers, like August Willich, who had been wounded and captured at Stones River, were also exchanged and began making their way back to the Army of the Cumberland.

The busiest branch of the army at Murfreesboro may well have been the cavalry. Though horses were in short supply, there were enough mounts for small patrols through Middle Tennessee. Rosecrans now had both the L&N Railroad and the Nashville & Chattanooga Railroad to protect. This was largely a job for cavalry. The mounted arm also had to protect the riverboats, for with the arrival of winter rains, the Cumberland River had risen enough for well-loaded steamers to proceed upstream and the Rebels were attacking them from shore. For the horse soldiers, it was a busy winter and spring. The biggest raid came during the third week in April when Colonel Eli Long of the 2nd Brigade, Stanley's Cavalry Corps, led a party of horsemen toward McMinnville. They destroyed sections and bridges of the McMinnville & Manchester Railroad, which was a Rebel supply line, and burned the railroad depot as well as some of the rolling stock. The raiding party captured 130 of the enemy and did not lose a single man in the doing. Hambright's brigade of Rousseau's division took part in another excursion, an eleven-day raid led by Major General Joseph J. Reynolds between Liberty and McMinnville in late April. It was a typically successful excursion in that it resulted in the destruction of cotton gins, grist mills, and stores of supplies useful to the enemy.

In a winter encampment of such long duration, the army naturally found some enjoyable diversions to relieve the work. Even the worried commanding general found recreation. Rosecrans' wife and daughter came to join him at Murfreesboro, but he did not neglect the need to maintain cordial relations with his officers and men. He played tenpins with Philip Sheridan and chess with Thomas L. Crittenden, and he hosted many visitors to camp. One of the most intriguing was the correspondent James R. Gilmore. Horace Greeley, editor of the *New York Tribune*, sent him down to query the general on the subject of the presidency. The question was: would Rosecrans consent to be a candidate in 1864? Rosecrans put an end to such talk. "My place is right here," he said. "The country gave me my education and so has a right to my military service, and it educated me for precisely this emergency. So this, and not the presidency, is my post of duty and I cannot, without violating my conscience, leave it." Besides, he had too high an opinion of the sitting chief executive. Rosecrans disagreed with the endless second guessing of Greeley and his reporter toward Father Abraham. He said, "You are mistaken about Mr. Lincoln. He is in the right place. I am in a position to know and if you live you will see that I am right about him"[10]

There were suggestions, too, that General Rosecrans might run for governor of Ohio, but he was not having any of it.

The men would have hated to lose Rosecrans to politics, for he remained very popular among them. He regularly inspected the many camps of his army at Murfreesboro, which was evidence of his concern for them and they loved him for it.

Like the officers, the men had their distractions, too. There was regular drilling and there were occasional forays into enemy territory, like the one described above. Rousseau's men could go to have their photograph made at their own divisional photography studio, a Cincinnati-based company called Butler, Bonsall & Co., Army Photographers, General Rousseau's Division. There were dress parades like the one the 1st Division conducted for Rosecrans and his officers on March 19. Rosecrans addressed the men afterward, praising them for their appearance and also for the orderliness of their camp — an important concern in an encampment of such long duration as this one at Murfreesboro. Alexander McDowell McCook complimented the men, calling it "the finest review" he had ever seen.[11]

Though his division won the approval of some of the top officers of the Army of the Cumberland, Rousseau himself was not present at the review held in General Rosecrans' honor. He did not return from Kentucky until March 29. In his absence, Brigadier General Robert Granger had temporarily commanded the 1st Division.

Soon after he resumed command, Rousseau was caught up in an event which was far less pleasant than dress parades, the execution of a trooper named David Blaser. Blaser had not only deserted, but had joined the Confederate army. A court-martial had sentenced him to die by firing squad and General Rousseau approved it on May 18. Twelve non-commissioned officers of the U.S. Regulars were chosen to carry out the execution on June 20.

In one other known instance, Rousseau had sanctioned an execution. After the Battle of Perryville, a captured Confederate with two paroles in his pocket was executed by Rousseau's men, but that man was an enemy. The condemned this time, though a deserter and a traitor, was one of their own and must have had sympathizers among the volunteer regiments. Perhaps that is why Rousseau selected the hardened professionals among his brigade of Regulars to carry out the sentence.

Military executions typically followed a similar protocol, and the June 20 execution was no different. The condemned man's comrades were marched out and formed into a hollow square, with one end left open. The provost marshal rode up on horseback, followed by a band playing the "Dead March." Twelve armed men — the executioners — came next in the procession, then a wagon carrying a coffin, and then the condemned man with a guard on each side, and a chaplain. There was a grave near the open end of the square and here the coffin was set down. The doomed man sat down on it and was blindfolded while the order of execution was read aloud. The firing squad raised their weapons. Rousseau himself gave the command "Fire!" The condemned man fell backward into his coffin. Rousseau then ordered the witnesses to march by the open casket and its gory, bullet-torn occupant and the men went back to camp with a new appreciation, one would think, of their duty as soldiers.

* * *

The men planted saplings along their regimental streets, and they drilled. They attended courts-martial and executions, performed dress parades, and went to have their photograph made until they were tired of it all. The weather was warm, the roads were drying out, and they were ready for General Rosecrans' order to go and challenge the enemy. The war would never be brought to an end while they sat in camp at Murfreesboro.

In this opinion, they were in perfect accord with Washington. Already vexed with his constant demands via the telegraph, the president and the War Department were beside themselves that his army remained in winter camp so late in the year that the men could have planted a corn crop.

Finally, in late June, Rosecrans was ready to move south. As he planned the campaign, each of his corps commanders would move along a different route in order to keep Braxton Bragg confused and distracted. On the west flank, Major General Gordon Granger leading the Reserve Corps and Major General David Stanley's Cavalry Corps would move in two separate columns south toward Shelbyville. There, they would turn sharply east to join the others at Manchester. General McCook would lead his XX Corps south toward War Trace. General Thomas would be on the Manchester Road, and over on the east flank would be General Crittenden's XXI Corps, moving east by southeast toward McMinnville. Past Bradyville, Crittenden would turn south toward Lumley's Stand. Whoever got to Manchester first, either Thomas or Crittenden, would proceed southwest from Manchester to get behind Bragg at Tullahoma and prevent his retreat. Bragg would have to fight and if he fought, he would be crushed by the converging columns of blue.

On June 24, the Tullahoma Campaign began. The columns moved out in a downpour. The rain continued for fifteen days, flooding every creek and river and melting the road into a muck so heavy that it took fifty men to move a wagon.

Thomas's corps was luckier than the others. The Manchester Pike was macadamized, so the men had easier marching of it. With Wilder's Lightning Brigade in the lead, General Joseph J. Reynolds' division moved out at 4:00 A.M., followed by Rousseau at about 9:00, and Negley at 11:30.

In late morning, Wilders' brigade easily took Hoover's Gap away from the 1st Kentucky Cavalry, CSA, and an artillery battery came up to help them hold it. This was one of the vital points along the Shelbyville Pike and no one was surprised when the Confederates launched a counterattack against Wilder later that afternoon. This was a tougher fight, even for men with seven-shot repeaters and gunners with double-shotted cannon. It grew so hot at one point that General Reynolds ordered Wilder to fall back, but Wilder refused. Reynolds threw his two other brigades forward and sent a request for General Rousseau to come up in support.

12. The Tullahoma Campaign

Rousseau's men had moved off the pike and gone into camp at Big Spring when Reynolds' call came. Proceeding to Hoover's Gap through the woodland trails was impossible, so Rousseau ordered his men back to the pike and they hurried to Wilder's aid. The 3rd Brigade, U.S. Regulars, arrived shortly after dark and, under fire, took up position on the west side of the gap; the other two brigades camped close enough that they could readily come up in support when the fight resumed on June 25. The Regulars suffered twenty-three casualties getting into position.

In the early morning hours, Rousseau ordered Scribner's 1st Brigade to move forward to relieve Wilder and Hambright's 2nd Brigade to move up as the reserve, but the Rebels disappointed them. There was no attack, only some sharp artillery fire from the enemy, which kept things lively for a while. Rousseau wrote, "The fire was very heavy and very accurate, the balls plowing up the ground all about [Scribner's] infantry and Loomis' battery, all in full view of the enemy, yet Scribner did not flinch, but received the fire without a tremor." The Yankee artillery responded, the Confederate guns fell silent, and this was the end of the contest for Hoover's Gap. The rapid taking of Hoover's Gap gave the Federals an unexpected gain in their schedule, but the advantage was wasted during a leisurely day after Hoover's Gap was won.[12]

On the third day, the march resumed. Rousseau's 1st Division and Major General John M. Brannan's 3rd Division made up for the previous day's inactivity, somewhat, when they pushed the Rebels down the Manchester Pike. Soon, they came to near Fairfield, where two brigades of the enemy, reinforced by some stray regiments, had taken up a strong position. Rousseau moved off to the right with his 1st and 3rd Brigades, intending to get around the enemy's left flank. The Regulars were officially under the command of Brigadier General John H. King, but he had been wounded in the hand at Stones River and was not yet healed, so the 3rd Brigade was led on the drive toward Tullahoma by Major Sidney Coolidge. No one knew how he would perform; some doubted his abilities, but on this day he erased all doubts. Supported by the other brigades in Rousseau's and Brannan's divisions, Coolidge's men charged across a soggy wheat field and gouged the enemy out of their positions on the left flank. The Confederates might have dug in farther down the road, but they were not interested in continuing the fight against Coolidge; they continued their retreat, with the Federals on their heels, until they were only six miles from Manchester.

The next morning, Wilder's Lightning Brigade dashed into Manchester, far ahead of the others. Rousseau's division did not get into town until about 1:00 A.M. on Monday, June 28.

By this time, Bragg had figured out what Rosecrans was up to and was falling back toward North Georgia. His impoverished army was able to move faster than the Federals, who were having a hard time keeping up the pressure — too many wagons and too much mud. The infantry and the artillery slowly slogged into Manchester, concentrating before renewing the chase after Bragg's graybacks. Wilder's brigade improved the time by a quick raid on Decherd, where they burned the railroad depot, broke up several hundred yards of track, and took eighty men prisoner. Then they returned to Manchester.

On July 1, the Federals learned that Bragg had given up the fight to hold Middle Tennessee. Now it was a matter of cutting off his retreat and defeating him. The enemy rear guard fought a stubborn delaying action beyond Manchester. Near Bobo Crossroads, the Rebels blocked the way forward. While General Negley's 2nd Division engaged them, Rousseau was ordered to turn off the pike and take a smaller road to the left in an effort to get across Elk River at Jones' Crossing. Rousseau's division got there in good time, but the enemy was guarding the ford and opened fire on the men as they approached. They might as well have saved their ammunition, for the river was so swollen by the interminable rain that it was "impassable for artillery, and barely passable for infantry," as Rousseau later remembered. The Federals stretched ropes across the river to provide the men hand-holds, and in this way Hambright's 2nd Brigade inched forward through the flood. "The passage, by reason of the strong and rapid current, was not only difficult but very hazardous, and much of the ammunition in the cartridge boxes of the men was unavoidably injured, the water running over their shoulders." It took all afternoon to cross this one brigade over Elk River. On the enemy bank at last, Hambright's men pushed forward three-quarters of a mile and ran into enemy fire once again, but the enemy faded back as the 2nd Brigade pressed them.[13]

Rousseau was able to cross his 1st and 3rd Brigades the next morning, but not the artillery. A day-long rainstorm caused the river to rise even more and the artillery did not get across until July 4. This was really the last day of the Tullahoma Campaign. The trailing unit of Bragg's army escaped over the rim of the Cumberland Plateau and reached Chattanooga. The order to stop pursuing them came down from Rosecrans at 2:00 P.M.

That night, in their camp near Decherd, the Army of the Cumberland had another reason to celebrate. They received the news that Robert E. Lee had been defeated by General Meade at Gettysburg and sent back to the Potomac River. Rousseau ordered that a salute be fired, "which was done with alacrity."[14]

Of the Tullahoma Campaign, Rousseau reported,

> This was the most remarkable march I have ever known. It began to rain just as my division was being formed to march out of Murfreesborough on the 24th ultimo, and it has rained heavily every day since but one. The roads have been in terrible condition, and marching was difficult and laborious, and the men who pursued the enemy, and fought during the day, through the rain and mud, laid down in the wet at night to rise in the morning to go through the same labor and fatigue and hardships, all of which was done without one single murmur.[15]

The campaign had been remarkable in a way that Rousseau did not mention. With a total loss of only six hundred Federal casualties (approximately fifty of them Rousseau's), General Rosecrans had inflicted two thousand enemy casualties and had maneuvered Bragg out of Middle Tennessee. The Army of the Cumberland had not been fast enough to block Bragg and force him into battle, but they had pushed him into the bottom tier of Confederate states and now that he was dispirited and his army demoralized, a final victory over them seemed in sight. The Union Generals celebrated with a feast on the Fourth of July.

There was no celebration of the Tullahoma Campaign in Washington, D.C. Secretary of War Edwin M. Stanton seemed to dismiss it as a mere prelude. His July 7 telegram to Rosecrans read, "You and your noble army now have the chance to give the finishing blow to the rebellion. Will you neglect the chance?" Stanton not only made a point of mentioning Meade's victory over Lee, but also Grant's successful conclusion of the Vicksburg siege on July 4. Rosecrans replied, "I beg in behalf of this army that the War Department not overlook so great an event [as the conquest of Middle Tennessee] because it is not written in letters of blood."[16]

Henry Halleck, the Army General-in-Chief, piled on next. On July 24, he wrote Rosecrans, "You must move forward immediately.... There is great disappointment felt here at the slowness of your advance. Unless you move rapidly, your whole campaign will prove a failure." The officials on the Potomac were worried that General Joseph E. Johnston was on the way to join Bragg.[17]

A second message arrived at Rosecrans' headquarters on July 24. This time, Halleck wrote, "The patience of the authorities here has been completely exhausted." And then there came a damning charge: "It has been said that you are as inactive as was General Buell and the pressure for your removal has been almost as strong as it was in his case."[18]

On August 4, there came another wire written in hard, official language: "Your forces must move forward without further delay. You will daily report the movement of each corps till you cross the Tennessee River." Rosecrans quibbled and wanted clarification. Washington warned him not to "stop to discuss mere details." Rosecrans protested that he was held in contempt and misunderstood. Buell! They had compared him to Buell![19]

Another ten days passed. As of August 14, Rosecrans had not taken a single step toward Georgia.

13

Chickamauga and Chattanooga

General Rosecrans was concerned about his supply line. He had advanced eighty miles from Murfreesboro. Nashville was thirty miles beyond that. He had crews out repairing the roads, but there were not enough men for both maintenance and campaigning. Until the lines were secure, he could not chase Bragg into the wilderness of North Georgia. The general's ever active mind had developed a plan, but it would require a sizeable commitment on the part of the Secretary of War and the General-in-Chief.

What Rosecrans wanted to do was to enlist ten thousand veterans into a new division to patrol and protect the supply lines. The veterans would be classified as mounted infantry and they would be armed with the best shoulder-arms available, Sharps or Spencer rifles. There was nothing especially new about the plan — he had essentially done it before with the Lightning Brigade. The main difference was that this new force of mounted men would be veterans, and that meant a net increase in the number of soldiers on the government payroll. Lovell H. Rousseau would command the division.

This time, to persuade the Washington authorities, Rosecrans decided not to rely on the telegraph; he dispatched two advocates to the Capital City, Colonel John Sanderson, 15th U.S. Infantry, and Major General Rousseau. They left in late July.

Rousseau had not seen the national capital since 1861, when the rebellion had barely begun. The city he saw now was transformed by war, an exciting place, a peculiar mix of the grand and the raw. The streets were still mud, which the free roaming, wallowing pigs enjoyed, but which the well-dressed men in their polished boots and the women in their dainty slippers did not. Ducks and chickens pecked about in the mire for grain that had fallen from the horses' feed bags. All the streets were this way, and the mess was unavoidable. Even Pennsylvania Avenue, one of the most famous streets in America, had only one sidewalk. Perhaps Rousseau and Sanderson visited Matthew Brady's photographic studio at the corner of Pennsylvania Avenue and 7th Street. If they did not see the White House when they first arrived, they soon would, for the War Department, where they had an appointment with Secretary of War Edwin Stanton, was just across the lawn from the Executive Mansion. Near there was a shantytown where contraband Negroes lived.

The city stank of animal droppings and wood smoke and drainage ditches where raw sewage flowed slowly down toward Chesapeake Bay. As always, Congress took care of itself first and the members did not contribute their bodily waste to the common flood of filth. The legislators' outhouse, in the shadow of the unfinished Capitol dome, was a magnificent edifice that had cost almost $250 to build.

The city was loud with the sounds of saloons, gambling dens, and whorehouses. In contrast were the city's three great and handsome hotels, the National, the Brown, and the Willard. The two officers from Rosecrans' headquarters undoubtedly stayed in one of these.

On or about August 16, shortly after their arrival in Washington, Rousseau and Sanderson went to see Secretary of War Stanton to present Rosecrans' plan for a veterans' division. The secretary had the well-earned reputation of being prickly even when things were going well and, in his view, things were not going well with the Army of the Cumberland and its whiney commander. He was annoyed at Rosecrans' eternal demands for more horses and weapons, at his excuses for not moving forward with alacrity against the enemy, at his continuing complaints that he was misunderstood and unappreciated. Now, here were this Rousseau and Sanderson with a scheme that would cost the government even more men and horses for a commander who had not performed up to expectations from the very start.

When Rousseau explained the reason for their visit, Stanton erupted. He declared that "Rosecrans shall not have another damned man." Sanderson wrote to his wife that Stanton was "bearish and unmannerly."[1]

A visit to General-in-Chief Henry Halleck was no more promising. Halleck blinked and scratched his elbows and said that he could see "no advantages" to the plan. Sanderson privately described Halleck as "bull-headed."[2]

Rousseau and Sanderson had one more hope. They went next to see President Lincoln. This was the second time Rousseau had met Lincoln and he would have noticed in the president's face the personal price of waging war. Lincoln's face was laced with more wrinkles. His eyes were sunk deeper in their sockets and the shadows were darker beneath the shelf-like cheek bones. The president might look more fragile than before, but his mind was vigorous, anxious to grasp new strategies to win the war. He liked the idea of giving Rousseau a mounted division of veterans. He ordered Stanton to see Rousseau and Sanderson again, which he did on August 17. Obviously acting on the president's instructions, but with no more enthusiasm than before,

Stanton agreed that Rosecrans could have his veterans division, after all. Stanton would have his little revenge, however. He seems to have wrenched a concession out of Rousseau that the division would not be mounted on horses, but on mules — a slight change from the original plan that would have to be approved by General Rosecrans. At least, that is the way the first sentence of Stanton's August 17 acknowledgment to Rousseau read:

> General: The proposition submitted by you today for mounting a division upon mules, subject to the approval of Major General Rosecrans, and arming them with Spencer or Sharps rifles, is favorably considered by this Department and its efforts will be directed to accomplish that object as speedily as it can be effected consistent with the engagements of the service. Directions will be given to the Ordnance and Quartermaster's Departments to make investigation and report in regard to practicability of furnishing the arms and mules and the period within which they can be procured. As soon as these reports are received they will be considered and you will be notified of the result.[3]

Aside from the change from horses to mules (which Rosecrans might not approve, thereby derailing the plan), one finds that Stanton's note to Rousseau is full of not-so-subtly coded phrases that lead a careful reader to the conclusion that the secretary was trying to sabotage the project which he had been ordered by the president to implement. Stanton said the proposition would be "favorably considered," an effort would be made "to accomplish that object as speedily as it can be effected," the departments would "make investigation and report," and "the reports will be considered." So, even after all the investigating and reporting and considering, the answer might still be "no." Rousseau plainly was not going to get his veterans division anytime soon. Stanton was playing for time. A great deal could happen in wartime that would make the idea obsolete or impractical before it could ever be effected.

* * *

Rousseau was at the height of his acclaim in 1863, and if Secretary of War Stanton did not realize that, others did. There was even a popular song dedicated to Rousseau, "The American Flag." The lyrics were written and the melody composed by William Shakespeare Hays, a man whose artistry is best judged by a glance at his toe-tapper written in honor of the tall Kentuckian:

> All hail to the star spangled flag of the free,
> The flag of our Union, the pride of our nation;
> Oh! Still let it wave o'er the land and the sea,
> America's emblem of truth, rank, and station.
> The thunders may crash

> The lightnings may flash,
> It shall fly wherever we send it;
> It shall ride on the wave,
> With the sons of the brave,
> Who will die in the cause to defend it.
> CHORUS:
> In peace or in war,
> Our flag is still there,
> We will never forsake it, no! never!
> Our motto shall be
> The American Union Forever.
>
> Lone Star of the West — Kentucky the brave,
> Thy sons and they daughters all join in communion,
> So long as the star spangled banner shall wave,
> Be true to yourselves, and the flag of the Union.
> The flag it is ours,
> Let no foreign powers,
> Ever trample upon it or take it;
> Wherever we are,
> In peace or in war,
> Kentucky! Oh! Never forsake it.[4]

There was another verse which described the flag and the majestic eagle hovering above it, but the sample above is enough to convey the talents of William Shakespeare Hays, an admirer, one presumes, of General Rousseau.

* * *

Rousseau did not return directly to Tullahoma. The evidence suggests that his mind was turning to politics again and that he made some public appearances while he was in the East. He gave at least one speech during this period, in Lancaster, Pennsylvania, and he collaborated with a man named Isaac Funk to publish in 1863 a collection of patriotic essays and speeches called *The Loyalists' Ammunition*. It was seventeen pages of text and was meant for "gratuitous distribution."[5]

Isaac Funk was a prosperous Illinois farmer, and one of his speeches was included, as well as such eclectic selections as a 1656 speech of Oliver Cromwell before Parliament and a resolution of the 115th Pennsylvania Infantry dated March 11, 1863. The regiment pledged continued devotion to the laws and government of the U.S. and condemned their enemies, whose claim of fighting for Southern rights was merely a euphemism for fighting to extend slavery. The resolution also stated the regiment's implacable hatred of traitors, both North and South.

The selection from Rousseau, called "The Words of a Patriot Soldier," was an excerpt from his Lancaster speech. He said:

My political creed is but a minute long. I am for the government of my fathers and the friends of that government, and I am against the enemies of that government, and all their friends, both North and South....

No matter what your political predilections may be, unite to save the country, and after that settle questions of policy. Let not your differences of opinion weaken the arm of the brave men who are fighting that you may be free. In the Army of the Cumberland, in which I have the honor of commanding a division, officers and men know only the cause of their country; all are united in a common work; no dissension or jealousies weaken their force.[6]

It is unlikely that a man as experienced as Rousseau actually believed that there were no dissensions or jealousies ebbing and surging within the Army of the Cumberland and flowing from that army through poisonous arteries of secret communications to the War Department. But, even if he did believe that, he was soon to get an education in army politics and learn what a crippling impact they could have on a loyal man's career. Rousseau returned to his division at last on the night of September 20.

* * *

As he was en route to his division, Rousseau must have heard of the terrific battle that was going on in North Georgia along the banks of a little creek called Chickamauga.

Rosecrans had pushed south after Bragg beginning on August 16. General Crittenden's corps had moved from McMinnville toward Chattanooga. General McCook's corps had stepped off from Winchester toward Stevenson, Alabama, with Gordon Granger's Reserve Corps trailing behind. General Thomas marched from Manchester toward Bridgeport, Alabama. General Absalom Baird, a Pennsylvanian with the elaborate whiskers of a maharaja, was temporarily commanding Rousseau's 1st Division. The Cavalry Corps under General David Stanley was far off to the west, screening the army's right as they rode from Fayetteville toward Huntsville.

Bragg would not stand and fight. He appeared to be disorganized and demoralized. The prisoners and deserters coming in from his army said the same thing. The Army of the Cumberland chased the Confederates across the Tennessee River and beyond, where the columns separated in an attempt to catch Bragg and cut him off. At its most widespread, Rosecrans' left (northernmost) flank was forty miles from the right (southernmost) flank.

Then, on September 9, Bragg turned. He had not been running scared, at all. He had been luring Rosecrans on, tempting him to spread out his forces so that they could be defeated in detail. Emerging from Stevens' Gap into McLemore's Cove, General James Negley of Thomas' corps found the whole valley in front of him filled with Rebels. If Bragg had fallen on Negley as planned, the 2nd Division would have been finished. Bragg's subordinates let him down, though; they failed to attack before Negley began to pull back. General Baird had only just moved up to support him, but now they both withdrew into Stevens' Gap where they could not be outflanked.

Rosecrans, who had been confidently hunting Bragg, now realized that it was he who was in the trap. He issued orders for his army to concentrate to the north. By September 18, it was done, but by that time, Bragg had begun to be reinforced by General James Longstreet's corps from the Army of Northern Virginia. Three brigades under General John Bell Hood had arrived just in time to join in a move against General Crittenden, on Rosecrans' left. Rosecrans saw the dust rising from their line of march and ordered Thomas and McCook to hurry north in closer support of Crittenden. They tightened up near Lee and Gordon's Mills on Chickamauga Creek. Thomas, in fact, passed behind Crittenden and took up position further north. Now, the XIV Corps was the Union left flank.

Early on September 19, Thomas sent out Colonel John T. Croxton's brigade of Brannan's division to bag a CSA brigade that was reported in their front. Croxton advanced and found the woods full of CSA brigades. Soon, he was tangled up in a real fight. Baird moved the 1st Division up to support Croxton; other units were thrown in piecemeal by both sides all the rest of that confusing day. John T. Wilder of the Lightning Brigade said of the fight on September 19, "There was no generalship in it. It was a soldier's fight purely." More of Longstreet's men arrived on the 19th, but too late to take part in the day's fighting. It was a good thing, too, for even without Longstreet's help the Rebels pushed Thomas back a mile and captured hundreds of prisoners. Only darkness saved the rest.[7]

In the evening, General Baird warned Thomas that his division, on the left flank, was in the air. He would need reinforcements to extend his line and anchor it. This was in Thomas' thoughts when Rosecrans called a council of war at his headquarters in the Widow Glenn's cabin. Thomas napped throughout, but kept waking up when he was asked a question to repeat one piece of advice. "I would strengthen the left," he said.[8]

In the hours after midnight, the council over, Thomas was back among his men, directing the building of breastworks and placing the reinforcements which Rosecrans shuffled over to him. The next morning, the fight resumed, as Thomas had predicted, on the left. John C. Breckinridge and Nathan Bedford Forrest slammed into Thomas' unexpectedly strong line and were beaten back. Bragg saw that his efforts on that flank had failed and ordered his whole line into action.

During a shift of the Union forces about 11:00 A.M., there developed a hole in the defenders' line. Longstreet hit that gap at precisely the right moment to shatter the entire Federal right. Philip Sheridan and Jefferson C. Davis abandoned the field, quickly followed by McCook, Crittenden, and Rosecrans, himself. Thomas was left to fight the whole Rebel army with his single corps, plus whatever regiments, companies, and individual soldiers he could snag out of the fast blue tide streaming toward Chattanooga. All the while, Longstreet on his right and Leonidas Polk on his left kept slugging away at General Thomas and the XIV Corps.

General Gordon Granger, commanding the Reserve Corps far to the rear, heard the sounds of Thomas' desperate fight and took it upon himself to send aid to the determined Virginian, beginning with Brigadier General James B. Steedman's division, who arrived on the field about 2:30 P.M. and immediately helped fight back an assault.

The last CSA attempt began about 4:00 P.M. Peter Cozzens wrote in *This Terrible Sound*, "It was upon Baird that the full fury of the Confederate attack fell." Baird was on the left of a tight semicircle that curled around the Kelly Farm. Baird's men — Rousseau's old division — had to remember their training now, and they did. They beat off the attacks of Brigadier General Lucius Polk and Brigadier General John Jackson.[9]

During the attack, Baird got the order to withdraw his division — a difficult order to carry out while the enemy continued to flail at them. Starkweather went first, followed by Scribner and King. Each retreating brigade meant more pressure on the ones who remained. Benjamin F. Scribner's men suffered badly trying to pull out. Polk's Rebels came pouring over the barricades, plunging among the bluecoats and capturing many. The encouraged Rebels tried even harder now. Fresh troops of Brigadier General George Maney's Confederate brigade charged King's brigade, the last of Baird's men on the firing line. It was too much. The Regulars broke and fled, and it might have been much worse for them if they had not dropped their rifles, which the Rebels stopped to pick up.

General Baird reported, "As my men fell back the enemy pressed after them, and in crossing the open field very many were struck down. They reached the woods, in as good order as could be expected, but they were uncertain which direction to take, and having no landmarks to guide them, many became separated from their regiments." Benjamin Scribner agreed, and wrote of the little knots of wandering men, disorganized and leaderless, "but not demoralized or panic stricken."[10]

It was during this retreat that Rousseau appeared. He had arrived at Rosecrans' headquarters on the night of September 20 and started to the front at 2:00 A.M. on the 21st. He would learn the details of how his division had performed later. For now, he was charged with the responsibility of bringing some order into these confused remnants of the army streaming into Chattanooga, to direct men back to their proper regiments and shepherd the whole into the city. Baird wrote, "Major General Rousseau arrived and resumed command of this, his old division, inspiring it with new life after the arduous duties it had performed." Rousseau's own 1st Division became the rear guard and, assisted by the cavalrymen of Colonel Robert H. G. Minty (the 1st Brigade of the 2nd Division of the Cavalry Corps), they skirmished all day with the pursuing Confederates. On the night of the 21st the Rebels made a stronger effort. The XIV Corps responded and fought the enemy off as their comrades in arms continued into the city. Late on the 21st, Rousseau was able to inform Rosecrans, "As directed by you I have gathered up and forwarded to their respective commands several hundred disorganized troops ... I find the troops in fine spirits and ready to restart the fight, though they have suffered severe loss. What is left is all right.... There are not many stragglers now." Rousseau continued to hold Rossville Gap until the wee hours of September 22, when he was ordered to rejoin the army in Chattanooga.[11]

Many of these soldiers had tried to get to Chattanooga back in 1862 when Buell made his march across Northern Alabama. They could not reach the city then; enemy raiders and drought had defeated them. Now, a year later, they had gotten to Chattanooga and, this time, found that the reverse situation prevailed; now, they could not get *away*. Bragg had followed them and entrenched on top of the surrounding mountains. Chattanooga was besieged.

Bragg's army occupied Missionary Ridge and Lookout Mountain and controlled the supply routes into the city. Yankee starvation was the result. Squirrels, rabbits, dogs, cats, and rats all disappeared into Federal cookpots. Men ate the kernels of corn that dropped from the horses' mouths and, when the horses died, paid top price for the offal and even the hooves. By the third week of the siege, the men trapped inside Chattanooga were down to one-quarter rations. There was only a single, inadequate wagon road, rough and out of the way, to bring rations and fodder into Chattanooga. The road was so rugged that its precise length was unknown — maybe sixty miles, maybe seventy-five. From Bridgeport, Alabama, the road ran northeast for about thirty miles through the Sequatchie Valley, then turned sharply southeast, crossed the Walden Ridge, and proceeded to Chattanooga. On Walden Ridge, the road was so narrow that a broken down wagon could stop the whole train and so steep that it took sixteen mules in harness to pull the wagons and even at that the men walking behind had to push and shove and grab hold of the wheel spokes to get the wagons over the top.

This one fragile line was keeping Bragg's siege of Rosecrans from being complete, so on October 1, he ordered the young cavalry commander Joseph Wheeler to remedy that. The Confederate "War Child" proceeded into the Sequatchie Valley to raid and burn. Wheeler enjoyed a small success the very next day when he caught and destroyed thirty-four Yankee wagons near Dunlop, but that was not a patch to the later victory at Anderson's Crossroads. There, Wheeler captured almost four hundred wagons with all their contents plus 1,800 animals. The official Yankee reports of this disaster noted that these wagons were the "trains of General Rousseau, General Sheridan, the Anderson Cavalry, and a small ammunition train of General Thomas' corps."[12]

It was not just rations and ammunition that Wheeler stole or burned, it was the warm coats and blankets needed to survive an icy Chattanooga winter. The Yankees were going to suffer without warm clothes. They had torn down most of the wooden houses of Chattanooga for firewood and shelter and there was a dangerous scarcity of wood.

Adding to the discomfort of the Federals on the valley floor was the daily shelling from Colonel E. P. Alexander's artillery on Lookout Mountain. Alexander, the famous young artillerist of Pickett's Charge at Gettysburg, had come west with Longstreet's corps. He judged the range with a professional eye and warned that this long range shelling from Lookout would be ineffective and it was. After a week, it was called off, the only Yankee casualty being a mule. It was an annoyance to the Yankees, though, and possibly a dangerous one. Maybe a mule was killed today; that did not mean that tomorrow it would not be a man's messmate, or even his general. Lieutenant Arthur Carpenter of the Regular brigade in Rousseau's division remembered that one Rebel gun crew seemed to pick out Rousseau's headquarters as their special target: "They commenced throwing their shells at General Rousseau's house about noon when the men were all in line to answer roll call, the first shell came over and struck right in the center of our camp ... it was a percussion shell and struck on a rock and exploded beautifully. Very fortunately no one was injured." Nor was any man injured during the rest of the barrage, though one round did knock over a water carrier.[13]

While the men in the ranks shivered and starved and ducked shells, the army hierarchy was in convulsions. Since the rout at Chickamauga, the power seemed to have gone out of Rosecrans' thinking. His mind was slack. He devoted hours to trivial headquarters duties. He sent rambling telegrams to Washington saying that if they but trusted in God, He would see them through these difficulties. President Lincoln said Rosecrans "acts dazed, like a duck that has been hit on the head." Even if Rosecrans had been in his right mind, he could not have retained his command. Chickamauga had been a debacle and someone had to pay. Rosecrans was finished.[14]

In retrospect, it looks inevitable, perhaps, that General George H. Thomas should replace Rosecrans as the new leader of the Army of the Cumberland. He had led his men with great steadiness in every contest of the rebellion, so far, and with a kind of determined genius on September 20. Thomas was celebrated across the nation as the "Rock of Chickamauga."

However, in the winter of 1863, it was not so clear that Thomas would be the man. The possibility of command was mentioned to Major General Rousseau, who was said to be ambitious to lead more than just a division. His elevation to command of the Army of the Cumberland was in no way a foregone conclusion, but he was being considered. It was an opportunity that must have been very tempting to the Kentuckian.

In the end, Rousseau dismissed the offer. He said that he would gladly accept any promotion outside of the Department of the Cumberland, but he "could not consent to become the successor of General Rosecrans because he would not do anything to give countenance to the suspicion that he had intrigued against his commander." So, the promotion went to Thomas, after all.[15]

The axe fell for Rosecrans on October 19, 1863. When he showed Thomas the telegram, the Virginian turned pale, but Rosecrans was gracious. He said to Thomas, "No one but you can safely take my place now, and for our country's sake you must do it." At Rosecrans' request, the news was kept from the men for a few hours; he did not think that he could bear to face them. Before dawn on October 20, Rosecrans quietly left Chattanooga.[16]

The promotion of Thomas left a vacancy at the head of the XIV Corps, and Rousseau would not have been human if he had not thought that he was the presumptive successor to Thomas as corps commander. When command of the XIV Corps went instead to Major General John M. Palmer, Rousseau was flabbergasted.

Rousseau, by this time, had won a certain acclaim among the men, his fellow officers, and the public at large. Troops who weren't even in his division cheered when he rode by. The appearance of a rabbit in a camp of men starved for fresh meat was always an uproarious occasion with lots of cheering, but there was an event that challenged it for joyous noise. When men suddenly began cheering in some unseen part of camp, it became axiomatic that it was "either Rousseau or a rabbit." Though from a southern state, the General hated secessionists. Furthermore, he had shown himself to be a natural born soldier. He had directed his men with great competence and personal courage at Shiloh, Perryville, and Stones River. He had arrived in the midst of the rout that followed the debacle at Chickamauga and he had skillfully brought order out of chaos.[17]

Yet, there were several factors that worked against Rousseau. First, he was a Kentuckian, which caused him to be viewed with caution — an attitude that also affected the career advancement of others from the Bluegrass State, such as General John Buford. Students of the Battle of Gettysburg remember Buford as the commander of the 1st Cavalry Division, Army of the Potomac, whose intelligent and determined defense of Gettysburg on July 1, 1863, not only prevented the Confederates from taking position on the high ground but also gave the rest of Meade's army time to arrive, so that they had the strength to defeat Robert E. Lee's Army of Northern Virginia and drive it out of the North. Buford's performance at Gettysburg was masterful, the latest in a commendable military record. Even so, promotions were slow to come for the Kentucky-born Buford. Kentucky, though a loyal state, was a slave state, and her sons had difficulty attaining the top jobs in the Union Army.

Also, Rousseau was known to be cool toward, if not openly critical of, the Emancipation Proclamation. He was on the wrong side of a question which had now been settled by administration policy, and that was not a path to advancement.

Third, Rousseau refused to seriously criticize Don Carlos Buell, even in the safe environment of the Buell Commission hearings, and had favored the policy of conciliation toward Southern civilians. Conciliation had been administration policy in 1862, but it was held in contempt in 1863, as were those who had practiced it in Mississippi, Alabama, and Tennessee.

One also cannot discount the jealousies and envies of other, less popular officers like Brigadier General John Beatty, who, in their whispering, behind-the-hand gossip, liked to over-emphasize (with a curiously prissy attitude for battlefield commanders) Rousseau's love of Kentucky bourbon, his occasional bluster, and his cursing.

However, there was one man among the critics who heartily disliked Rousseau and was in a position to really hurt him. The man was Charles A. Dana, a former newspaper man who was now employed as a spy for Secretary of War Edwin Stanton. Dana's job was to roam the camps and pick up colorful and damaging information for Stanton and, in the camp of the Army of the Cumberland, Rousseau came into Dana's sights. What Dana had against Rousseau has never been known. What is known is that he had a receptive audience in Stanton, who was bitter toward Rousseau for going over his head to see President Lincoln in the matter of the veterans mounted division. Dana admitted that Rousseau had "extraordinary talent, quickness, and energy," but nevertheless referred to him as "unfit" to command and applied a nonsensical but catchy phrase to Rousseau that has stuck ever since. He said that Rousseau was "an ass of eminent gifts."[18]

So, Rousseau was passed over for command of the XIV Corps in favor of John M. Palmer, a man whom he outranked in seniority and, by all evidence, in talent and temperament as well.

Secretary of War Stanton went further. He removed Rousseau from command of the 1st Division and reassigned him to command the District of Nashville. General R.W. Johnson got Rousseau's division.

In an unbelievably short span of time, and without any failure on Rousseau's part to justify it, one of the most skilled division commanders in the West had been stripped of his field command and assigned to an administrative position, far from where the war was being won. In this re-assignment, he was placed in the same group as McCook, Crittenden, and Negley, who also lost their field commands after Chickamauga. The great difference was — they were failures. Rousseau was not. But, like them, Rousseau was gone.

Rousseau was in Chattanooga long enough to see the October 23 arrival of General Grant to coordinate the relief of the Army of the Cumberland. Four days later, the Federal takeover of Brown's Ferry on the Tennessee River opened up one end of a new supply route, remembered in history as the Cracker Line. Two detached corps of the Army of the Potomac, moving east from Bridgeport, Alabama, under General Joseph Hooker, opened up the other end and, on October 29, full rations began to be delivered into Chattanooga.

In the last week of November, one group of Federals under Hooker won Lookout Mountain and another group under Thomas chased Bragg's army off of Missionary Ridge. Rousseau was not there to see or take part in the breakout.

Two weeks earlier, on November 13, Rousseau had left for Nashville. He addressed his troops one final time. Many of them were weeping when they heard him say:

> A year and a half ago I succeeded the gallant and patriotic General O. M. Mitchel in the command of the 3rd Division — now the 1st — of the Fourteenth Army Corps.
>
> In yielding up my command for one in another field of duty, I feel that I am severing one of the strongest ties that can exist between friends and brothers in arms.
>
> In taking leave of those who have dared danger and death by my side, who, without murmur, have borne the "pitiless peltings" of the elements, and bravely breasted the storm of battle, I must be allowed to say, I feel honored in having commanded you.
>
> I leave you with regret — with heartfelt sorrow — for there is not an officer nor soldier of my command to whom I do not feel grateful for his

gallantry and soldierly bearing. In the future, as in the past, I know your services and your chivalric deeds will challenge the admiration of your countrymen; I shall exult then, as now, in the recollection that once you were called "Rousseau's Division."

Good-by, my brave comrades in arms, and may God bless you.[19]

14

The Great Alabama Raid

Nashville was still Nashville, only more so. The streets were jammed with uniformed officers and men, but in addition, there were upwards of eighteen thousand non-military personnel who had come to work on behalf of the army — mechanics, carpenters, wheelwrights, teamsters, and so forth. There were more hospitals than ever, filled with the wounded of Chickamauga and smaller battles. There were five newspapers and two theaters. One of them, the Nashville Theater, had booked the young Shakespearean John Wilkes Booth for an extended engagement in January and February of the coming year.

The waterfront was lined with military warehouses, the river loud with the whistles of steam transports, most of them riding low in the water from the weight of the cargo they carried. In the first two weeks of February alone, steamers carried to Nashville from the docks of New Albany, Indiana, and Louisville, Kentucky, a staggering amount of provender: two million pounds of pork, thirteen thousand barrels of flour, eighty-four thousand bushels of grain, over three thousand tons of hay and this tally did not include the stores that also arrived in the city via the L&N Railroad. The indigent received a portion of the military foodstuffs; in March 1864 about forty thousand rations were distributed to needy citizens of the city.

The post commander at Nashville was General Robert Granger, a balding man with a boxer's nose, and a moustache that extended east and west from jawbone to jawbone. Rousseau knew him as the man who had temporarily commanded his division while he was in Louisville testifying before the Buell Commission.

As post commander, Granger learned the peculiar challenges of running a military base inside of a large city. The problems included as many social as military questions and sometimes they overlapped. Because the government had seized their sanctuaries for use as warehouses and magazines, church congregations had to meet wherever they could find space. The public schools were closed, many of them had become military hospitals. There was an outbreak of smallpox in November and since the disease was no respecter of uniforms, Granger ordered the whole population, military and civilian alike, to be vaccinated.

By far, the most serious health threat to Granger's garrison was venereal disease. Prostitution thrived in wartime Nashville, feeding on the regular pay and the carnal lusts of an army of young men, not only the permanent troops, but also the ambulatory convalescents, and those who were passing through on furlough. The women who served the men in uniform ran the gamut from streetwalkers whose boudoir was a dark alley, to elegant girls with perfumed hair and fancy dresses who lived in well-run houses on lower College Street. They were gathered in neighborhoods with such colorful names as Slabtown and Smoky Row. This red light district was in the eastern quarter of the city, near the Cumberland River. Army veterans teased recruits that a man who had not done a tour of duty in Smoky Row was no soldier — and by this boyish challenge wrecked the health and well-being of many a young man, for venereal disease was as common in Nashville as a change of shirts.

Authorities tried in the summer of 1863 to reduce the health risk of a soldier's stay in Nashville by rounding up the white prostitutes (curiously, the order was applied only to the whites) and loading them on a steamboat for Louisville, but Louisville sent them right back. During their brief absence, black prostitutes had come in great numbers to take advantage of a suddenly wide open market, so now Nashville had more whores than ever. The order to round up prostitutes was rescinded, the experiment a failure.

Still, something needed to be done. The provost marshal, Lieutenant Colonel George Spalding, had the idea to fight the problem not through prohibition, but by intelligent regulation. Spalding appears to have been an exceptionally clear-thinking young officer. As provost marshal, he possessed considerable legal authority, an amount of power that went to some men's heads, but not Spalding's. He did not lose sight of the enduring ideals for which the war was being fought and did not use the excuse of wartime to cancel the constitutional rights of the accused, even if they were Southerners. He insisted upon the necessity of the writ of habeas corpus and resisted the practice of holding accused persons for indeterminate periods of time without ever bringing them to trial.

In the matter of the prostitutes, Spalding instituted a system consisting of regular medical inspections of the prostitutes coupled with the mandatory purchase of a special business license. The inspections were to begin on August 17 and repeated every two weeks.

Spalding issued 300 licenses by January 1864. A year later, that number had nearly doubled. The growing numbers of fancy businesswomen was not matched by a similar increase in cases of venereal disease. Syphilis continued, of course, but at a much slower pace — the regular examinations were working. Girls who tested positive were quarantined and could not spread the disease wholesale.

A V.D. hospital was established for victims of syphilis on the west side of town and a second hospital for women was begun in a building the government seized on Market Street.

General Granger was undoubtedly on more familiar ground as a post commander than a social engineer. Though the Confederate lines were further south than ever before, the city was more heavily fortified than ever, ringed by forts and redoubts and the railroad bridges were guarded by blockhouses. Important streets were barricaded. The lawn of the state capitol was covered with white shelter tents, and squads of men with bayoneted rifles patrolled the grounds. Ten thousand soldiers garrisoned the city — they were all white at first, but that began to change about the time that Rousseau was assigned to the District of Nashville. Enlistment of blacks was legal beginning in the fall, and an office to handle Negro enlistment was opened on Cedar Street. The first blacks in blue uniforms paraded in Nashville on October 2.

It was a sight that was shocking to both the military personnel and also the southern civilian population of Nashville. The Emancipation Proclamation had added another dimension to the war. After January 1863, the U.S. was fighting not only to preserve the Union, but also to win Negro freedom. Many soldiers who had believed they were going into the army to restore the Union were unhappy with the idea of fighting for the Negroes, but the idea of serving *alongside* blacks in the earthworks, the thought of being put on an equal plane with them, inspired a more violent negativity. It was more than many men in the ranks could bear, and was the cause of increased numbers of desertions. The idea of blacks in the army was a detriment to recruiting and to the effort to get soldiers to re-enlist. Even some officers resigned because of the policy and others were pushed to the brink of mutiny by the idea of serving with blacks.

An example is that of Lieutenant Colonel John H. Ward. Ward had helped to recruit and had led since the beginning of the war the 27th Kentucky Infantry. The 27th was in the Army of the Ohio, but Ward's father was Brigadier General William T. Ward, an officer in Rousseau's department.

In response to an order that blacks should report to officers in Knoxville, Loudon, or Kingston (cities in eastern Tennessee, where the 27th was serving), Lieutenant Colonel Ward composed a letter of protest to Major General John G. Foster at headquarters. He said, in part, "I consider this a wide departure from the legitimate cause for which we fight, an insult to every true soldier ... I cannot endure the sight of my flag ... carried by such hands." He said that these were the sentiments of his regiment and that if he ever saw the American flag being carried by black troops, he "would lead the Regiment and rescue our flag from such disgraceful custody."[1]

Then, young Ward wrote to his father in Nashville, telling him what he had said in the letter. Brigadier General Ward saw the letter as a career-killer, at least, and perhaps worse. He advised his son in a letter dated February 4, 1864, to take back the note to General Foster.

The next morning, Ward sent a second letter to his son. He said, "After writing to you last night I concluded to show your letter to Genl Rousseau and consult with him about the best course for you to take under the circumstance now surrounding you, we both agree that you had better take back the communication to Genl Fosters adjutant General; obey the order reenlist your men and fight throughout this war ... my dear son take your note back."[2]

Appended to General Ward's letter to his son was a long note from General Rousseau. He wrote:

> I have carefully read over this letter of a brave and patriotic father to his brave and no less patriotic son and concur fully in every suggestion made. I think the son should take back his communication referred to. By his own showing the time is not come for him to act for he is not yet called upon to serve by the side of negroes in the army and may never be. For myself I think the negro the horse and the hog had as well die for the old Government as I and there were moments at Perryville and Murfreesboro in which if negro troops had been there I had said with alacrity "Cuffee go in."[3]

Rousseau then pointed out that Andrew Jackson had fought alongside blacks at the Battle of New Orleans and had never felt himself disgraced by the experience and that the pioneers of their home state of Kentucky had fought alongside blacks in their struggles against the Shawnee and the Cherokee. Concluding, Rousseau wrote:

> My opinion is this That negroes serve the enemy in the rebellion and should be taken from them and used by the Government in this bloody struggle for existence. How shall this be done? We Kentuckians say in building Fortifications. In handling supplies and perhaps in guarding both and why not? But in doing this you expose the negro to death, unarmed, for the enemy comes and cuts his throat. Mercifully arm him and then let him at least defend his own life. This he may do with a big or little gun, as an artillerist or a musketeer or rifle man.
>
> I think it well enough that the negro shall guard the railroad bridges and depots of supplies while the white man fights the battle of the country. In that way less white blood will be shed on our side and if the rebels

don't want to lose their blood let them quit and like honest men live up to the laws of the land.[4]

Rousseau advised Lieutenant Colonel Ward to wait and see if having to serve alongside Negroes would ever come to pass — then would be the time to raise an objection. In the meantime, the young officer should not worry his head. Ward accepted Rousseau's advice. He remained in the service and led the 27th Kentucky Infantry until near the end of the war, leaving the regiment only when he was assigned to post duty in Louisville. Other officers who suffered a crisis of conscience over enlisting and leading blacks made different choices.

In Nashville, the large number of non-military blacks was a problem that grew more acute as winter approached. They came as refugees from the plantation to a city which was poorly equipped to give them food or shelter. Fuel was scarce and since civilian craft were forbidden on the Cumberland River, and the railroads, too, were restricted to military use, no large quantities of firewood could be brought into the city for civilians. There were no jobs for the refugees and little room. Humanitarians warned that either these indigent blacks would be sheltered and cared for, or they would turn to crime in their desperation. The army was slow to respond, but a contraband camp was finally begun over Governor Andrew Johnson's objections in February 1864.

Housing for army officers was as easier problem to solve — they simply seized private homes. The practice was so widespread that on December 3, 1863, shortly after he assumed command of the District of Nashville, General Rousseau asked his superiors for a clarifying order. Rousseau pleaded on behalf of the homeowners, saying that "families should not be put out of their dwelling houses to give quarters to officers" and that such practice should be "conveniently avoided." The Official Records do not reveal whether Rousseau got the clarification he ordered, but the complaints continued. The new post commander (as of January 1864), General John F. Miller, tried to protect the property of loyal citizens from outrages, even to the point of posting military guards around civilian homes.[5]

Of course, Rousseau's responsibilities were manifestly more complicated than the subject of housing for the homeless and for officers. Not only did his command include the Post of Nashville and Granger's brigade, but also the detachments at Murfreesboro, Duck River Bridge, McMinnville, Clarksville, Fort Donelson, Elk River Bridge, and Bridgeport, Alabama — and all the railroads in between. To make secure this wide-flung area, Rousseau had an aggregate of approximately 108,000 men, plus over four hundred artillery pieces. In Nashville alone there were six forts, not to mention scattered camps, seventeen pieces of heavy artillery, and twenty field pieces.

14. The Great Alabama Raid

Since the city was so thoroughly protected, it is no wonder that the Confederates did not attack it. Instead, they attacked outlying areas, focusing their attention on the railroad links to Louisville and also points south, though they were also well defended. Rousseau reported on May 12, 1864, "When the works at Stevenson [Alabama] shall be finished, I am of the opinion every garrison on the road between Nashville and Lookout Creek will be able to defend itself till aid can reach it." There were water tanks at each blockhouse and the officers were ordered to keep five days' worth of rations stored. The men of each garrison were provided with two hundred rounds of ammunition apiece and were armed with Enfield rifles or equally good shoulder arms.[6]

As guerrillas continued to operate against the railroads and riverboats, and to harass loyal citizens, Rousseau tried a method that other district commanders were using, namely, assessing rebellious civilians in the area where guerrilla activity had occurred. In other words, because of the guerrilla's deeds, the nearby civilians were fined and the tax money used to fund repairs to bridges, railroad depots, and the like. The method was as unsuccessful for Rousseau as it was for other commanders. The guerrilla raids continued.

New troops arriving in Nashville were quickly shuffled off to reinforce vulnerable points in Rousseau's district, but there were still incidents of sabotage. In fact, at times, it was necessary to suspend overland travel because of guerrilla raids. Very often they were attributed to Forrest, Morgan, or Wheeler.

One of Rousseau's many responsibilities was coordinating communications between the army in Tennessee and Georgia and the commanders in Kentucky. On June 14, 1864, for instance, Rousseau conveyed the news from Governor Thomas E. Bramlette that General Stephen Burbridge had whipped that old pest John Hunt Morgan at Cynthiana and that Morgan was moving south. The telegraph lines from Tennessee to Kentucky were so unreliable that Rousseau resorted to sending messages by rail and had at least one dispatch carrier take the train each day to Bowling Green.

Every sort of complaint and request, both civilian and military, came into Rousseau's office. A man named J. T. Hollis had been arrested at Gallatin in September 1863 and $13,000 taken from him. He was sent to Nashville and placed under the authority of Provost Marshal Spalding, who released him on a $10,000 bond and ordered him to report every twenty-one days. Hollis wrote to Rousseau on March 25, 1864, to say that he had taken the oath of allegiance only the day before and now wanted his money back.

Felix Prince Salm-Salm, Colonel of the 68th New York Infantry, wrote to Rousseau to recommend that an acquaintance named A. Friedlander be allowed to start a business in Nashville and "as your high authority and your protection is a necessity," Salm-Salm asked that Rousseau extend the same to Friedlander.[7]

One of the most intriguing letters that arrived on Rousseau's desk was from the discredited Major General Robert H. Milroy. Until recently, Milroy had commanded approximately five thousand men in Winchester, Frederick County, Virginia. In June 1863, CSA General Richard Ewell was moving north through the Shenandoah Valley on his way to Gettysburg and Milroy moved out to block the way. Milroy was confident, but ineffectual. Repulsed by Rebel general Jubal Early, he fell back to a speck on the map called Stevenson's Depot. There, he ran into General Edward Johnson, who finished the job Early started and destroyed or captured Milroy's whole command. Only about two hundred men, including General Milroy, escaped; four thousand others were taken prisoner, and over four hundred were killed. By their victory, Early and Johnson also obtained for General Ewell's use in Pennsylvania over twenty cannon and three hundred tightly packed wagons. Inevitably, Lincoln removed Milroy from command. The general had actually been placed under arrest for a time.

On June 26, 1864, Milroy wrote to General George Thomas, through Rousseau. Milroy wanted another field command, believing that it was only on the battlefield that he could restore his reputation as a soldier. In his cover letter to Rousseau, Milroy wrote, "I would as soon serve under you as any other general in the North, if you were in the *right place*, that is in front of the enemy."[8]

In this regard, Rousseau tended to agree with Milroy that he was not exactly in the right place. It was not that Rousseau lacked a talent for district command. Indeed, the truth was just the opposite; he was a gifted administrator. William Sumner Dodge wrote in 1864 of Rousseau's "strong practical intellect, strengthened by his experience as a legislator — his innate honesty — his calm and dignified address — his firmness, independence, disposition to do justice without fear or favor — his policy of dealing with secessionists with ungloved hands — [and] his sound discrimination between military and civic duties." Even so, this was not the type of duty that Rousseau had joined the service to perform. Anxious to return to the field, Rousseau saw the opportunity he was looking for in events that were unfolding further south.[9]

Since May 7, General Sherman had been advancing slowly on Atlanta in three columns, each one made up of a separate army. On the right was the Army of the Tennessee under General James Birdseye McPherson, whom Sherman considered to be one of the most promising young officers in the Federal service. The middle column was the Army of the Cumberland under General George H. Thomas. The team of Grant and Sherman had never cared much for Thomas nor for his style of fighting, but he was as solid an officer as wore the blue uniform and his army would do most of the hard fighting of this campaign. Had things broken better for Rousseau after Chickamauga, he would have been leading one of Thomas' corps. The left column, the smallest of the three, was the Army of the Ohio, fresh from East Tennessee, led by bald-headed, wispy bearded John Schofield. Opposing them was the Confederate General Joseph E. Johnston, who had succeeded Braxton Bragg after the Federals did the nearly impossible and broke out of the Confederate trap at Chattanooga.

The battles around Chattanooga had ended once and for all Rousseau's hope of leading a division of mounted veterans; so many horses and mules had died that there were none to spare, so Secretary of War Stanton got his way, after all. But, Rousseau had another plan.

By late June, Sherman had shoved Johnston backwards from the Georgia-Tennessee border toward Kennesaw Mountain, only a few days' march out of Atlanta. Since the Confederates who were so stubbornly opposing Sherman's advance were being partially supplied by the railroad running from central Alabama east to Atlanta, why not break up that railroad? This was the idea which Rousseau advanced first to General Thomas and then, with permission, directly to Sherman. From his headquarters of the recently renamed District of Tennessee, Rousseau telegraphed Sherman on June 19, 1864:

> With 3,000 men I could go down and destroy fifty to one hundred millions' worth of property belonging to the rebel government, including a portion of the important road between Selma and Atlanta. There are several long trestles on that road within twenty-five miles of Selma, and at that place there are manufacturing establishments far more extensive and important than they have at Atlanta, while between here and Selma there are five or six of the most important iron works there are in the Southern Confederacy. With Thornburgh's brigade ... and Colonel Harrison Eighth Indiana Cavalry ... and the Second Kentucky Cavalry, I could make the trip. The last two regiments are here to be mounted.[10]

Rousseau went on to describe how he could make his way back to the Union lines at the end of his raid and said, "I hope you will think of it and allow me to try it."[11]

On June 27, Rousseau again wired Sherman about his plan, and two days later Sherman tentatively agreed. He said, "Of course, go on and make all the preparations but do not start ... until I have pushed Johnston across the Chattahoochee.... Don't move until I give specific orders."[12]

On June 30, Sherman wired Rousseau a long message in code. It advised Rousseau to pick good officers to lead 2,500 men, to arm the men well, and to take pack mules "loaded with ammunition, salt, sugar, and coffee, and some bread or flour." He expected Rousseau to find meat for the men and forage for the animals along the line of march — the Rebels themselves would be made to feed the raiders who were savaging their country. Sherman advised Rousseau as to his route and warned him to avoid as much fighting as he could. Finally, he told him that if he found his way back to Union lines blocked, he should make for the Gulf Coast. At Pensacola, Florida, Major General Edward R. S. Canby would have supplies for Rousseau's men, if needed. The raiders could leave the horses at Pensacola and embark for New Orleans and "come round to Nashville again."[13]

On July 2, Thomas removed one of the concerns of the men planning this raid when he informed Headquarters that Nathan Bedford Forrest was going to be occupied in Mississippi. General A. J. Smith had been sent after "That Devil Forrest" and a fight between them was shaping up near Tupelo. This left the way through Alabama open for Rousseau. There would be no Confederates to oppose him aside from some militia and the small force of Alabama infantry commanded by Brigadier General James H. Clanton. With Thomas' concurrence, Sherman sent a telegraph to Rousseau later that same day, "Now is the time for the raid on Opelika. Telegraph me whether you go yourself or who will command."[14]

On July 3, Rousseau answered, "I shall go in person."[15]

The wires hummed with communications between Rousseau and Sherman over the next several days. On July 7, Rousseau sent word that he was leaving for Decatur the next day and would begin his raid from there, leaving at daylight on July 9.

Sherman, with his characteristic attention to detail, remembered one more thing he wanted to tell Rousseau. He sent another wire that afternoon. In it, he shared with the Kentuckian the trick to destroying railroads: "Burn the ties in piles, heat the iron in the middle and when red hot let the men pull the ends so as to give a twist to the rails. If simply bent, the rails may be used, but if they are twisted or wrenched they cannot be used again."[16]

Rousseau was one day and nine hours late in leaving Decatur. July 9 was spent attending to last minute details while the last of the regiments arrived. By early morning, July 10, some of the regiments still were not ready, and the pack mules were acting like mules, but the column moved out, nevertheless, about 1:00 P.M. "I go sixteen miles today," Rousseau informed Sherman.

The cavalry Rousseau finally chose to ride with him were nine companies of the 2nd Kentucky Cavalry (Companies A through I), the 4th Tennessee Cavalry, the 8th Indiana Cavalry, the 5th Iowa Cavalry, and the 9th Ohio Cavalry. In addition to the above named regiments, Rousseau took two ten-pounder Parrott guns of Battery E, 1st Michigan Light Artillery and five ambulances. Two companies of the 2nd Kentucky Cavalry were Rousseau's escort.

To many of these men, who had known Rousseau since the Camp Joe Holt days, it must have been good to be serving under the tall Kentuckian again. A correspondent named W. F. G. Shanks wrote a long article about Rousseau that appeared in *Harper's New Monthly Magazine* in November 1865 and described the man these troopers again saw before them as "fully 6'2", perhaps 3 inches high and otherwise Herculean in build and strength. When mounted, he always rides great, ponderous, and invariably blooded horses — he displays to great advantage, and no more graceful and impressive figure can be conceived than Rousseau mounted ... his elegant manners are as natural as his bravery and his high sense of honor are intuitive." There was no shame and considerable pride in serving under such a man as this.[17]

On the first night out, July 10, the raiders rested on a plantation near Somerville, seventeen miles south of Decatur. They moved out at 5:30 A.M. on the 11th and made thirty miles before camping at an old mill near Summit. Only the second day out and already the men had found an abundance of horses, mules, bacon, and some tobacco. Several Confederate prisoners were caught and paroled. One of them provided a good deal of amusement.

In the afternoon, a lone Confederate was captured. Rousseau showed up a few minutes later and decided to have some fun with the scared young Southerner by pretending to believe that he was a spy sent out to count the passing Union regiments. "We'll just hang you and save further trouble," Rousseau said. "Major, where's that rope?"[18]

The grayback was no Nathan Hale. He pleaded innocence, he begged for his life. Rousseau played the hardnose for some time before agreeing to a compromise — he would let the man run to save his life, away from the road and out of sight of the Yankee raiders, but if he looked back, he would be gunned down. The Rebel, his life almost reprieved, took off running, while behind him, the amused Rousseau shouted that he had better run faster. Until the very end of the raid, Rousseau would parole every prisoner his men took, though rarely would he get as much fun out of one as the quick-footed runner of the second day.

On the 12th, the column began breaking camp at 5:00 A.M. Within moments, shots were fired. The Rebels had arrived the night before and prepared an early morning surprise for the Yankees. The enemy attack was startling, but not very determined, and the Rebels were nudged aside as the column proceeded.

About midmorning, Rousseau's raiders reached a plantation and here one can get an idea of the kind of haul the men could expect from such a fine Southern estate, for the General kept a careful count of what was taken: three hundred pounds of meat, two hundred shocks of oats, and three hundred pounds of salt. In addition, the men filled their canteens with molasses. It is notable, though, what the men did not take. There was no promiscuous looting — Rousseau allowed the men to take only what they needed for their march. These men would not be seen with satin dresses draped over the cantle of their saddles or with jewelry boxes in their hands.

Proceeding to Blountsville, the raiders opened the jail to free some Rebel deserters and runaway slaves and burned some cotton before moving on toward Ashville. They collected cattle through the afternoon and looted the farm of Mr. James Brown. At dark, they came to Blount Mountain, an elevation so steep that the ambulances and gun carriages had to be eased down with ropes. They went into camp outside of Ashville. Though it had been a lot of miles and many hours since "To Horse" sounded that morning, there was still work to be done. Rousseau sent a few officers and men of the 4th Tennessee on into town. They skirmished with a small Rebel force there, but it was worth the fight. After the graybacks were driven away, the Tennesseans found a good supply of commissary stores and forage, which were distributed the next day.

On July 13, the men moved out at 6:00 A.M., but rode only five miles to Ashville before they stopped. Already, the horses need to be re-shod. While the farriers worked, the men explored the town and, as was becoming customary with them, opened the jail. They also looted the post office. Some seized the pressroom of the local paper (called, humorously, the *Vidette*) and printed a circular to be distributed among the brigade detailing Rousseau's orders for the march. The amateur journalists also printed one thousand special editions of the *Vidette*, which reported all the latest news of Union victories and announced the visit of Rousseau to Ashville as if it were an item in the social column. The *New York Times*, in reporting the incident, laughed, "The *Vidette*, in the hands of the raiders, doubtless turned a complete somersault."[19]

It was early afternoon before the raiders rode out of Ashville, leaving a bonfire of all the supplies they could not use. They rode until they reached the west bank of the Coosa River. As the rear of the column came into bivouac, a small party of Rebels attacked them and killed one officer and badly wounded another of the 5th Iowa Cavalry. The Rebel skirmishers got away and that night the men dressed the wounds of Captain J. C. Wilcox and buried the first man to give his life on the raid, Captain William Curl.

From independent evidence given years later by Confederate colonel

James Q. Chenoweth, the men who killed Captain Curl must have been part of the command of General Adam "Stovepipe" Johnson, who was crossing Northern Alabama on the way to make a raid in Kentucky. In Johnson's autobiography (which included sections written by contributors other than Johnson, himself) Colonel Chenoweth wrote that he was riding ahead of Johnson's column when "we came near running into Rousseau's cavalry." Chenoweth and the others returned to make their report to Johnson, who sent the colonel back with three other riders to make a reconnaissance.[20]

Colonel Chenoweth continued his account:

> Noiselessly nearing the road, we concealed ourselves in the thicket not twenty feet from the clattering column, as it dragged along stretched out with artillery and wagon train, miles in length. We crouched in our hiding place for quite an hour and until we believed the whole of the Yankee raiders had passed.... In this we were deceived. Just as we had risen upon our feet and were about to beat a retreat, we heard voices on the road and two officers appeared in sight, riding leisurely abreast ... we fired upon the horsemen, and in all haste broke for the rear.[21]

The Federals chased Chenoweth and his party, who escaped only by leaping their horses over a high-banked creek. Later, Chenoweth read in a captured newspaper that two of Rousseau's raiders had been killed in North Alabama — a report that turned out to be only half true.

* * *

Rousseau took the opportunity at the Coosa River to tighten his command. In his report, Rousseau wrote, "I here ordered a thorough inspection of the command to be made, and about 300 horses being reported in unfit condition for the service required, they were sent, together with the ineffective men, to Guntersville, forty miles distant, at which point the detachment crossed the Tennessee River, and reached our lines in safety. The effective force of the command was now reduced to less than 2,300 men."[22]

Worried about the security of the far bank, Rousseau also ordered Major Thomas Graham to lead two hundred men of the 8th Indiana, the two Parrot guns, and four of the ambulances over the river and establish a beachhead. The ferry boat could only carry about a dozen men at a time, but by midnight the advance force was across the Coosa.

At 5:00 A.M. on July 14, Rousseau began to move down the west bank of the river to the Ten Islands ford, where the brigade would cross. Those men of the 8th Indiana who had crossed the night before moved down the east bank at the same time, but they didn't get far before running into the enemy — 200 Alabama cavalrymen, plus some militia.

As the main part of the column began crossing the ford downstream, they also came under attack, suffering what Rousseau described as "severe fire from the enemy posted on the east bank, sheltered behind rocks and trees." The 4th Tennessee took position on Woods Island, the largest of the many at the ford, and the 5th Iowa spread out on a smaller island upstream.[23]

Woods Island was the better of the two positions, since it was not only bigger but also thick with driftwood and boulders. Still, a Rebel bullet dropped one Yankee and another ripped a stick from Rousseau's hand. These Rebels were not going to fade away like the others on this raid had done.

To persuade them, Rousseau brought three more regiments — the 2nd Kentucky, the 5th Iowa, and the remaining companies of the 8th Indiana — over to Woods Island. Lt. Colonel Fielder Jones of the 8th Indiana volunteered to lead a charge to drive away the Rebels and relieve Graham who, at this time, was still hotly engaged on the east bank upstream. Rousseau valued Jones and was reluctant to see him go, but finally consented to let him lead his men from the island back to the west bank and ride north to the ferry and, from there, relieve Graham. Rousseau sent Jones off with a gesture and the one word order: "Go."[24]

Jones encountered a Negro man on the road and learned from him of a crossing point between the ferry and the Ten Islands. This would save miles and be a surprise to the Rebs. The end of another hour later saw Jones' men on the east bank, riding hard for Graham, but Graham's men had already scattered the 6th Alabama and were themselves on a rescue mission; they were riding south to attack the Rebels who were stopping Rousseau at Ten Islands. The Rebels of the 8th Alabama were focused on the men on the islands in front of them when Graham's men unexpectedly burst upon them on their right flank. The surprised Southerners broke and ran.

As soon as the enemy fire from shore began to diminish, the men with Rousseau started to cross. A few slugs from the retreating Confederates zipped harmlessly past them as they splashed toward the shore. Captain Thomas C. Williams was dazzled by the pageantry of the sight. He wrote, "The long array of horsemen winding between the green islands and taking a serpentine course across the ford — their arms flashing back the rays of the burning sun and guidons gaily fluttering along the column, formed a bright picture."[25]

Another writer who may have been inspired by the sight of Rousseau's cavalry crossing the river — an imagined sight in his case — was the poet Walt Whitman. In an article that appeared in the fall 1999 issue of *Alabama Heritage* magazine, Dr. Betty Barrett argued persuasively that Whitman's short poem called "Cavalry Crossing a Ford" was a free verse account of Rousseau's men at Ten Islands. The geographical clues do match and the point of view is not first person, which was typical of Whitman, but third person, just like the war correspondent W. F. G. Shanks' reports of the crossing. Much of the language is identical to Shanks'. In its entirety, the poem reads:

> A line in long array where they wind betwixt green islands,
> They take a serpentine course, their arms flash in the sun—
> hark to the musical clank,
> Behold the silvery river, in it the splashing horses loitering stop to drink,
> Behold the brown-faced men, each group, each person a picture,
> the negligent rest on the saddles,
> Some emerge on the opposite bank, others are just entering the ford—while,
> Scarlet and blue and snowy white,
> The guidon flags flutter gaily in the wind.[26]

The poem appeared in Whitman's *Drum Taps*. The matter is best left to literary critics, perhaps, but the poem is arguably a better contribution to Civil War verse than "The American Flag," William Shakespeare Hays' song which was dedicated to Rousseau in 1863.

* * *

On the east bank of the Coosa River, the Federals found a decidedly unpoetic sight; they counted fifteen of the enemy killed. Forty were estimated to have been wounded and there were eight prisoners. The bluecoats lost only one wounded, a trooper in the hard fighting 8th Indiana. Rousseau praised Major Graham for his gallantry in his report of the raid.

Five miles beyond the ford came the first real destruction of enemy property, so far. The Cane Creek Furnace was an important iron-smelting complex. It once provided iron for such noble building projects as the Alabama capitol. Now, its production was turned over to military use. Iron plates from Cane Creek were said to have been used in building the ironclad C.S.S. *Virginia* (known for its inconclusive battle with the U.S.S. *Monitor*), and it also supplied sheet iron to the manufactories in Selma. Cane Creek Furnace was blown up and the surrounding complex of wooden buildings burned. Five miles away, the not-yet-completed Janney Furnace was also destroyed. From there, the men proceeded south along rutted roads through an afternoon that was undoubtedly the warmest that some of the young Hoosiers and Buckeyes had ever seen. As they rode on, the men added to the heat of an Alabama July day by burning barns and cotton gins.

The weather being like it was, the men were surprised in the afternoon to see a sad looking woman and a girl plodding toward the Coosa River in a rickety wagon with digging tools in the bed. David Evans relates in his excellent book *Sherman's Horsemen* that a trooper "playfully" called out to them, "Where are you going?"

"To Ten Islands," the old woman answered, "to bury our dead."[27]

* * *

The men rode to Martin's Mill that evening and some of the men rested, while others followed orders to smash one of the Parrott guns. Hauling two guns was slowing the raiders down; but just one piece, double-teamed, might be able to keep up. At 10:00 P.M., the men moved out and rode another four hours, fighting a skirmish en route. They stopped as Eastaboga for what was left of the night.

The men were up at 4:30 A.M. No time was allowed for breakfast. The great danger in a raid of this sort was that, the longer it went, the more enemy forces would gather, and a great noose would begin to tighten, invisible at first and fully visible only when it was too late to escape. A prudent commander took notice of the signs. From the increasing severity of the skirmishes and the women on the road, it was obvious that word was spreading of the raiders' presence in the Heart of Dixie. Making good time was essential now.

The raiders arrived at Talladega at about 8:00 A.M. A few shots were exchanged with the enemy, but the men quickly had possession of the town. Guards were posted to protect private homes while others went on to the work of destruction. Smokehouses, barns, and stables were looted. As usual, a visit was paid to the post office and the jail, but the great prizes in Talladega were the railroad depot and the military warehouses, which were full of flour, wheat, salt, bacon, shoes, and tobacco, as well as other goods. When every useful item was removed from the buildings, the townspeople were invited to come take a share. Then, the men with the torches came. Because Dr. Charles Smith, a local man, urgently pointed out to Rousseau that burning the warehouse would put the entire town at risk, that building was spared. Likewise, two nearby gun factories were not burned, though the machinery inside was broken up. But, the depot and some railroad cares were torched, and the water tank and the switches were destroyed.

Rousseau earmarked some supplies for Dr. Smith's hospital in hopes of guaranteeing good treatment for Private John Matz who had been shot through the face at the Coosa River crossing and was going to have to be left at Talladega.

Some of the raiders were riding fresh mounts when they left Talladega at 10:00 A.M. A short distance out of town, a trooper of the 9th Ohio, James Doran, who had gotten drunk on confiscated whiskey, made a violent nuisance of himself and challenged Rousseau's adjutant, Captain Thomas C. Williams. The two got into a fistfight and were slugging it out when Rousseau stepped forward to put a stop to it. The belligerent Buckeye still had not had enough, so Rousseau decked him. The watching soldiers suddenly had a renewed admiration for their General as a fighting man, for Doran was a noted brawler.

Discipline seemed to take a small holiday after Talladega. Despite strict orders to the contrary, a few stragglers remained in the town and three of them paid a heavy price for whatever plunder they found — they were captured and now would be sitting out the war at Andersonville or some other Rebel prison camp.

Rousseau's men had no way of knowing what a panic their raid had loosed in Montgomery. The rumor was spreading that 3,500 Yankees were on their way. Every able-bodied man in town was asked to help protect the capital city, and those who did not volunteer were forced to comply, some of them at the point of a bayonet. The local soldiers' payroll, which had just arrived in Montgomery, was hurried, along with some bullion, into a hiding place outside the city and the specie of the Central Bank was sent to the railroad and placed on a guarded rail car which was hooked to a locomotive for a quick getaway when the raiders appeared. The money was, in large part, the funds of the banks of Atlanta, which had been sent to Montgomery for safekeeping.

The raiders were not heading for Montgomery, though they were on the Montgomery road. They were riding instead for Mardisville and beyond. The countryside was fertile, a good country for plantations, which meant a large slave population. Slaves were often told horror stories by their masters and ministers about what to expect if the Yankees passed by, but the slaves in east central Alabama had not listened to the propaganda; indeed, they proved to be so friendly that they began to tag along with the cavalrymen despite the rapid clip. Colonel William Hamilton of the 9th Ohio, remarked with typical nineteenth century gentility, "We found the niggers everywhere to be our friends."[28]

The horse soldiers proceeded through Mardisville and Winterboro, and arrived at Sylacauga an hour before midnight. Still, they were not done. They rode for two hours more and, finally, they bivouacked, closing a thirty-nine mile day. The rear element of the column, the 5th Iowa, reached the camp about 3:00 A.M., only an hour before the next day's ride began.

The men were ordered up at 4:00 A.M. on July 16 and a half hour later cantered out of a camp some of them had barely seen. The men were bone-tired, bleary-eyed and too tired to talk. They must have been glad to see the plantation of Patrick McKinney near Socopatoy — Rousseau would probably halt for a rest there, if his usual pattern held true. The General did not disappoint them, and the men ate and settled down to sleep beneath the shade trees.

Before Rousseau's raiders rode on at 4:00 P.M., they looted the McKinney plantation and those of his neighbors, but some of them forgot to keep a sharp eye. Nine were captured, more proof that the Confederates were closing in around them.

About 6:00 P.M., Rousseau's men reached Youngville. They relieved the town of its grain and bacon and pressed on to Stowe's Ferry on the Tallapoosa River. The one artillery piece, the ambulances, and the pack mules were left there to cross by boat, but the mounted men rode on to a ford a half-mile up. It was after sundown before the last of them began across. The ford was rougher than had been expected and so deep that the horses had to swim. Crossing here in the dark turned out to be a hard business and there was one drowning—a black youngster who had attached himself to the raiders died in the Tallapoosa River that night, having lived free only one day in his life.

It was early morning of the 17th before the last of the soldiers got across the river. Even then, their rest was disturbed. A Rebel scouting party of four men approached and was fired upon. Two of the men were captured, and one escaped, but their captain was shot through the head and killed.

Rousseau's column broke camp at 8:00 A.M., a later hour than usual. Rousseau had done the best he could for his raiders. He knew the men were exhausted, but they had a job to do: "Being within a day's march of the railroad, I decided it important to press forward," the General later said.[29]

Beyond De Soto, the column veered toward Loachapoka, a town on the Montgomery and West Point Railroad. They arrived at 6:00 P.M., seven days and 240 miles from their starting point. If they had arrived a bit sooner, they might have captured Braxton Bragg, who was on the last train that passed through Loachapoaka—the last train, in fact, that would pass through Loachapoka for some time to come. The raiders had missed Bragg, but they were nevertheless in position to do some real harm to the Confederates; they could break the railroad supplying the Confederates near Atlanta from the west.

The railroad turned out to be strap-rail, a mere strip of iron nailed on top of a pitch pine rail. T-rail, which was solid iron, would have been harder to destroy. While videttes were posted on the approaches to town, other men went to the work of destruction. Work gangs of twenty men or more used fence rails to gouge up entire sections of track at a time—fifty to one hundred feet of rails and crossties—which were piled up and burned. Rousseau wrote, "The dry pine burned so readily and produced such an intense heat that the iron was warped and rendered worthless and the ties burned off where the track rested on them, making the destruction complete."[30]

The bonfires also produced constellations of sparks which set fire to the railroad depot and threatened the private residences of Loachapoka. The *New York Times,* in reporting Rousseau's raid, noted that "the adjacent houses were saved by the personal exertions of the General and his soldiers — the latter putting their own wet blankets on the roofs." In some reports, Rousseau *posted* soldiers on the roofs to snuff any sparks that fell. In this way, the fire was contained to the railroad buildings.[31]

(In a curious twist, the Southern papers found something ominous in what the *New York Times* applauded. The *Montgomery Advertiser* ran a piece several days later, on July 25, which said, "Let no one be deceived by Rousseau's pretended regard for private property and the rights of citizens ... he wants your negroes, provisions, and stock kept undefended until the larger armies of the enemy shall come to take them.")[32]

A group of Confederate militia and convalescents came out from Auburn and traded gunfire with some of Rousseau's scouts while the other men were busy at Loachapoka, but it was only a nuisance. There was no Confederate follow up. By daylight of the 18th, six miles of M&WP RR was demolished and the men rode out. Rousseau divided them into separate work parties and sent each of them to attack a section of the thirteen miles of track between Chehaw Station and Loachapoka. The 2nd Kentucky Cavalry was ordered to destroy track between Loachapoka and Notasulga and they were good at their work. Rousseau stayed with the regiment during the morning and later remembered, "The alacrity with which Lt.-Colonel [Elijah S.] Watts and the officers and men of his regiment entered upon this duty and the effectual manner in which they performed it, came upon my personal observation and deserves honorable mention."[33]

There had been plenty of warning signals during the past few days that the Confederate strength was growing against Rousseau's raiders. Now, while Rousseau watched the 2nd Kentucky Cavalry at work near Notasulga, the enemy struck at another of his work parties, the one at Beasley's Station near Chehaw. A band of 450 Confederates led by Major Bryan M. Thomas arrived by train, disembarked, and formed up for battle in front of the surprised men of the 5th Iowa. The dismounted Yankees hurried for cover near a cotton gin house on the south side of the tracks and began to fire at the Southerners. The Confederates were mostly teenagers, many of them cadets from the University of Alabama, but what they lacked in years they made up for in grit. They moved bravely forward and pushed the Federals back into some woods. The students had brought with them a small cannon and they might have really punished the Yankees with it, except that the horses pulling it became spooked and galloped off, pulling the wildly bouncing field piece behind, until it overturned and dropped into a gully. It came to rest upside down and the horses got loose from their harness and ran away.

Even without this reassuring bit of artillery support, the Confederates pushed forward. Yankees on horseback raced up to block the Rebel advance. Major Thomas ordered his young Rebels toward the left to outflank them, but the cavalrymen saw what was happening and rode away before the enemy could get into position.

As they re-dressed their lines, Major Thomas had the engineer back his train up to Chehaw Station and blow the whistle, hoping to fool the Yankees into thinking that enemy reinforcements were arriving. Perhaps it was the very simplicity, the lack of guile, that made the Federals fall for the Rebel trick. Rousseau received a message in a few minutes that the 5th Iowa was being attacked by Rebels who were arriving by the multiple trainload.

Rousseau sent six companies of the 8th Indiana under Colonel Tom Harrison to ride to the Iowans' rescue. Arriving, they dismounted north of the track and advanced until they could see the Rebels drawn up in a clearing between the gin house and the woods, the space the Yankee horsemen had vacated minutes before.

Two companies hurried forward to bulk up the left flank of the Yankee line and Lt. Colonel Fielder Jones led the other four companies to the right flank which was advancing just then, pushing against the Rebel left. The Rebels adjusted their lines to meet the newly arriving Yankees and for the next hour the two sides slammed away at each other, neither side giving any ground. Finally, the quick fire of the Yankees' Spencer carbines was too hot for the Rebels—they began to falter, to fall back, and soon the entire enemy line was abandoning the field.

Earlier, while the gunfire in the distance increased, Rousseau had become visibly upset. W. F. G. Shanks said that it was the only time the General was ever "known to betray any considerable nervousness under fire." He was heard to say, "I shouldn't have got into this affair. I'm very much afraid this isn't judicious."

He ordered Captain Thomas Elkin forward to see how the fight was going for the Federals at Beasley Station. Elkin arrived in time to see the Rebels retreating. He rode back to Rousseau and reported, "There's no reason to be uneasy about Harrison."

"Uneasy about Harrison?" Rousseau roared. "Tom Harrison can whip all the militia in Alabama. But what shall I do with my poor wounded boys? We are a thousand miles from home and no way to carry them comfortably."[34]

The General's fears for his wounded turned out to be exaggerated. Two men were killed and were beyond help; another was mortally wounded. One trooper was captured. Six of the wounded men were so badly hurt that they would not be able to continue. They would have to be left at the Confederate hospital at Camp Watts. This is where the merciful treatment of civilians along the way and the effort to spare private homes from the torch would pay off—his wounded men, now, had every reason to expect mercy. Further, Rousseau used the young prisoners his own men had captured as a bargaining chip. He paroled them and told them, "Boys, go home and tell your parents that Rousseau does not war on women and children; and, mark you, do you see that they don't make war on wounded prisoners."[35]

Meanwhile, the 2nd Kentucky's work at Notasulga went on. Before leaving the area, all the railroad buildings and the water tank were destroyed. About 4:00 P.M., the raiders rode away.

The 5th Iowa was not the only regiment that came under fire this day. Colonel William Hamilton's 9th Ohio Cavalry had run into the enemy while moving toward the railroad near West Point. Seeing them ahead, Hamilton had his buglers blow "Charge!" and, with sabers drawn, the Yankees plowed through the enemy, who had no stomach for cold steel. They dashed for the woods behind them. Hamilton sent in dismounted troopers to find them and once they did, the rest of the Yankees charged again and emptied the woods of Confederates.

For the rest of the day, half of the men stood guard while the other half destroyed railroad, prying up, piling up, and burning up sections of track. Every now and then, the workers and the videttes would switch roles. In this way, three miles of track were turned to ash and twisted iron by 11:00 A.M.

Approaching Auburn, they learned that the townsmen were arming and deploying on the outskirts to protect their city. Hamilton responded with his usual vigor, dashing in with guns blazing and, as earlier in the day, the enemy fled to the woods. When Hamilton and his men rode into Auburn, it was a town of women. The only opposition the raiders faced at all was when Captain T. H. Francis, commander of the Confederate post, marched eighteen men armed with shotguns out to demonstrate in front of the Yankees. The stalwart eighteen fired one sally and retired.

Isabelle Wood Johnston Shacklette was a young girl living in Auburn in 1864 and she denied that the townsmen had prepared any defense at all. In her short memoir of the visit which Rousseau's men paid on that Sunday morning, she claimed the bluecoat cavalrymen were fooled by the sounds of carriages racing about on the streets of Auburn which were "very rocky and stoney." It was this clatter that caused the Yankees "as we afterwards heard, to think we had cannons and men preparing for defense."

She continued, "We had a large hospital with many wounded and sick soldiers who were being hastily removed, though not all in time, for Rousseau's men suddenly dashed in shouting and firing at everyone in the streets and into the hospital, the wounded and sick running in every direction for shelter."[36]

Hamilton's troopers helped themselves to supplies at the Rebel warehouse and then invited the women to come pick over what was left. Rousseau had done the same thing at Talladega.

Isabelle Shacklette said that the soldiers also entered private homes. She wrote, "Then ensued a terrible time of carnage, thieving and destruction. The lady I was boarding with was ordered to bake bread for sixty men or he would 'burn the house down over our heads.' She replied to the officer he could have everything in the house, that there was a negro cook in the kitchen whom he could command to prepare it for him, as she would not."[37]

Outside the house, Mrs. Shacklette remembered hearing the soldiers shout "that the whole town would be burned down because it was near the home of William P. Young, the great secessionist, his plantation being just a mile out of town. They burnt his dwelling house, but not the houses in town."[38]

The men down by the railroad soon heard a train whistle — a load of Rebels coming from Atlanta, it was said. Company L of the 9th Ohio under Captain Asbury Gatch went east to investigate, while others began barricading Auburn's streets.

Company L found the train two miles out. After it passed, Gatch and his men poured out of the underbrush and tore up the track behind it. The engineer saw them and quickly reversed the train to escape, but too late. The train backed into the break and jumped the track. The engineer and two crewmen were brought before Gatch. Questioned, they said that they had come from Columbus, Georgia. They were carrying no soldiers and no troop train was behind them.

The alarm over, Hamilton's men gave up on the barricades and went to burning: the depot, warehouse, supplies, a tannery, even six tons of lead, all torched. Though the townspeople had been rudely talked to, even threatened, and their town looted and some of it burned, there was no killing. Even Mrs. Shacklette, who was certainly no friend of the invading Yankees, did not mention a single life that was lost among the civilian population of Auburn while Rousseau's men were there.

As Hamilton's men left Auburn, they destroyed the locomotive which Captain Gatch had derailed. Then, they moved on down the track, tearing it up.

Rousseau and the others were following. It was raining. At midnight, they caught up with the men of the 9th Ohio, who were still tearing up track.

Rousseau rode up to the colonel and asked him in an amused way, "Hamilton, are you going in to Atlanta tonight?"

"I don't know," Hamilton answered, "my orders ... were to keep at work till I heard from you."[39]

Rousseau let Hamilton know that it was time to quit for the night. He thanked the colonel for his role in helping to make the "expedition" a success and then went up to a house with a porch where he could sleep out of the rain.

One would think that a day of tearing up nearly twenty miles of railroad, plus burning all the railroad and government property between Notasulga and Auburn and beyond, would have left everyone too tired to think of anything but sleep. But some had plunder on their minds. That night, a few slipped back through Rousseau's pickets to Auburn where they robbed citizens and stores. Mrs. Shacklette mentioned this in her narrative. She said, "People were robbed of everything they possessed and the awful carousing continued through the night. In the morning the alarm was sounded that the Confederates were coming in force to capture them. Then I looked out of my window and such a hurrying and scurrying to mount and haste away I never saw."[40]

If Mrs. Shacklette did look out her window and see the raiders mounting up, she must have seen it by firelight, for Rousseau had his men up before dawn. By 4:00 A.M. they were riding east toward the sunrise. Once again, the General divided his command into separate work gangs and sent them to destroy the railroad in and around Opelika.

Later that morning, when Rousseau reassembled his men on the banks of Sougahatchee Creek, they feasted on the bounty of Opelika's warehouses including, to the delight of many, thirty boxes of chewing tobacco. The warehouse and depot were fired about noon, along with some other buildings and some boxcars, and the men continued east toward the Georgia state line. They veered north at Rough and Ready, Alabama, riding quietly through the woods, trying to escape the attention of the Rebel cavalry. That night, by the light of a full moon, they bumped into a squad of enemy horse soldiers and had to cut their way through to Bethlehem where they stopped at 2:00 A.M., July 20. After two hours, they were in the saddle again, headed for Carrollton. The horses were suffering, dropping dead in their tracks, and the men unstrapped the saddles and carried them until they could acquire fresh horses by the usual method. They stopped for dinner at Rock Mills. There, they found a guide named Green Harper, who led them across the state line about 2:00 P.M. Seven hours later, thirty-one miles inside Georgia, the men stopped for what one accurately remembered as "the first good night's rest we have had on this trip."[41]

As they passed through Carrollton about 2:00 P.M. the next day, the raiders did not stop to plunder or burn, but a civilian foolishly took a potshot at them and they killed him. Sixteen miles further, at Villa Rica, they captured two Rebels who, this time, were not paroled but taken along, now that the men were so near the end. The raiders slept that night fewer than 25 miles from Marietta.

Another sign that they were near the end of the raid came the next morning. The men slept until dawn and then, were allowed the time to cook breakfast. They rode out at 6:00 A.M. At Powder Springs, they met a platoon of men from Major General George Stoneman's 14th Illinois Cavalry, who saluted the raiders as they passed by. Continuing, they rode by the flank of Kennesaw Mountain and noted the wreckage of the recent battle there.

The men stopped for a rest at 1:00 P.M., five miles shy of Marietta, but Rousseau and his staff rode on. At Marietta, the General wired Sherman, announcing his safe arrival. He added:

> I have torn up and destroyed nearly 30 miles of railroad between Montgomery and Opelika and three miles of it between Opelika and Columbus and two miles between West Point and Opelika also the Y and the turntable and the depots filled with stores at Opelika and many depots of supplies in other points.
>
> My trip was entire successful in all respects. I destroyed 30 miles of railroad in 36 hours. My command will be here [Marietta] in three hours. My whole loss does not exceed 12 killed and 30 wounded. I captured 400 fine mules and 300 horses.[42]

He did not mention the three hundred Negroes who came in with him, nor the sixty-one prisoners he had captured and paroled, though he remembered to include both in his official report.

The raiders began arriving in Marietta, the last of them coming in about 8:00 P.M., July 22. Before they slept, the men fed their horses.

The men got a chance to briefly rest before they returned to duty, but not Rousseau. Sherman ordered the General to proceed without delay to the railroad bridge over the Chattahoochee River below Turner's Ferry to relieve General Stoneman. By the time the order arrived, the energetic Rousseau had already left for the front. He got Sherman's message at General George Thomas' headquarters and proceeded to Sherman's. The scruffy, fidgety Ohioan greeted Rousseau warmly and then said, "I didn't expect to see you back."

Rousseau asked, "Why not?"

"I expected you to tear up the road," Sherman answered, "but I thought they would gobble you."[43]

15

The Defense of Middle Tennessee

That Rousseau and his men had not been "gobbled" was a tribute to Rousseau's leadership. Sherman told Rousseau that he had done well and was amused enough by a story that Rousseau told him that he included it in his autobiography. As Sherman recounted it:

> He said he was far down in Alabama, below Talladega, one hot, dusty day, when the blue clothing of his men was gray with dust; he had halted his column along a road, and he in person, with his staff, had gone to the house of a planter who met him kindly on the front-porch. He asked for water, which was brought in, and as the party sat on the porch in conversation he saw, in a stable-yard across the road, quite a number of good mules. He remarked to the planter, "My good sir, I fear I must take some of your mules." The planter remonstrated, saying he had already contributed liberally to the good cause; that it was only last week that he had given to General Roddy ten mules. Rousseau replied, "Well, in this war you should at least be neutral — that is, you should be as liberal to us as to Roddy (a rebel cavalry general)." "Well, ain't you on our side?" "No," said Rousseau; "I am General Rousseau, and all these men you see are Yanks." "Great God! Is it possible? Are these Yanks? Who ever supposed they would come away down here in Alabama?" Of course, Rousseau took his ten mules.[1]

Yet, by the time Sherman wrote his memoirs, he had changed his mind about the ultimate effectiveness of Rousseau's Raid. He wrote, "The expedition ... must have disturbed the enemy somewhat; but, as usual, the cavalry did not work hard, and their destruction of the railroad was soon repaired."[2]

Modern historians have agreed with Sherman's first evaluation, that Rousseau did well. Shelby Foote wrote that General Sherman authorized additional strikes on the railroads around Atlanta in hopes that Rousseau's raid had "established the model" for the kind of cavalry operations Sherman required. The railroad Rousseau had broken would not be repaired for a month. Mark Fretwell, an early student of Rousseau's raid wrote, "In some respects the Alabama Raid was without parallel in the war." He emphasized that the raid was swift and sharp, with only one objective: that it penetrated deeper into the Confederacy that any other and with an unusually large number of men; and that it inflicted great damage at just the right moment. It was, said Fretwell, "an essential, important, and timely strike." Edwin C. Bearss agreed. He wrote, "Rousseau's Raid on the Montgomery and West Point Railroad was one of the most successful cavalry strikes of the entire Civil War.... In the entire annals of this bitter conflict, it would be very difficult to discover another cavalry operation of this type where so much damage was inflicted upon the adversary, at such a small cost to the side undertaking the raid."[3]

Historian David Evans, who wrote the best and most comprehensive account of the raid, praised Rousseau's swing through Alabama as "the most daring, most successful expedition since Colonel Benjamin H. Grierson's sweep through Mississippi in the spring of 1863" and noted that, "unlike Grierson, Rousseau had succeeded in reinforcing a Federal army in the midst of an important campaign."[4]

Further, Evans said, "There are men like Lovell Rousseau, who inspired confidence and enthusiasm wherever he went.... He was conspicuously brave, a self-made man who inspired other men to follow him, and he led them on one of the most successful cavalry raids of the war." Indeed, Sherman would never find another like Rousseau. In the three subsequent raids which Sherman ordered around Atlanta — those of Edward McCook, George Stoneman, and Judson Kilpatrick — the results would be far less satisfying. In each case, there were more casualties, more men lost to Confederate capture, and much less destruction to the CSA transportation system. In the case of Kilpatrick's expedition, the Rebel trains were operational again and pulling into Atlanta almost before the raiders themselves got back.[5]

There are still others whose opinions shed light on the effectiveness of Rousseau's Raid. The people of Alabama have never forgotten it, as some of the collateral descendants of Rousseau have discovered for themselves. Rousseau's relative Verna Rosecrans was told by another family member that in Cherokee County, Alabama, even today, "the people would not let you picnic in their Cow Pasture if you are a relative of his."[6]

* * *

In those days following Rousseau's Raid, when Sherman was still enthused with the results, it seems that he would have wanted to keep Rousseau in the field. However, for reasons that are not understood, Sherman returned Rousseau to Nashville. He left on July 25 to resume command of the 4th Division of the 20th Army Corps, the District of Tennessee — and fell sick of a fever there.

This was no time for the commander to be sick, though. The CSA "War

Child," General Joseph Wheeler, was moving into Tennessee to try to destroy Sherman's supply line, just as Sherman was trying to cut those of the Confederates at Atlanta.

Wheeler left Covington, Georgia, on August 10 with 4,500 officers and men. He enjoyed a success almost immediately when he captured at Calhoun a drove of 1,700 cattle, which was sent back to General Hood at Atlanta.

Further north, trouble developed. At Tilton, Wheeler was attacked by Major General James B. Steedman and badly stung. The diminutive Rebel proceeded to Tunnel Hill near Chattanooga where he tore up track, but inexplicably failed to destroy the tunnel itself, an act that would have interrupted Sherman's flow of supplies for weeks to come. Instead, Wheeler contented himself with breaking up track.

Heavy August rains had swollen the Tennessee River so that Wheeler was forced far to the east to find a crossing. He crossed the Hiawassee at Athens, where he captured a load of supplies. Still searching for a crossing point on the Tennessee, he led his men closer to loyal Knoxville and came under frequent attacks by Federal soldiers and even Unionist guerrillas.

Beyond Knoxville, he finally got his raiding party across the Holston and the French Broad Rivers and headed, at last, for Middle Tennessee, his original destination. He had been forced to detour for two hundred miles and was way behind schedule. By this time, the Federals knew full well what Wheeler was up to. General Thomas warned Rousseau by wire to watch Wheeler, which the Kentuckian had been doing, already. Rousseau sent a wire to General Robert Granger (former post commander at Nashville) at Decatur, saying, "Wheeler has crossed the river above Knoxville and will be upon us. All our cavalry should be ready to move at any moment." A similar message went to General Robert H. Milroy, the discredited former commander at Winchester, Virginia, who now commanded the three brigades defending the Nashville & Chattanooga Railroad from his headquarters at Tullahoma.[7]

Wheeler destroyed two trains on the Nashville & Chattanooga Railroad and seized still more supplies at McMinnville, after a fight with Milroy, but the Yankee pressure was constant and increasing around him. On September 1, Rousseau, leading both infantry and cavalry, slammed into Wheeler head-on and forced him into a fight near Murfreesboro. Wheeler escaped, but Rousseau fought him again later that day at LaVergne, and the next day at Franklin. Immediately after the latter named fight, Rousseau wired Brigadier General J.D. Webster, his chief-of-staff at Nashville, "We are out of ammunition and must wait for it.... If ammunition be sent on the railroad to this place we can get it, I hope, in time to pursue tonight. After the fight to-day, the enemy went down the pike to Columbia.... With the infantry and artillery I can whale Wheeler out of his boots."[8]

Rousseau must have received his ammunition, for he kept after Wheeler, slashing at him, until the Confederates decided to give up their objective of Nashville and turn back south. Rousseau kept up the pressure from behind and there was a Federal garrison in every town ahead — the retreat took on the nature of an escape. Wheeler was forced to fight again and again. Even the men in the commissary departments and the convalescents in the towns were taking arms to meet Wheeler, should he be bold or foolish enough to dash into their towns. On September 3, General J. D. Webster at Nashville wired Major General Halleck in Washington, "General Rousseau has fought Wheeler two days, driving him.... He will probably give us but little more trouble."[9]

Wheeler was losing men and horses at an alarming rate as he reeled toward the Alabama line. Rousseau captured five hundred of his horses, but worse, he drove an impenetrable wedge between Wheeler's main column and Colonel George Dibrell and a detachment of several hundred men. Permanently lost to Wheeler for the rest of this raid, Dibrell linked up with General John S. Williams further east.

Wheeler had hoped to demolish a section of the Alabama & Tennessee Railroad, but was able to inflict little or no damage, he was so weak and harried. Still, Rousseau kept up the chase. It was reported on September 7, "Rousseau is pursuing with effect and is said to have taken many prisoners. Hundreds of Wheeler's men are deserting." A second report from later that day said, "Wheeler's force was met and whipped by Rousseau near Manchester, Tennessee and the rebels disbanded." Other running fights followed at Campbellsville and Lawrenceburg.[10]

At Athens, on September 8, General Rousseau linked up with Generals Steedman and Granger and hurried toward the Tennessee River. Sherman wired Halleck the next day, "I think General Rousseau and Steedman are stirring up Wheeler pretty well, and hope they will make an end of him." Despite their effort to cut off his escape, Wheeler was able to get across the state line on September 12. On that day, Rousseau wired the news to his corps commander General Thomas. Rousseau was anxious to return to Nashville, but he had had enough of the saddle for awhile. Rousseau's acting adjutant general sent a wire to district headquarters later on the 12th saying, "General Rousseau will start for Nashville as soon as a train can be obtained, and wishes to have one sent out from Nashville as far as the break in the road to meet him." The General arrived back in Nashville on the 13th.[11]

The month of September was a productive one for the Union. On the second day of the month, General Sherman occupied Atlanta. On the 4th, John Hunt Morgan was shot and killed in Greeneville, Tennessee. And now Fighting Joe Wheeler had been sent stumbling back into Alabama. Accounts of the successful repulse of Wheeler spread through the army and won Rousseau the praise of his superiors both near and far. From Missouri, where he had been assigned after losing command of the Army of the Cumberland, Major General William S. Rosecrans took the time to write Rousseau a long personal letter dated September 14. "My Dear General," it began, "I have had my blood stirred by your expedition across the Tennessee River and on the RR in Ga. and more recently by the big raid of Wheeler. John 'Horse thief' Morgan has ceased to trouble us forever — I hope 'point Wheeler' the little ruffian may fall before my friend General Rousseau."[12]

"The little ruffian" Wheeler had not fallen, but he and his men were used up. He stopped at Tuscumbia to allow his troopers a chance to rest and recuperate. There were fewer than half as many men with Wheeler now as had begun the raid. The little bit of damage that he had done was quickly repaired by Rousseau's work crews. Raiding behind Yankee lines was not the lark that it had been in 1862.

But there was another who wanted to try it. Nathan Bedford Forrest was on his way to test his luck in Rousseau's domain.

Nathan Bedford Forrest was an unequaled Confederate threat. Looking back from a distance of a century, Shelby Foote considered him one of the authentic geniuses of the war, and Forrest's contemporary William T. Sherman would not have disagreed; he believed that it would be worth almost any number of men to stop him. He was the "Wizard of the Saddle" and he was on his way.

Forrest had hoped to link up with Wheeler, but after seeing the War Child's ragged remnant at Tuscumbia, Forrest reported to his superiors that though he could "expect but little assistance" from Wheeler's "demoralized" men, he would "nevertheless go ahead." He hoped that he would be able to pick up some of Wheeler's stragglers as he moved through Tennessee. Two days after he gave up on Wheeler, Forrest was reinforced by nine hundred men from General Phillip Roddey (whose name was often misspelled in Federal reports as "Roddy"). Now, Forrest had over four thousand men and eight guns.[13]

Forrest led his men toward Tennessee the following day. Two days later, he attacked one of the Yankees' prized railroad forts at Athens. The commander, Colonel Wallace Campbell (110th United States Colored Troops) held out, even against Forrest's artillery, hoping for help from Robert S. Granger at Decatur. In fact, Granger did send a rescue party toward Athens—

portions of the 102nd Ohio and the 18th Michigan, led by Lieutenant Colonel Jonas D. Elliott — but Forrest had anticipated such a move and sent the 21st Tennessee to meet them. The rescue party was defeated and captured. Convinced that Forrest had ten thousand men and nine artillery pieces, Colonel Campbell finally surrendered, but not before losing a third of his men either killed or wounded. Two nearby blockhouses also surrendered, one with no resistance whatsoever and the other after a short barrage from Forrest's artillery.

Unwilling to be burdened with the plunder of these early successes (which included wagons, ambulances, and huge quantities of quartermaster and commissary stores), Forrest sent it all back to Florence and continued toward Pulaski.

On September 25, at Sulphur Branch, Forrest again employed his artillery to advantage and after two hours, captured the two blockhouses which guarded the large railroad trestle on the Nashville & Decatur Railroad. It was a repeat of Athens, in regard to the amount of weapons and stores that were captured, but he also captured one thousand prisoners. The next day, Forrest approached Elk River. Colonel George Spalding had been resisting Forrest's advance as best he could since Sulphur Branch, but the Rebels were too powerful for him to stop. Knowing that they were making for Elk River, Spalding rode ahead, ordered an indefensible blockhouse south of the river to be abandoned and used the garrison to reinforce the other two blockhouses which guarded the Elk River Bridge. As the enemy appeared and began to deploy, Spalding saw that his small cavalry force was about to be enveloped. He sent for the officers commanding the blockhouses and, as he remembered, "moved them to hold the blockhouses at all hazards ... and told them also I would be obliged to withdraw my cavalry or Forrest would have me surrounded before daylight. They promised to hold the blockhouses until they were knocked to pieces." Reassured, Spalding led his cavalrymen toward Pulaski.[14]

At daylight, he stopped to gather intelligence of the enemy and learned to his astonishment, that "the negro soldiers and their officers that I had left to hold the bridge had abandoned the stockade and had been in advance of the cavalry all the morning, having evacuated the stockades without firing a shot." Colonel Thomas N. Pace, who had commanded one of the blockhouses, reported afterward that Forrest had seven thousand men and three full batteries. Pace hoped, no doubt, that the exaggeration made the defenders' quick retreat excusable, if not admirable. Forrest burned the Elk River blockhouses and the bridge. At Richland Creek, he burned another bridge.[15]

Now, Federal forces stronger than Spalding's cavalry were gathering against him, coming from as far away as Memphis. Rousseau sent 1,300 cavalry south toward Pulaski from Nashville and followed "with all the other forces that can be spared from here" about 10:00 on the night of September 25, and General George H. Thomas was coming north from Georgia. Forrest was elusive, and two weeks later the chase was still afoot, but one can sense from the dispatches that hope was growing among the Federal commanders that the end was coming at last for Forrest. Thomas was riding a swelling wave of excitement; even a week and a half later, on October 4, Thomas would wire instructions to Rousseau, "Push Forrest to the death, holding your troops well in hand and snugly to the work." Then, in a second wire later that day, "I think you will never have a better chance to capture Forrest."[16]

Rousseau reached Pulaski while Forrest was still at Richland Creek. In truncated language, Rousseau wired his chief-of-staff at Nashville, "Arrived here half an hour since ... I think Forrest will go over to the Nashville & Chattanooga Railroad by way of Fayetteville; this is but conjecture. Have scouts out to see where he goes. If comes this way will be ready for him."[17]

The next morning, Forrest approached Pulaski and Rousseau went out to meet him. They fought all day. The Federals lost eighty men, and were slowly pushed back into Pulaski's defensive works, but Forrest did not have the numerical strength to force their surrender. "I have driven the enemy ... into the fortifications at this place and find General Rousseau with heavy force well fortified," Forrest reported. "I will move to Nashville & Chattanooga Railroad. My loss today about one hundred wounded.... Enemy concentrating heavily against me," he said. He slipped away that night, leaving his fires burning bright to lure the Federals into an empty camp.[18]

Rousseau, however, had guessed his enemy's next move and sent a party of horse soldiers to follow Forrest toward Tullahoma. Rousseau himself returned to Nashville on September 28, leaving in Pulaski two regiments of Tennessee cavalry and portions of the 9th and 10th Indiana Cavalry—an aggregate of about 1,500 horse soldiers—plus three pieces of artillery and "also two companies of demoralized colored patriots who ran away from blockhouses below Pulaski."[19]

At Nashville, Rousseau prepared immediately to go Tullahoma. Before nightfall on September 29, he had departed with "seven trains of troops" while his cavalry moved cross country. Along the way, Rousseau and General Thomas were in constant telegraphic communication, though Rousseau explained, "Believing the wires are tampered with I have been careful to telegraph nothing that would aid the enemy." He may have said this as a way of warning Thomas to be careful, too, of what he included in his messages.[20]

By September 30, Rousseau was in Tullahoma, dispatching troops in response to the reports that were flying at him from all over the Tennessee map. A good many of them showed an unmistakable degree of panic on the part of the local commanders: at Lynchburg there were five thousand enemy and sixteen artillery pieces. Forrest was massing for an attack at Decherd: "As sure as you live Forrest [was] at Spring Hill at 3 this PM; General Lyon is with him." Five thousand Rebs were approaching Columbia and a large infantry column was threatening Pulaski again. And so it went. Rousseau sent scouts to confirm the reports and none of them found anything of the enemy. Thomas was annoyed that Rousseau kept forwarding to him the messages from his excitable subordinates. Rousseau admitted that "most of the dispatches I have considered worthless though I felt it my duty to send them to you ... I think the efforts of the secessionists are to create a stampede by magnifying the rebel forces."[21]

Forrest got no nearer to Tullahoma than Mulberry. He reported, "At this place I learned from my scouts and from the concurrent testimony of reliable citizens that the enemy was in strong force at Tullahoma, and at all other vulnerable points on the railroad in that direction." He was able to do but little damage to the N&C Railroad before he had to withdraw. Rousseau's defensive buildup at Tullahoma had caused Forrest to cancel his intended destruction of the N&C Railroad. The Kentuckian returned to Nashville to organize his cavalry and infantry for a quick move toward Forrest.[22]

By October 2, it was clear that Forrest was retreating. The Confederate later reported that one of the main reasons for the withdrawal was that he had expended too much of his artillery ammunition and now he was perilously low on shells. He divided his command into two parts—Abraham Buford took one group toward Huntsville while Forrest led the other toward Columbia. There, four more blockhouses and three bridges were burned. Columbia itself was too heavily defended, so he turned toward Lawrenceburg and, from there, toward Florence, Alabama. Any further damage would be incidental; now the object was to get safely south of the Tennessee River.

Rousseau left Nashville on October 3 and reached Franklin by nightfall; by the next night he was in Mt. Pleasant. The skies had opened up and heavy rain had caused the Tennessee River to rise four feet in twenty-four hours. This was mixed news. It was hoped that the rain-swollen river would trap Forrest on the north bank, but at the same time, the inclement weather was hindering Rousseau, too. The enemy was only forty-eight hours ahead, but Rousseau could not close the gap. On October 7 he was still twelve miles north of Florence and on the 8th progressed only four miles.

Forrest had reached Florence on October 5 and had hoped to cross the river there—as General Buford, returned from an unproductive strike toward

Huntsville, had already done — but the river presented a nearly impassable obstacle. It took Forrest thirty-six nervous hours to get his artillery and most of his troops across. The only boats at his disposal were three small ferries.

There were still a thousand of Forrest's raiders on the north bank of the Tennessee when reports reached Forrest that the Yankees were approaching. Forrest ordered one regiment to remain behind to fight a rear-guard action while the rest swam to an island in mid-river.

Forrest himself helped in ferrying his men from the island to the southern bank. After holding back the Federals for three days, the rear guard crossed and Forrest's Tennessee Raid was over.

Forrest had escaped and all that was left now was a mopping up operation. Thomas wired Rousseau on October 8, "I understand that there are about 500 of Forrest's men scattered through the country in your vicinity, who have been unable to get away with him. I wish you to see that none of these men escape if it is possible to secure them." Thomas also ordered Rousseau to destroy every ferry boat and crossing on the river between Decatur and Eastport before returning.[23]

Five days later, Thomas ordered Rousseau to return to Nashville and "to consult with me in the reorganization of the troops in this district."[24]

The destruction wrought by Forrest in his September raid was summarized in a report made on October 13 by Brigadier General D. C. McCallum, Director General and Manager of Military Railroads, Military Division of the Mississippi:

> One engine and twelve cars burned on a trestle near Decatur Junction, all destroyed; three cars burned between Huntsville and Stevenson. All the bridges and trestles between Pulaski and Athens, a distance of thirty miles, destroyed. This embraces Elk River bridge and the most formidable trestle on the Decatur and Stevenson line, 1,100 feet long, and almost 90 feet high; and about two miles and a half of track, partially destroyed. Between Spring Hill and Columbia, three bridges destroyed and two to three miles of track.[25]

It took six weeks to put the Tennessee and Alabama Railroad back in operation, but the Nashville and Chattanooga was still running. McCallum reported of the N&C Railroad that it was uninjured "excepting the tearing up of one or two rails."[26]

More seriously, Forrest had captured over 2,300 Federals and killed 1,000 more. He had burned 11 blockhouses and their bridges, captured 7 guns, 800 horses, 2,000 rifles and 50 loaded wagons.

Rousseau himself had fought Forrest in only one engagement — that one at Pulaski — and had been pushed back by him. But on a larger scale, Rousseau had defeated Forrest. By the earlier strategic preparation of defenses at the critical points in his department and his rapid and intelligent deployment of Croxton at Franklin, Milroy at Tullahoma, Granger at Decatur, and all the other forces from the posts under his command, Rousseau had prevented Forrest from inflicting a rear-echelon disaster on the Federals.

* * *

Whether he knew it or not, Forrest had been contending with the man who might have been the running mate of Abraham Lincoln in the 1864 election. The Radical Republicans had held their own convention at Cleveland, where they nominated John C. Frémont, but President Lincoln's more moderate faction, renamed the National Union Party, had held its convention at Baltimore in June. The delegates re-nominated Lincoln, but several names were considered to share the ticket with him as his vice presidential candidate. In addition to the sitting vice-president, Hannibal Hamlin of Maine, there were Joseph Holt, General Benjamin Butler, Schuylar Colfax, Lovell Harrison Rousseau, and Andrew Johnson. Rousseau got twenty-one votes, all from Kentucky's delegates. It is hard to know how closely Rousseau was able to follow the progress of the convention as he developed his plans for the Alabama raid or the degree of disappointment he felt when, in the end, Johnson was selected.

General Rosecrans wrote Rousseau, "I wish you had been nominated V.P. instead of the one who was."[27]

Rousseau was intensely interested in the presidential election. In addition to the Radical faction's hero Frémont, the Democrats' own George B. McClellan, former commander of the Army of the Potomac, was challenging Abraham Lincoln's bid for a second term. Of the three candidates, Rousseau favored Lincoln and seems to have had tentative plans to campaign for his fellow Kentuckian. On October 26, James Speed of Louisville wrote Rousseau a letter which mentioned without specifics the possibility of Rousseau making a speech "before the election." Speed said, "I think a speech [on behalf of Lincoln] from you in Louisville will do more good than from any man I know. The mention of your name always 'brings down the house.' Make us a speech if you possibly can."[28]

There is no evidence that Rousseau ever gave the pro–Lincoln speech. The military situation in Middle Tennessee was too uncertain and Rebel activity was increasing ahead of a late-year invasion of the state by the main CSA army under General John Bell Hood. Rousseau's responsibilities in Middle Tennessee were more pressing than ever and his presence was essential.

In the end, Lincoln won his re-election (though not Kentucky) without

Rousseau stumping for him. The hopes of the Southerners for a McClellan victory and a negotiated end to the war were dashed. The war would be fought to a conclusion and it was looking increasingly unlikely that the winner of that contest would be the exhausted South.

* * *

Confederate general John Bell Hood was a crippled man. On the second day at Gettysburg in July 1863, he had been struck in the left arm by a shell fragment while leading his men against Devil's Den. It was thought that he might lose the arm. Surgeons were able to save it in the end, though it hung useless and Hood had to carry it in a sling. Then, at Chickamauga in September of the same year, Hood received a bone-shattering wound in the right leg. Surgeons had to amputate the leg, very near the torso. To dull the pain of two such traumatic wounds suffered in less than a year, Hood took large doses of opiates, which also dulled his powers of reason.

But, incapacitated though Hood was in body and mind, President Jefferson Davis had confidence in the drug dependent general and called upon him to take command of the Army of Tennessee in place of Joseph E. Johnston. Johnston had allowed Sherman to push him beyond the Chattahoochee, the last natural barrier between the Federals and Atlanta and President Davis was furious. He dismissed Johnston on July 18 and replaced him with Hood.

Hood knew what was expected of him and soon proved that, in spite of his incapacities, he was still a dangerous man. William Tecumseh Sherman found this out at Peachtree Creek, at Ezra Church, and at Jonesboro, and though Sherman eventually won Atlanta, Hood escaped with forty thousand men. With such an army behind him, an aggressive general like Hood could do a lot of damage. But on what front, the Confederate general had to ask himself, would his army be able to inflict the worst damage on the Federals?

What Hood hit upon was a plan so extremely peculiar, so dreamily optimistic, that some historians have speculated that it was developed while Hood was in the reverie of a laudanum-induced euphoria. The plan was this: he would abandon Georgia and drive north for Tennessee and Kentucky. Sherman would be forced to abandon Atlanta and follow, for he could not allow Hood to maneuver freely along his supply line. During the pursuit, as Sherman's larger army became more and more strung out, Hood would be able to double back, attack the weak spots, and defeat the Yankee army in detail. If everything worked perfectly, Hood might even reach the Ohio River and cross over to Indiana or Ohio and carry the war to a northern population who had not felt the sharp sting of war like the Georgians had.

The plan was so eccentric that it caught General Sherman completely off guard. On October 1, Hood's Rebels slipped quietly away behind their cavalry screen. It was two days before Sherman knew the Confederates were on the move. On October 4, Hood struck the Western & Atlantic Railroad at Big Shanty and Acworth. Sherman's supply line had suffered its first break, eight miles of ruined track. The next target was the large Union supply depot at Allatoona.

Sherman, awake at last to what was happening, was now on Hood's trail. The Federals pressed so hard and skirmished so frequently with his rear guard that Hood was unable to do the damage he had hoped for. His move toward Tennessee became a move to get *away* from Sherman. At Dalton, Georgia, Hood turned west and struck out for Alabama. On or about October 17, Hood got across the state line and Sherman called off the chase. He returned to Atlanta, for he had business down South.

* * *

Hood, of course did not stay in Alabama. On November 19, he advanced from Florence toward Waynesborough. General Thomas wrote, "My only resource [did he mean recourse?] then was to retire slowly toward my re-enforcements, delaying the enemy's progress as much as possible, to gain time for re-enforcements to arrive and concentrate." One town where troops were concentrated was Columbia, and another was Murfreesboro. Rousseau was at Murfreesboro, trying to refurbish Fortress Rosecrans, the old earthworks from the Federal winter encampment of 1863. He was directing the erection of a blockhouse and of gun platforms and was placing his artillery: three short howitzers, a James rifle, a Wiard gun, and four pieces he had brought with him under the direction of Colonel Cyrus Loomis. Rousseau was angry with Loomis because of "an inexcusable blunder"—he had neglected to bring the tangent scales, which were used in sighting the guns. Reinforcements began coming to Rousseau at Fortress Rosecrans from Athens, Decatur, and Huntsville on or about November 23, ordered there by the reliable sub-district commander, General Robert Granger. A week later, General Milroy abandoned Tullahoma and joined the defenders of Murfreesboro. All of these reinforcements brought the artillery from their posts with them until Rousseau had fifty-seven guns mounted on the walls of Fortress Rosecrans.[29]

On November 24 and 25, General John Schofield skirmished with Hood's cavalry at Columbia, but the next day the Rebel infantry arrived and Schofield saw that he could not continue to single-handedly oppose the enemy there. On the night of the 27th, he retired to the north bank of the Duck River.

There was a day of rest for Schofield's Federals on the 28th, but the next day the Confederates crossed the Duck River, forcing Schofield to continue his retrograde movement, beginning after nightfall and slipping by Hood at

Spring Hill. He might have gone all the way to Thomas in Nashville, but at Franklin he discovered that the bridges over the Harpeth River were down. He had no choice but to stop. As his infantry prepared defensive works south of the town, his engineers and teamsters did manage to get his supply wagons, at least, across the river to the north bank.

Hood was furious at his generals for having allowed Schofield to bypass them at Spring Hill and decided that Franklin was the place to discipline an army that had grown too lax — he ordered a frontal assault on Schofield's line. The attack began a little after 4:00 P.M. on November 30. As the Rebels advanced over two miles of ground, they kept flushing coveys of quail from the dead autumn grass. More than one young Southerner must have wished that he, too, could fly away from this. But, they kept moving forward, while the Yankees watched. The long rows of butternut and gray beneath the blood red battle flags were a sight to see. One Federal officer said, "For the moment, we were spellbound." Then, the Rebels were within rifle range and it was time to go to work.[30]

A volley staggered but did not stop the advancing enemy, who crashed into the center of the Union line. At first, it looked as if Hood's long gamble would pay off. The center of the Yankee line gave way. The men were fighting at point blank range, and then grappled in hand to hand combat before fresh regiments in blue were hurried into the break and the Confederate attackers who had pierced the Federal line suddenly found themselves in a terrible trap. Those who could fall back did so, reformed, and tried again. All along the Rebel line they tried, fell back, reformed, and tried again until 9:00 P.M. Twelve times they tried and every time they failed. When it was finished, Schofield pulled confidently out of his works and marched across newly laid pontoon bridges for Nashville with 2,200 fewer men than had started the day. That was a big number, but Hood had lost more than 6,200 men and five generals, including the great Patrick Cleburne. Five more general officers were wounded and one was captured.

Schofield joined General Thomas in Nashville in the early morning hours of December 1 and took his place on the left of Thomas' developing defensive line. John Bell Hood did not have much back-up in his nature and he did not back up now. He led his crippled army on to heavily fortified Nashville.

During this time, Rousseau was at Murfreesboro, preparing defenses. He anticipated that the Rebels would try to drive a wedge between Thomas and himself. He wrote to Thomas on November 29, "It may be that communication between this and Nashville will be disturbed and it might be well for you to give me instructions to govern my actions in that case."[31]

Thomas replied, "In the event of communications being cut off between us, I want you to hold Murfreesborough secure."[32]

Rousseau's fears were well-founded; the Rebels were on their way to Murfreesboro. On December 2, John Bell Hood issued an order to corps commander Major General Benjamin F. Cheatham to detach General William B. Bate's division (the least ravaged of the divisions that had fought at Franklin) and send it, with one battery of artillery, over to Murfreesboro and "destroy the railroad from Murfreesboro to Nashville, burning all the bridges and taking the block-houses and then burning them."[33]

Bate had only one thousand men with him when he left Hood. In his report, Bate revealed that Confederate intelligence was woefully lacking; seven miles from his destination, he learned "that Murfreesboro, instead of being evacuated, as was supposed, and as the nature of my order had led me to believe, was occupied by a strong force estimated from 6,000 to 10,000, commanded by Major General Rousseau, which fact I reported to army headquarters on the morning of the 4th." Hood disputed Bate's higher figure, but did admit that reports confirmed as many as five thousand Federals in Murfreesboro and promised to send some of Forrest's cavalry to reinforce him.[34]

On December 4, Bate moved forward to Overall Creek and attacked the blockhouse there. The Confederates fired seventy-four shots, which did no damage at all. Three regiments of Federal infantry under General Milroy soon arrived and slammed into the Rebels, with results that remain uncertain, even today. Bate, in his report, admitted that the Yankees turned his left flank, but claimed that his artillerymen trained their pieces on the enemy and fired double charges of canister into them "scattering them in all directions and securing fifteen or twenty of their horses." A second attack was likewise turned back and the Rebels held the field.[35]

Rousseau, in his report of the same action, said that his infantry "attacked and routed the enemy, showing great spirit and courage ... although we took possession of the field, night closed in at the end of the fight and I ordered our forces to return."[36]

The problem with reports of Civil War engagements is that, too often, both generals claimed victory. Whatever the true result of the fight at Overall Creek, the blockhouse was not reduced and Bate lost eighty-seven men he could ill-afford to spare. His losses were made good that night, however, when the first elements of Forrest's cavalry began to arrive.

The next day, as Bate's men worked at ripping up the railroad, Forrest himself showed up at the head of two divisions of cavalry and two infantry brigades with a full complement of artillery. Since he outranked Bate, For-

15. The Defense of Middle Tennessee

rest assumed command, ordered Bate to quit his railroad demolition, and began immediately to plan for an attack on Rousseau. Bate disagreed with Forrest's decision to do battle at Fortress Rosecrans. He wrote, "The order to keep in view the object of my mission, viz, 'to destroy the railroad,' seemed to be revoked, and offensive operations against Murfreesboro assumed, which did not accord with my judgment, as I was satisfied there were 8,000 or 10,000 Federals within, with twice our numbers, I, however, readily gave cheerful cooperation." Bate's estimate of the number of Union soldiers inside the fortress was correct; Rousseau had eight thousand men.[37]

The next day, as Forrest directed, Bate ordered his skirmishers and sharpshooters to creep toward the earthen wall of Fortress Rosecrans and lost sixteen more men in the doing. "I dug pits for skirmishers and built defenses for my main line," Bate said.[38]

On the 7th, however, Forrest ordered Bate to redeploy his entire command on the Wilkinson Pike, three miles northwest of Fortress Rosecrans. There, the Rebels piled up logs and rails to make temporary defensive works. Before they were quite finished, seven regiments of Union infantry, six artillery pieces, and a small detachment of cavalry appeared. It was Milroy again, sent out by Rousseau.

Milroy had left Fortress Rosecrans at 10:00 A.M. and swung west, driving away a Rebel vidette within a half mile of the fort and a stronger force of three hundred at Stones River, near the "fine residence" of a Mr. Spence. Milroy called a halt there and learned from Mrs. Spence that "General Forrest and Bate, with a large force of infantry, artillery, and cavalry, were north of me on Wilkinson Pike ... I deemed it best to turn my attention in that direction."[39]

For the information he had received, Milroy repaid Mr. and Mrs. Spence by stealing their hogs. Milroy said, "I detailed a company and sent them back with a drove of sixty fine, fat hogs, belonging to Mr. Spence," giving the excuse that they "would have fallen into the hands of the rebels if left."[40]

Within a half mile of Wilkinson Pike, Milroy ran into Rebel skirmishers and soon came under artillery fire from a battery in some woods across a field. Milroy ordered his own artillery to respond, but they had not come prepared for such a duel and after thirty minutes were out of ammunition. There was a lull in the fighting as Milroy retired into some woods and sent back for more ammunition for his field pieces. Hidden from the sight of the Confederates, Milroy decided to slide his line to the right in order to threaten the enemy left and also to get in better position between the enemy and Fortress Rosecrans. Then, he ordered his infantry forward. They emerged from the woods and advanced quickly across the field toward the Rebels' aforementioned log and rail barricade. Directing the fire of both his flanks to converge on the CSA works, Milroy proceeded across the field to the fringe of the enemy-held woods. The effect of the fighting was elemental, in Milroy's mind, and best compared to a force of nature. The general said that the sound "was like the thunder of a volcano" and that his line "wavered as if moving against a hurricane."[41]

The middle of his line was sagging, but the left flank was scarcely engaged, so Milroy ordered it to come over in support "on the double-quick," and also ordered the second line forward into action. At the same time, the front line surged forward on its own initiative and spilled over the enemy barricade. The Rebels flew to the rear, with the Yankees in close pursuit. Forrest and Milroy were on horseback in the middle of the rout, perfect targets, bravely trying to stiffen the spines of their frightened men. Forrest reported, "I seized the colors of the retreating troops and endeavored to rally them, but they could not be moved by any entreaty or appeal to their patriotism. Major General Bate did the same thing, but was equally as unsuccessful as myself."[42]

The Federals captured many prisoners, as well as "one battle flag and two fine pieces of artillery (12-pounder Napoleons), with their caissons." The fresh supply of artillery ammunition arrived at this moment and the big guns opened up on the retreating Rebs. Rousseau said in his report that the enemy was "utterly routed and driven off in great confusion, Forrest's cavalry making the finest time, to the right, across and down the Nashville road, I have seen in many a day."[43]

The Rebels had lost nineteen killed, seventy-three wounded, and 122 missing. The Federals had lost thirty killed and 175 wounded at the fight on Wilkinson Pike.

Rousseau had been busy himself. As Milroy's fight was going on three miles to the northwest, CSA general Abraham Buford with his division of cavalry charged into Murfreesboro. They reached the town center, set up their guns, and began throwing shells, "knocking the houses to pieces." Rousseau counterattacked with an infantry regiment and artillery and gouged Buford out of position and out of Murfreesboro, "and I have not heard any more of them in any direction since," he said.[44]

In his response to General Rousseau's report of the action at Murfreesboro, General Thomas' Assistant Adjutant General Robert Ramsey said, "Your report has been read with a great deal of pleasure by the major general commanding." Thomas sent his "highest commendation and hearty thanks" for the efforts of Rousseau and his men.[45]

No officer had been more active than General Milroy, who only a few months before had been so disgraced and discredited that he had to beg

Rousseau and Thomas for a field command. He did not forget what they had done for him. Milroy concluded his own report of the action on December 7 by saying, "I avail myself of this opportunity to tender to the major-general commanding the District of Tennessee my most grateful acknowledgement for his kindness in affording me the two late opportunities of wiping out to some extent the foul and mortifying stigma of a most infamously unjust arrest, by which I have for near 18 months been thrown out of the ring of active, honorable and desirable service."[46]

The two Napoleons that Milroy had taken away from Forrest and Bate were added to Fortress Rosecrans' defenses, but they were never needed. Bate's Rebels spent the next day destroying a few more yards of railroad, but the day after that they were ordered to join Hood in Nashville. Forrest remained behind and continued to wreck sections of the N&C Railroad. His men caught a few outlying Federal supply wagons, but on the 15th they were ordered to move closer to Hood. On the 16th, new orders arrived for Forrest to retire toward Pulaski — the Confederate army was evacuating Nashville. Hood's attempt to capture the Tennessee capital and destroy Thomas had failed miserably; it was Hood who was destroyed, utterly destroyed. After two days of fighting, the disorganized remnants of his army were hurrying down the roads toward Alabama. The Confederate Army of Tennessee had essentially ceased to exist. Some of the surviving units would make their way to the Carolinas and join with General Joseph Johnston in his small and useless effort to stop Sherman as he moved north from Savannah. The fighting in North Carolina and Virginia would rage for a few more months, but the struggle in the Western Theater was at an end, except for the manhunt for a few incorrigible guerrillas. It was that effort which would occupy much of Rousseau's attention in the spring of 1865. But first, there was a campaign of a different nature which demanded Rousseau's attention. Some of Kentucky's leading politicians were calling his name.

16

Nashville and the End of the War

On December 30, 1864, Major General Rousseau sent from his Nashville headquarters a request to General Thomas. Without elaboration, he asked, "I greatly desire to be in Kentucky for a few days on business of vital importance to me. Can I go?"

Thomas's replied through his assistant adjutant general, "You are authorized to go to Kentucky, as you desire."[1]

The matter of vital interest seems to have been his pursuit of the U.S. Senate seat being vacated by Lazarus W. Powell. In those days before the Seventeenth Amendment to the Constitution provided for the direct election of Senators, they were selected by the state legislatures. There was very little personal campaigning on the part of the candidates; they simply let it be known that they were willing to serve, while their friends advocated on their behalf among the legislators. In Rousseau's case, this included the Speeds of Louisville. It can be inferred by the timing of Rousseau's terse request to return to Kentucky that he wanted to meet and strategize with this important and influential family.

The General Assembly met to select the new Kentucky senator on January 11, 1865. In a close vote of sixty-five to fifty-six, Rousseau lost the U.S. Senate seat to his part-time ally and part-time opponent, the Democrat James Guthrie, president of the L&N Railroad. Among those who lamented Rousseau's loss was Major General Stephen G. Burbridge, commander of the Military District of Kentucky. He wrote Rousseau on February 13, "Allow me to congratulate you upon the excellent race you made for the U.S. Senate. I am truly sorry (and so are all Union men) that the Election could not have been postponed for a few days. You would undoubtedly have been elected." Burbridge's speculation that a postponement of a few days would have made a difference in the outcome is curious, but he may have provided a clue elsewhere in the letter, for he closed by saying, "Trusting you have regained your usual health." Had Rousseau once again been afflicted by a sudden and serious winter illness, one that raised questions about his health or which prevented him from meeting with some of the power brokers in Kentucky politics? There is no way to know for a certainty.²

In any case, Rousseau would not be going to the Upper House of the U.S. Congress. He returned to Tennessee and the many difficulties facing a district commander as the war was winding down.

* * *

In Nashville, politics was also taking precedence over army matters, at least for the present. Tennessee voters ratified the state constitutional amendments that allowed it to be re-admitted to the Union on February 22, 1865. The next day Governor Andrew Johnson scheduled elections for March 4 to fill state offices and Tennessee's U.S. congressional seats. On February 24, Johnson left Nashville for Washington, D.C., where, on the same day as Tennessee's elections, he would be inaugurated as vice president of the United States.

When the Tennessee election was held, the old East Tennessee Unionist William "Parson" Brownlow was elected as governor. He took his oath of office on April 5 amid a galaxy of stars: Generals Thomas, Rousseau, Milroy, and post commander Brigadier General John F. Miller, among them. That same day, the legislature ratified the 13th Amendment to the U.S. Constitution, ending slavery in Tennessee. A new day was dawning in the South.

That the war was lost and the Southern world was changing forever was evident, too, in the number of prominent Tennesseans who were stepping forward to take the amnesty oath. They included Andrew Jackson Donelson, Old Hickory's nephew, and also John Overton, Jr., the once-ardent secessionist, who was the son of President Jackson's friend and trusted advisor and the wealthy owner of Traveller's Rest plantation.

It was plain that Tennessee's leaders knew that the game was over. The fabric of society had loosened and unraveled, though, and these same leaders no longer had the influence to guide the actions of their fellow citizens. The best of them — the most thoughtful, the most patriotic, the bravest — were dead or scattered and what were left were the dregs who used the war as an excuse to vandalize, steal, and settle old scores by murdering those against whom they held a grudge. Styling themselves guerrillas, they had little in common with the great partisan rangers of the past like Francis Marion or Andrew Pickens. They were simple outlaws and they were operating for personal gains and largely at the expense of the citizenry, though they would ambush military targets. On February 15, fifteen guerrillas hit a wood train of thirteen wagons outside of Nashville. This was the kind of action the guerrillas liked, an attack not on regular troops but on a bunch of weakly defended woodcutters. Even more to their liking were attacks on civilians, who would be less well-armed than woodcutters. Guerrillas attacked a passenger train at Spring Hill on February 16, derailed another train at Mitchellsville on March 1, and robbed and burned another train across the Kentucky line at Glasgow on March 15.

They were not the kind of opponent Rousseau was used to fighting. There were no Forrests or Cleburnes, or Wheelers among these roving gangs of men. But, they were a threat in his district and they had to be dealt with.

With its passion for renaming and renumbering, the army had reorganized Rousseau's district again. It was now the District of Middle Tennessee and it encompassed all of Middle Tennessee and North Alabama, "with all the lines of the railroad and water communication therein." Included were the District of North Alabama (Brigadier General Robert Granger, commanding at Decatur); the First Sub-District of Middle Tennessee (Major General Robert Milroy, commanding at Tullahoma); the Second Sub-District of Middle Tennessee (Brigadier General R. W. Johnson, commanding at Pulaski); the Third Sub-District of Middle Tennessee (Colonel C. R. Thompson, commanding at Kingston Springs); the Fourth Sub-District of Middle Tennessee (Colonel James Gilfillen, commanding, no headquarters given); and the Fifth Sub-District of Middle Tennessee (Colonel A. A. Smith, commanding at Clarksville). Rousseau had an aggregate of 29,681 officers and men with which to suppress the guerrillas.[3]

While the guerrillas continued to challenge Rousseau's forces throughout Tennessee, more conventional forces were laying down their arms. Robert E. Lee surrendered to U.S. Grant at Appomattox on April 9. In celebration, General George H. Thomas ordered Rousseau on April 13 to "cause a salute of 200 guns to be fired at meridian tomorrow, and every post within the District of Middle Tennessee and North Alabama which is prepared to fire such salute, in honor of the capture of the rebel Army of Northern Virginia and of the raising of the old flag over Fort Sumter. General [John F.] Miller will be directed to fire a salute of 200 guns from each of two points of the post at Nashville." Plans were quickly put together for a city-wide celebration on the 15th.[4]

Saturday, April 15 dawned bright, but by mid-morning the sky was shrouded with heavy clouds. The festivities were planned to begin at 10:00 A.M., with military bands and a parade led by Generals Thomas and Rousseau that would begin at Fort Negley and proceed to the town square. The streets were lined with excited citizens who were hoping that it would not rain, waiting for the parade to pass by. There was an unaccounted-for delay. Then the news crackled through the crowd — President Lincoln had died that morning of a gunshot wound. John Wilkes Booth, the actor, had shot the president at

Ford's Theater the night before. The news of Lincoln's death arrived by military telegraph just before the parade was to begin. Now, there was not going to be a parade. The celebration was cancelled and a day of joy was suddenly drenched in sorrow.

On April 19, the national day of mourning, Nashville had a symbolic funeral procession beginning at Fort Negley, as the celebratory parade would have done, and proceeding downtown. The church bells tolled while the catafalque, drawn by twelve horses and followed by soldiers on foot, officers on horseback, and civil authorities of the state and the city. The sad procession passed by the public square and the capitol. At the end of the parade on Harding Pike, there was a field and there a speakers' platform had been set up. The catafalque was placed and the soldiers went into formation as thunder rumbled in the distance. General Rousseau and Governor Brownlow spoke to the crowd to conclude the ceremony and the people went home.

Rousseau's emotions must have tumbled over one another in a complicated mix — he would not have been human, otherwise. His fellow Kentuckian, a man he had met and liked, as well as being the president whom he had served through four years of hardship, had died a violent death at the moment the nation was celebrating the return of peace. Another man, one he had worked with closely in an effort to keep wartime Nashville safe and orderly, was now the chief executive. And, if things had gone differently at the Baltimore Convention back in June 1864, he, Rousseau, might have now been in Andrew Johnson's place as the seventeenth U.S. president.

* * *

After Appomattox, all but the most hardcore guerrillas began inquiring of the local authorities about the conditions under which they could lay down their revolvers and shotguns. The sub-district commanders referred the question to Rousseau, who referred it to General Thomas. He, in turn, referred the question to U.S. Grant, who replied on May 5, "I would advise as a cheap way to get clear of guerrillas that a certain time be given for them to come in, say the 20th of this month, up to which time their paroles will be received but after which they will be proceeded against as outlaws." By the time of Grant's reply, Thomas had already instructed his commanders to proceed essentially along the same lines. Those guerrillas who surrendered would be given the same terms as Grant had given Lee.[5]

It was a workable plan and a remarkably generous one, considering that many Northerners were demanding blood for the death of Lincoln.

The number of paroled CSA solders, both regulars and guerrillas, passing through Nashville increased after Joseph Johnston surrendered to William T. Sherman on April 26.

For those, like the notorious East Tennessean Champ Ferguson, who still refused to accept the end of the war, General Thomas had no patience. On May 16, Rousseau passed on to Milroy at his Tullahoma headquarters the corps commander's attitude in a dispatch that read, "In accordance with orders heretofore published by the major general commanding the Department of the Cumberland, Champ Ferguson and his gang of cut throats having refused to surrender are denounced as outlaws and the military forces of this district will deal with and treat them accordingly."[6]

Ferguson, who was infamous for having killed wounded Yankees on the battlefield at Saltville and even in the hospital afterward, was still a stone in the Federal boot on May 25, when Rousseau was ordered to send the 4th Tennessee Mounted Infantry on a sweep of White, Overton, Fentress, and Montgomery Counties in an effort to trap Ferguson.

Rousseau himself may have been set to lead a second attempt to snare Ferguson when the guerrilla was caught on May 30. Ferguson was tried in Nashville, convicted there, and was hanged for his crimes on October 20.

With so many guerrilla bands trying to surrender (Ferguson's notwithstanding), there was bound to be confusion. General John S. Williams' brigade of Rebel cavalry surrendered at Augusta, Georgia, and the men were allowed to keep their horses, in keeping with the Appomattox model. Confederate cavalrymen provided their own horses and were compensated by their government (theoretically) at a rate of 40¢ per day. At Chattanooga, Williams' men were stopped and arrested and their horses taken by the Federal quartermaster. Williams wrote a four-page letter of protest to General Thomas' Assistant Adjutant General, Brigadier General W. D. Whipple. The matter landed on Rousseau's desk and was rectified.

In another matter involving horses, a group of Confederates who had been paroled stole enough saddle mounts to carry them to Kentucky and were hot on the road when Rousseau received orders to "stop that band of paroled rebels and take their stolen horses from them if possible.... They can be permitted to walk home, provided they take the oath of allegiance, otherwise not."[7]

Then, there were some commanders who became too carried away by the spirit of leniency. When Colonel John W. Horner, commanding the post at Huntsville, declared that no passes were required of citizens passing to or from Huntsville or through the county and, furthermore, were allowed to carry guns either for self-protection or "hunting and gaming," Rousseau had to step in to rescind the policy.[8]

So it went as the Confederate belligerents came in, individually or in small bands of seventeen or thirty-seven or forty-eight. The General's advice and consent were constantly required.

16. Nashville and the End of the War

In late June, Rousseau took a furlough from his responsibilities and General R. W. Johnson took temporary command of the district in his absence. Once again, it was politics that drew Rousseau away from Nashville — he was running to represent the 5th U.S. Congressional District, which included not only the city of Louisville, but also the outlying areas of Jefferson County, Oldham County, Henry County, and Owen County. On June 28, 1865, Joshua F. Speed wrote to James Speed, "Our Congressional canvass had commenced. Rousseau has been speaking in the country — with what effect I can't learn. I do not think that there is much enthusiasm for [Robert] Mallory. If Rousseau is a good man at organization he can carry the city by 1200 votes."[9]

Then on July 11, Speed wrote again to his brother, "Rousseau is making a spirited canvass. He will carry the city by an overwhelming vote."[10]

In his campaign speeches, Rousseau identified himself as the Union candidate and stated in advance what he expected to do in the House of Representatives: "I will advocate and help to enact, if elected, all those measures that are more likely to root out the remnants of rebellion, and to prevent the leaders and promoters from again obtaining the power to repeat their experiment. I will work to establish and perpetuate a Union of free and equal states ... I will do my share toward reestablishing the credit of the Union, such as it was before this Democratic, pro-slavery rebellion, that has just gone down to its inglorious grave ... I will also tell you beforehand that in most of these things I expect to co-operate with Andrew Johnson, who is now occupying the White House."[11]

Having subtly introduced the subject of slavery, Rousseau then addressed Kentucky's resistance to the Thirteenth Amendment. He mocked, "In the whole Christian world there remains but three slave States: Cuba, Brazil, and Kentucky." He argued that the war of the last four years had cost more in blood and treasure than all the profits that slavery had ever generated, and reviewed the many ways that slavery was an inefficient and wasteful system. Then, though he admitted that it was unfashionable to do so, he laid out a simple theological argument against the Peculiar Institution. He said, "God, in his wisdom, has arranged the world so that in the long run a system of wrong will not and cannot pay."[12]

The *Louisville Daily Democrat* opposed Rousseau and teased, "General Rousseau holds the office of Major General in the service of the U.S. He was, whilst a Major General, a candidate for the Senate and now wants to go to Congress. One office at a time, General."[13]

In spite of the *Democrat*'s opposition, Rousseau decisively won his August election. The initial totals were Rousseau: 4370, Mallory: 1720, and a third candidate, Marc Mundy: 125. The totals were later adjusted upward slightly for all three candidates.

Rousseau's movements between the election and November are uncertain. It stands to reason that he returned to Nashville to attend to the final details of command before his resignation from the army on November 30, 1865.

He then returned to his Louisville home and his family as a private citizen for the first time since 1861.

17

In and Out of the House of Representatives

The Rousseau family had changed and grown in his absence. His oldest son, Richard, was nineteen and George was thirteen. The mysterious daughter "B" was eighteen and daughter Mary was a married woman of twenty-one. Her husband was Brigadier General Louis Watkins, who had served in Rousseau's district and, presumably through a warm social relationship with his commander, had become acquainted with Mary, whom he wed in August 1864. Their married life was made considerably easier when Watkins was made the post commander of Louisville in April 1865.

Perhaps the greatest familial change was that there was now a third generation in the household. By the time Lovell Harrison Rousseau rejoined his family in November, he was a grandfather of five months; Louis and Mary Watkins had had the first of their three children, a son whom they named Lovell Rousseau Watkins.

Rousseau had to approach the difficult task of how to be a father to his younger children, who had come into the difficult teenage years without his guidance, and how to co-exist with a wife he had seen only infrequently during the past four years. She had undoubtedly established her own routine as head of the house and had serious adjustments of her own to make with her husband's return from the service.

There were a good many changes Rousseau had to make aside from getting used to his family again. In his whole routine there must have been a sensation of sudden decompression. The day was not regulated by bugle calls and the volume of desk work was minute; more than that, none of it involved matters of lawlessness or life and death. Black or dark blue broadcloth replaced the wool uniform, a stickpin and watch fob took the place of shoulder-boards, and a rattan walking stick filled his hand now instead of the engraved officer's sword.

Rousseau took his seat as the representative from Kentucky's 5th Congressional District on December 6, 1865, one of only thirteen members of the

Unconditional Unionist Party. There were no representatives from the Southern states, for even though the Confederacy (except for Texas) had rejoined the Union under Johnson's Reconstruction plan, and had elected senators and representatives, the Radicals refused to seat them. It was easy to bar the Southerners since the Republicans held a majority in both houses.

The new congressman from Kentucky was appointed to serve on the committee on military affairs and also the committee on roads and canals. He had come to Washington at a momentous time and did not serve long before he learned that the government, like his own family, had been struggling before his arrival and was still struggling to make some difficult adjustments in response to a new, post-war United States.

An invalid pension law had to be passed, for example, and the army had to be reorganized. In addition, answers had to be found to some questions that had no precedent in American history. How should the states of the conquered South now be considered? How should they be readmitted to the Union? What protections should be offered to the former slaves? It had seemed, immediately after Lincoln's death, that the president and the Congress were in accord and would be able to work together. Upon Johnson's ascension to the presidency, the radical Benjamin Wade had said, "Johnson, we have faith in you. By the gods, there will be no trouble now in running this government."[1]

In the weeks after Johnson took office, however, the Radicals began to get a glimmer that the new president was going to be a disappointment. He appeared ready to deprive Congress of any role at all in "running the government," at least, as far as Reconstruction was concerned. He was willing to follow Lincoln's 10 Percent Plan, with only a few changes. Under Lincoln's plan, four states (Louisiana, Tennessee, Arkansas, and Virginia) had already been readmitted to the Union. On May 29, President Johnson issued a proclamation which organized North Carolina's provisional government, there was every indication that others would quickly follow. The fear began to grow in Radical hearts that Reconstruction would become an accomplished fact while the Congress was still on its summer and fall recess.

On that same May day, Johnson issued his amnesty proclamation which offered broad pardons for those former Rebels (who took the loyalty oath) and restoration of their property, except slaves. Only high Confederate officials and those whose wealth exceeded $20,000 were exempt — these must make "special application" to the president in order to receive their pardons.[2]

The Radicals were displeased and were even less pleased in passing months as reports began to filter north of violence toward the former slaves and the codification of repression of blacks with the passage of the Black Codes. It appeared that Johnson's Lincoln-like leniency was interpreted by the Southern legislatures as a license to return to the *status quo ante bellum*. Northern support for President Johnson began to dissolve, even among those who had been inclined to go along. By the start of the new year, a good many of those serving in Congress had decided that Reconstruction made no sense, as Johnson was guiding it. In order to seize a greater role in Reconstruction, the radicals in Congress proposed to send to the president two bills. One was a civil rights bill which would protect freedmen from the various Black Codes by declaring *all* persons born in the United States (except Indians) to be citizens and eligible for all the accompanying rights and protections. It also strengthened the authority of the courts to punish anyone guilty of restricting said rights.

The other Radical measure was a new Freedman's Bureau bill. The Freedman's Bureau had first come into being in March 1865 for the benefit of the former slaves, and, under the provisions of the original bill, was to continue for one year after the conclusion of the war. Now, the Radicals wanted a new bill to both strengthen and extend the life of the Freedman's Bureau.

These bills represented a bitter divide between the president and the congressional Radicals, and it was into this breach that Rousseau stepped when he entered the House of Representatives in December 1865. By his words and by his votes in the months ahead, Rousseau showed that he was an ally of President Johnson.

On February 3, 1866, Rousseau was recognized by Speaker Schuyler Colfax and stood to make some remarks regarding the new Freedman's Bureau bill. It was a long speech. He opened by saying that he was not a Republican, but belonged to the Union Party. However, he had acted with the Republicans to suppress the Rebellion and to preserve the Federal government. He had believed that the Republic would prevail in the struggle and it had done so. He said, "There is not in the whole of the United States one single armed rebel to-day ... [therefore] the existing state of things in the country affords no excuse for the passage of a bill of this description, outrageous in all its features.... At one blow it sweeps away the constitution and laws of Kentucky." The bill, he argued, made it possible for juries, sheriffs, and justices of the peace to be arrested "by agents of this bureau and fined and imprisoned not exceeding a fine of $1,000 and imprisonment for one year" on the mere charge that they had violated the rights of a Negro. Even ministers of the gospel who declined for whatever reason to perform a marriage between Negroes might be fined and imprisoned. He believed that such autocratic power might actually work to the detriment of the black race, because whites would be embittered by the excessive protections contained in the bill.[3]

Rousseau talked about the many unjust arrests made by the head of the Freedman's Bureau in Louisville. "He would arrest any man, no matter whom, the most inoffensive and the most loyal, on the *ex parte* statement of a negro." Then, he gave an example.[4]

In Louisville, a Mrs. Blevins got into a disagreement with a Negro servant, "not one who had belonged to her as a slave." Mr. Blevins took the side of his wife and the Negro woman went to the head of the Freedman's Bureau, a Major McCaleb, who sent two soldiers to arrest not only Mr. and Mrs. Blevins, but also their little girl. Mr. Blevins appealed to Rousseau, who went to the post commander, his son-in-law, General Watkins. Watkins pleaded that he was powerless. He said, "This Freedman's Bureau, it is said, is over all; what can I do?"[5]

The next morning, Rousseau saw Major Blevins and told him, "If you want to protect the freedmen of this community I am with you heart and soul; I will stand by you in all measures; but if you intend to arrest white people on the *ex parte* statements of negroes and hold them to suit your convenience for trial and fine and imprison them, then I say that I oppose you."[6]

Then, he went on to tell the House of Representatives a remark he had made to Major Blevins that would rebound in unexpected ways: "If you should so arrest and punish me, I would kill you when you set me at liberty; and I think that you would do the same to a man who would treat you in that way, if you are the man that I think you are, and the man you ought to be to fill your position here."[7]

Rousseau's remarks opposing the Freedman's Bureau bill went on for several more tightly printed pages in the *Congressional Globe*. The text shows that he accepted and answered some questions from other members, but it was mostly Rousseau. He repeated and sharpened some points ("You may take away the liberty of any man, woman, or child without warrant of law, without affidavit, but upon the *ex parte* statement of any vagabond negro who strolls through the country"), he reviewed his own military career, and he also drifted into the question of the status of the Southern states. Thaddeus Stevens and other Radicals justified their pet Reconstruction measures by saying that the Southern states were out of the Union. This offended Rousseau's sense of logic. He said that the North had fought the war to prevent secession, that the North had won the war; therefore, secession had never occurred. Yet, it was now claimed by the Radicals that the states *had* seceded. He charged, "These gentlemen insist that the insurrectionary States are out of the Union, as Jefferson Davis has insisted for the last five years."[8]

Rousseau also insisted that the war had never been regional. He said, "The war recently closed never was a war between the North and the South; it was the United States against its domestic enemies.... Not a battle has been fought in the West, and not one in the East, without some southern blood enriching the soil, blood freely poured out for preserving the integrity of the Union."[9]

He had exhausted his time, but Democrat George S. Shanklin of Kentucky's 7th District yielded some of his own time to allow Rousseau to conclude. Rousseau ended after another couple of pages of tight script, by saying that seven-tenths of the people would side with President Johnson in his opposition to the bill. "They want and will have a united, harmonious, and a prosperous nation and they will not permit one half of the nation to rule and trample upon the other half on any pretext whatever. While the Union Party holds to this position it will be triumphant, when it abandons it, it will fail and ought to fail."[10]

On February 5, Josiah B. Grinnell rose to respond to some of the remarks made by Rousseau. Grinnell was a Republican representative from Iowa, the founder of the town that carried his name, a lawyer, a promoter of railroads. Grinnell slightly misrepresented Rousseau's remarks to Major McCaleb of the Louisville Freedman's Bureau as "if he were arrested on the complaint of a negro and brought before one of the agents of this bureau, when he became free he would shoot him." Grinnell then said, "I care not whether the gentleman was four years in the war on the Union side or four years on the other side; but I say that he degraded his state and uttered a sentiment that I thought unworthy of an American officer when he said that he would do such an act on the complaint of a negro against him."[11]

Rousseau was not present in the House on February 5. It was a regrettable absence for, in reporting Grinnell's comments to Rousseau, the Kentuckian's friends got the wording slightly wrong, as gossips sometimes will. They reported to Rousseau that Grinnell had said that he "did not know whether Rousseau had fought four years on the rebel side or the Federal side."[12]

When Rousseau returned to the House on February 6, he took his turn in this developing fuss-fight. He objected to Grinnell's characterization, saying, "I did not use the language imparted to me by the member from Iowa and I pronounce the assertion ... that I have degraded my State and uttered a sentiment unworthy of an American officer to be a vile slander, and unworthy to be uttered by any gentleman upon this floor."[13]

Grinnell replied that if he misunderstood Rousseau's language, then he apologized, but "if I understood his language correctly I make no apology for my criticism of it." He added, "I stand upon my rights, as a member of the House ... and when I characterized the language of the gentleman as I did, it was because I believe it was unworthy of an American officer and unworthy of his noble state."[14]

Rousseau had an answer: "I am a new member here, but I have always endeavored to deport myself with the utmost courtesy and kindness toward every gentleman upon the floor. And it does seem to me that it came from exceeding ill grace from gentlemen who have sat in their houses, who have remained in the bosoms of their families in that safety in which we were fighting in the battlefield to come here and ... proceed to assail [another member] first by putting words in his mouth he did not use, and then offer him an insult on account of those words."[15]

Grinnell's words grew more personal as he stood to respond. In part, he derided the Kentuckian as a braggart and said, "The gentleman has paraded his profession of arms before this House."[16]

The exchange continued on February 8. Grinnell said, "I give the member the full benefit of an explanation of his declaration that he would kill a white officer acting under oath and in the discharge of his duty, if that is a less unworthy act than to shoot an American citizen of African descent. That may not have been degrading to his State, and whether it was, as I said, language unbecoming an American officer is a question which I will refer to the gallant soldiers of the State of Iowa who never fought, thank God! but upon one side."[17]

Rousseau, in his response to Grinnell, tried to return to the original matter of his remarks to Major McCaleb. He said that he meant that if his wife and children were arrested in the night (as apparently had happened to the Blevins family) on the testimony of a negro and taken away "between bayonets," that in that case he would seek revenge in protecting his wife and family "and if bloodshed came of it, let it come." He also said that Grinnell "may attempt a fling at Kentucky by talking about fighting on both sides of this question. Kentucky does not care what he may say; and I must say I do not care one cent about anything he may say. But I will tell him one thing, that whether on the Union or the rebel side, he cannot point to a Kentucky man who ever turned his back upon danger, or who has ever dishonored or degraded himself by deserting or failing to defend the cause he espoused." He characterized the words Grinnell had used as "unnecessary and uncalled for ... discourteous and unkind, and against the rules of the House." He did not know what else to do but to rise and "pronounce it false and a vile slander.... And I think he should have done the same against me, if I had assailed him in like manner. And what I accord to other men, I must and will claim for myself."[18]

There, the matter came to a temporary rest. Grinnell, as a man who had lived his life in the North did not know, perhaps, how prickly was a Southern man's sense of honor, but he had trampled upon Rousseau's honor in a way that the Kentuckian could not forget.

In his excellent book *Southern Honor*, Bertram Wyatt Brown identified five essential components to the quality of honor, as the Southerner understood it: (1) personal bravery, (2) the "opinion of others as an indispensable part of personal identity and gauge of self-worth," or in other words, honor was reputation, (3) "physical appearance and ferocity of will," (4) "defense of male integrity," and (5) "reliance upon oath-taking." Brown did not have Rousseau in mind, but in his discussion of the elements of honor, he painted a perfect picture of Rousseau, the internal man.[19]

Grinnell had unwittingly, perhaps, challenged Rousseau on each of the above points and, in doing so, he was treading on perilous ground, for a Southern man was expected to take physical action (dueling, in its most extreme expression) in response to an insult. Rousseau may have been giving him a subtle warning in his comment that Grinnell could not "point to a Kentucky man who ever turned his back upon danger or who had dishonored or degraded himself by deserting or failing to defend the cause he espoused." But, if the remark was intended as a warning, Grinnell missed it, to his eventual regret.

* * *

While the small, personal drama was unfolding between Rousseau and Grinnell, the matter of the new Freedman's Bureau Bill had not been forgotten, entirely. The bill passed both Houses and was sent to President Johnson for his signature. Instead, on February 19, the president vetoed it.

Rousseau had hopes that Johnson's Reconstruction plan would prevail. He wrote to Judge W.S. Bodley on March 16, "We are gaining ground here. The extremists are growing weak and becoming alarmed. In a little while we will have a majority, I hope, though the radical party has been as hard and firm as a rock ... I *know* Johnson and his friends will triumph." Later in the same letter he explained his desire for a moderate approach to Reconstruction in more personal terms:

> I went into [the war] on principle and to accomplish a great purpose and somehow I stand clear of the heart-burnings and hate which so many had and suffered from. I fought my own people — my friends and kindred, my section — and now that the war is over I would heal up the wounds it has made and restore all to the old health and vigour. And this will be done. All will be right. We shall have a struggle — a hard struggle — but the right will prevail.[20]

During the spring, Rousseau continued with his official committee duties. On April 10 he recommended to the House passage of a bill to grant land to build a military road in Oregon and an appropriation of $15,000 for constructing the road. And, in June, he presented a bill for the relief of Ellen

Sanderson, the widow of Colonel John P. Sanderson, provost marshal general of Missouri. But he had not dismissed Grinnell from his mind and made occasional public references to his simmering dislike of the Iowan who, as he believed, had insulted not only himself, but Kentucky, as well. In a spring speech in New York City Rousseau reportedly made a joking reference to Grinnell from the podium. The crowd laughed and cheered, but later, when he heard about it, Grinnell fumed.

The verbal feud had been on low heat since February, but it boiled over in the House chamber on June 11 during a discussion of the status of the Southern states and the seating of representatives from those that had re-entered the Union under Johnson's Reconstruction plan. Rousseau said that the House of Representatives "has held restoration in the palm of its hand. A half hour's work would have been sufficient to accomplish it. If the Lincoln-Johnson policy had been adhered to by this House ... restoration would have been accomplished. Instead of that, we have spent all our time in the denunciation of rebels in provoking sectional strife."[21]

He pointed out that, while he agreed that secession was a crime, it did not originate in the South, but in New England. Years earlier, Josiah Quincy had suggested New England secede over the annexation of Louisiana and even the admired John Quincy Adams had argued — in the case of Texas annexation — that New England had the right to protest by leaving the Union.

Rousseau said, "Now, sir, I should be ashamed of myself if I should come upon this floor to arraign the people of Massachusetts, to denounce and abuse them for any opinion which may have been held by the leading men of that State; I should be ashamed of myself as a member of Congress, or as a private man, if I should do so unworthy a thing. But, sir, how often have we had these flings at the State of Kentucky."[22]

He had opened the door a crack and the always-lurking subject of Grinnell crept in. "I said, sir, a while ago, that flings had been constantly made at my native State, in my hearing, upon this floor; and last and least of all things and everybody, let us give a moment's attention to the member from Iowa {Mr. Grinnell} who first assailed her here. Shortly after Congress assembled he assailed my State and myself; he charged that I had degraded my native State by saying that I would defend my family against the agents of the Freedmen's Bureau. That member was pleased to say on the floor, in answer to a suggestion of my colleague {Mr. Smith} that he did not know whether I had fought four years on the rebel side or on the Federal side in the late war."

Grinnell said, "Mr. Speaker..."

But, Rousseau said, "No sir; I cannot be interrupted now." He returned briefly to the subject about which he had begun speaking, and said, "If you will only allow it, the lately belligerent sections will embrace and be friends. If Congress will but stand aside, the contending factions will come together and restore the Union. All has been done but one thing, namely, the admission of representatives from the State lately in rebellion; and Congress will not do that, but upon a hearing the people will direct this to be done, and then this war will not have been fought in vain."[23]

Grinnell got the floor and said to the speaker, "I desire to give notice that when my colleague {Mr. Price} shall have concluded his remarks I shall claim the floor for a personal explanation in reply to some remarks of the gentleman from Kentucky {Mr. Rousseau} who, I hope, will remain here and listen to what I may have to say."

Rousseau replied, "I shall remain, and endeavor to hear patiently what may be said."[24]

Grinnell had to wait for several tense minutes while a report about the claims of U.S. citizens against the government of Venezuela was submitted, followed by the remarks of several other Representatives about Reconstruction policy. Then, Grinnell had the floor. He began by confessing his "reluctance" to say anything personal about Rousseau — and then went to it enthusiastically. Among other things, he said, "When any man, I care not whether he stand six feet high, whether he wear buff and assumes the air of a certain bird that has a more than usual extremity of tail, wanting in the other extremity, says that he would not believe what I utter, I will say that I was never called to stand under an imputation of that characterization in the company of gentlemen." Regarding Rousseau's four years in the Federal army, he mocked, "But his military record, who has read it? In what volume of history is it found?" He made fun of the story of "Rousseau or a rabbit" and implied that it meant Rousseau ran from battle. He said that Rousseau had never commanded any regiments from Iowa. He denied, however, that he had ever said that he did not know on which side Rousseau had served during the war.[25]

As he went on to complain about the New York speech in which Rousseau named "one Grinnell," Abner C. Harding of Illinois interrupted to ask the speaker if these remarks were in order. The speaker allowed Grinnell to continue. In a moment, Nathaniel P. Banks of Massachusetts raised the same question as Harding. Banks said, "I do not understand that in giving consent to the gentleman from Iowa the House gave consent to him to make personal allusions which are not justified by the rules of the House." The speaker, upon reconsideration, agreed with Harding and Banks that Grinnell was out of order and cautioned the Iowan.[26]

The House clerk recorded Rousseau saying at this point, "If the Speaker does not protect me from such remarks I must protect myself." About this time, there seem to have been several members speaking at once and it may be that Rousseau said it even as the speaker was calling Grinnell out of order, and that the Iowan did not hear Rousseau.[27]

Despite the speaker's admonition, Grinnell was unable to restrain himself, for a moment later he was back on the attack: "The gentleman remarked that he did not care a fig about what I said; but when he goes and proclaims the matter in a great city in the presence of thousands of people, I conclude that he does not rest altogether well satisfied under the well proven charge of having declared that he would shoot an officer of the United States on duty under certain circumstances. And then the member whines off with a woman's plea, taking refuge under feminine skirts, as a certain other gentleman in rebellion went off in disguise." By this sarcastic reference to "a certain other gentleman in rebellion" Grinnell meant Jefferson Davis, who was falsely rumored to have tried to elude capture by dressing in a woman's garments. His implication was that Rousseau was both a traitor and a coward. When the Chair once again ruled Grinnell to be out of order, the congressman said, "I have nothing further to say."[28]

Rousseau answered, "The member has been pleased to-day to make some personal allusions to me. I will not resent anything he can say, because, as I understand, he declares that he cannot be insulted. With such a man I can have no quarrel, and because I look with utter contempt upon anything he could say." He spoke of his military career, mentioning that he had, indeed, commanded Iowa troops during the war, including the 5th Iowa Cavalry, who went with him on the Alabama raid in 1864. It was a detachment of that regiment that had fought so bravely at Beasely Station. He explained the meaning of the "Rousseau or a rabbit" joke, but added that, of his service record, he had, "never dreamed of making a parade of it, and certainly not when I call upon *par excellence* stay-at-home patriots upon this floor, who denounce the friends of the President as lickspittles, to know in what manner they have served their country except in denouncing rebels, filling offices, and drawing salaries."

Rousseau concluded, "I hope now that I have heard the last of the member from Iowa. I hope I shall never have occasion to refer to the subject again. Whatever glory he has gained in this contest, I am content he should have."

Grinnell insisted on the last word. He jumped in to say, "The occasion is no fault of mine."[29]

And at 4:58 P.M., the House adjourned.

* * *

Rousseau said he hoped he had "heard the last of the member from Iowa," but there was one thing more Rousseau wanted to hear from Grinnell — an apology. When Grinnell still had not come forward by the end of the House session on June 14, Rousseau decided to take action.

A crowd drifted out of the Capitol to the East Portico. It was raining and the people hesitated under the canopy before going out to get wet. Grinnell was one of them. Rousseau stepped up to Grinnell and said, "I have waited for four days for an apology."

Grinnell said, "What of it?"

Rousseau answered, "I will show you what of that," and began hitting Grinnell over the head and shoulders with his rattan cane. He backed Grinnell up against a column.[30]

As the surprised crowd in the portico watched, Rousseau rained down stinging blows on Grinnell. During the beating, Rousseau occasionally stopped and chided Grinnell. "Now, you damned puppy and poltroon, look at yourself."

Grinnell whimpered, "I don't want to hurt you."

The tall Kentuckian, who was in no danger at all of being hurt, answered, "I don't expect you to hurt me, you damned scoundrel, but you tried to injure me on the floor of the House. And now look at yourself; whipped here, whipped like a dog, disgraced and degraded. Where are your 127,000 constituents now?"[31]

A few more blows of the cane followed, until the rattan broke and Rousseau walked away.

The conversation during the beating was testified to by witnesses who were called before the Select Committee on Breach of Privilege that was appointed to look into the assault. The committee consisted of Rufus P. Spalding of Ohio (chairman), Nathaniel P. Banks of Massachusetts, John Hogan of Missouri, Henry J. Raymond of New York, and James K. Moorhead of Pennsylvania.

The committee heard testimony from witnesses until July 2, when it finished both a majority and a minority report. The majority report concluded that Rousseau was guilty of assault and therefore "forfeited his privileges as a member of the House and is hereby expelled." As to Grinnell, his remarks had violated the rules of the House and merited disapproval. No other action against the Iowan was recommended.[32]

The minority report disagreed with the majority in that it recommended that Rousseau be reprimanded, not expelled, considering that he had been grossly provoked and that Grinnell had not been hurt.

The reports were read to the House on July 14, exactly one month after the assault. During the hot week that followed, when temperatures inside the House chamber reached ninety degrees, the members debated the proper action to take. Those who defended Rousseau, such as Robert Hale of New York, argued that the speaker had not protected Rousseau and that the Kentuckian's actions were not out of proportion to the insults he had suffered. Henry J. Raymond, one of the select committee members and another New Yorker, summarized a history of violence in the Congress. He pointed out that many brawls had broken out through the years. He referenced Matthew Lyon of Vermont, who spat in the face of Roger Griswold of Connecticut during debate; Preston Brooks who had beaten Senator Charles Sumner to the floor with a cane and nearly crippled him; and, Sam Houston, who had challenged William Stanbery of Ohio to a duel, had approached him in the foyer of the House chamber and would have done violence to him if James K. Polk had not intervened, and who later slammed a hickory cane across Stanbery's skull outside the Brown Hotel. None of these men was expelled, said Raymond.

Among those who spoke against Rousseau was an old acquaintance from the Army of the Cumberland, James Garfield of Ohio. He admitted that Grinnell's words were offensive, but said that Rousseau had a remedy; he would have been protected if he had exercised the right to call Grinnell to order. "If he [Rousseau] desired any more protection, he ought to have asked the Speaker for more," Garfield said.[33]

Ironically, while the discussion dragged on, a fistfight broke out in the basement of the Capitol. The commotion could be heard in the chamber above.

In the end, the majority failed to get the two-thirds vote necessary for expulsion. Instead, the House decided in favor of a reprimand. The resolution read: "Resolved, That Honorable Lovell H. Rousseau be summoned to the bar of the House and be there publicly reprimanded by the Speaker of the violation of its rights and privileges of which he was guilty in the personal assault committed by him upon the person of J. B. Grinnell, a member of the House from the State of Iowa, for words spoken in debate." Rousseau was ordered to appear and accept his punishment on July 21.[34]

On that day, Rousseau had a few remarks of explanation to make. He said that the arguments that had been made against him were both unfair and unjust and sounded as if a criminal case were being prosecuted. He said that he thought — had been informed — that Grinnell was going to give him a written apology on June 12 and that he waited for three days before deciding that, since neither Grinnell or the House had taken action, "I thought the matter had assumed an entirely personal aspect and, as such, my only remedy was in my own hands."[35]

Then, he resigned.

This sudden and unexpected action ignited another little firestorm. Now that Rousseau was no longer a member of the House, was it proper that he should still face a public reprimand? Rousseau was made to leave the chamber while the argument over this question went on; he waited in the lobby. It was finally decided that he must appear and accept his reprimand. Summoned, he entered with the sergeant-at-arms and presented himself at the bar, where he heard the speaker read: "General Rousseau: The House of Representatives have declared you guilty of a violation of its rights and privileges in a premeditated personal assault upon a member for words spoken in debate. This condemnation they have placed on the Journal and have ordered that you shall be publicly reprimanded by the Speaker at the bar of the House. No words of mine can add to the force of this order, in obedience to which I now pronounce upon you its reprimand."[36]

It was a mild admonishment, but to a Southern man, it was an insufferable affront to his honor. A private citizen once again, Rousseau returned home, where the people understood these things.

18
Rousseau and an American Alaska

Rousseau published, in the form of an eleven-page booklet, his own account of the events leading up to his resignation. In his *Address of Hon. Lovell H. Rousseau to His Constituents*, the former congressman said that he hoped to correct the "brief, detached, and often partisan statements of the press."[1]

The *Address* was an often verbatim retelling of the dispute, drawn from the *Congressional Globe*, but he added some new descriptions of Grinnell, "that pestilent member." He said, "With those who personally know Mr. Grinnell, in and out of Congress, what he could say as an individual would be scarcely worth attention; but as a member of Congress, a representative who uttered the obnoxious sentiments of men of more note, and remembering that those sentiments go upon the records of the nation, his remarks were entitled to some consideration.[2]

"It was this that prompted me to give my attention to his repeated assaults upon the people of Kentucky, as well as myself." He went on to call Grinnell a "blusterer" and a "wanton and voluntary libeler and assailant." He spoke of Grinnell's boasting of his own courage, and said that he and Grinnell both knew better than that. "We attained this knowledge on the eastern portico of the Congress," he said. He mocked Grinnell, who was scarcely hurt in the caning, for claiming later in testimony before the select committee that he "was crippled in the left shoulder and hand by the rattaning and could not use them."[3]

He wrote, also, of James A. Garfield, who had repeatedly proclaimed his friendship for Rousseau while explaining all the reasons he should be expelled. "Save me from all such friends and friendship," Rousseau said. As to Nathaniel Banks, Rousseau said, "His voice, cultivated and attuned to that of an ambitious baritone, lacking only the Italian melody and finish, rang out in full, but unvarying and monotonous notes, and penetrated every nook and corner of the amphiteatered hall, resounding back from the futherest galleries and heard by everybody in and about the building—except perhaps by the two chaps engaged in the sanguinary fist fight in the basement."[4]

Rousseau suggested to his constituents that there was a secret motive behind his punishment. It had been told to him that since Southerners were soon to be re-seated as members of Congress, the Radicals wanted to make an example of him as a warning to them to be meek.

He concluded, "You have thus, fellow citizens, a general conversational account of what occurred and I have returned to you the trust you confided in me. I have no regret for my conduct in the matter. I would have chastised Grinnell at every hazard, and would do it again tomorrow under similar circumstances, with impunity ... and on this issue I submit the case to your hands."[5]

* * *

Five days before Rousseau was reprimanded by the speaker of the House, the new Freedman's Bureau Bill passed over President Johnson's veto. The bill had failed once, but was submitted again and, on the second try, succeeded. It was a sign of President Johnson's eroding power. Relations between the chief executive and Congress were decaying rapidly.

On June 13, 1866, Congress passed the 14th Amendment and sent it to the states for ratification. The 14th Amendment restated the Civil Rights Act, in that it defined citizens as anyone born in the U.S. (except Indians, again), but it had four other sections. Former Federal office holders who had supported the Confederacy were prevented from returning to fill an office in the United States government. Any state that restricted the vote among adult males would, as a penalty, lose part of its representation. The U.S. war debts would be paid, but none that were incurred by the Confederacy. Section Five simply said that Congress would have the power to enforce the amendment. President Johnson urged the states to reject the 14th Amendment.

Realizing (a little too late) that he needed to shore up his support both among the people and in Congress, the president decided to go on a public relations tour. He would go on a long, winding train trip from Washington, D.C., to Chicago and back, a trip which came to be known as the Swing Around the Circle. To draw crowds and show the kind of men who supported him, Johnson traveled with an impressive entourage of heroes from the war. Among them were Lovell H. Rousseau; U.S. Grant; Admiral David G. Farragut; Secretary of State William Seward; Secretary of the Navy Gideon Welles; General James Steedman, who was one of the heroes of the Battle of Chickamauga; General George Crook; and the "Boy General," George Armstrong Custer. Along the way, Johnson would explain his point of view to the people and support local candidates who opposed the Radicals' harsh "conquered province" form of Reconstruction. One of those candidates was the Kentuckian in the entourage, Lovell H. Rousseau, who had responded to the calls for him to run to fill the seat in the House of Representatives that had been made vacant by his own recent resignation.

Luckily, Johnson's route took him through Indianapolis, near enough to Louisville that he could drop south of the Ohio River for a few hours and lend support to his old friend Rousseau. There had been rude crowds in Cleveland and Indianapolis who "by their boisterous manner and infernal clamor" had prevented the president from speaking, according to the *Louisville Daily Courier*, but he had reason to expect a better reception in Louisville. The *Courier* called him "the hope of our nation." Perhaps the crowd would agree and be more receptive.[6]

At 3:00 P.M. on a sunny September 11, 1866, Johnson and his collection of celebrities crossed the Ohio River in three ferry boats. When the ferries landed at the foot of 1st Street, the city's fire bells rang thirty-six times. The procession that had gathered to accompany the president's carriage to the city's center included the regimental band and an armed escort of the 2nd U.S. Infantry, plus national, state, and city dignitaries, followed by the Knights Templar and the Masonic Lodges, Temperance Societies, baseball clubs, fire companies, and "cars and wagons from the country and the city." The buildings were decorated with flags and cheering crowds lined the streets. There was a frightening moment when a rough-looking character dashed out of the throng toward the president's carriage. He was no assassin, though. He was a well-wisher who shouted over the noise of the crowd, "God bless you, Andy Johnson — I fought four years and was shot three times to keep the rebel states in the Union and now the traitors up North want to say they're out yet. But, President, keep your ground — the soldiers are with you!"[7]

A tiered platform ("beautifully and tastefully decorated") had been erected in front of the Willard Hotel, facing the courthouse and an assembled crowd of 25,000 people. The dignitaries arrived about 4:00 P.M. and mounted the platform. Senator James Guthrie introduced the president to a square filled with seventy-five thousand people or more. Seward was introduced next. The crowd could see for themselves the ravages to the old man's face. On the night Lincoln was murdered, an attempt was made on the secretary's life by one of Booth's co-conspirators, who had attacked Seward with a knife and sliced up his face horribly. The jagged scars never faded.[8]

Rousseau stepped forward next. The applause was described as "boisterous." The caning of an insolent whelp like Grinnell seemed not to have hurt his reputation in his hometown. He introduced Welles, Farragut, Steedman, Crook, and Custer, but when the crowd called upon him for a speech, Rousseau uncharacteristically declined, saying that since leaving Washington with the president, he had made it a point to decline to speak at every point.

It does seem that he might have made an exception in his home town, but he did not. Perhaps it was because he knew the president's visit would have to be a short one.

The introductions concluded, the party proceeded to the Louisville Hotel for a $10 a plate banquet. The fundraiser was well-attended and perhaps as many as 250 dined with the president and his guests, despite the exorbitant fee charged for the privilege. The *Daily Courier* reported that the president and his party, "pitched into the viands with a hearty good will." The dignitaries left Louisville at 8:00 P.M., and ferried across the river, their visit to Louisville at an end.[9]

The Radicals knew how to play the dirtiest kind of political tricks and they continued to use them all as the president's party continued east across Indiana, Ohio, and Pennsylvania on the final stretch of the tour. They drowned out Johnson's message by hiring thugs to disrupt his whistle-stop speeches and planted outrageous stories against him in the local newspapers. Worst of all were the hecklers with Republican money in their jeans who, at every stop, pricked Johnson's Achilles' heel — his inability to turn aside interruptions with grace or humor. He responded angrily, which made him look intemperate and fed the narrative in the newspapers that he was continually drunk.

The Swing Around the Circle was a disaster. Johnson's reputation suffered lasting damage and the congressional elections of 1866 went strongly to his enemies. But, in the 5th Congressional District of Kentucky, Lovell Harrison Rousseau, without opposition, was re-elected to his own seat in the House of Representatives.

* * *

One would give a lot of money to see a photograph of the faces of the other members of the House of Representatives when the Honorable Lovell H. Rousseau walked into the chamber to take his oath on December 3, 1866. One would give a lot to read a letter from Rousseau, describing his emotions on the occasion. Sadly, no such photograph exists, no such letter has come to light, and one can only visualize the chagrin the House members felt when the tall Kentuckian strode in and imagine the sense of satisfaction that hummed behind Rousseau's gleaming eyes as he took his seat in the familiar hall.

Rousseau was assigned to the same committees he had served in during the first session, but one gets the impression that the returning congressman was more interested in the vindication his re-election represented than in the actual work of a committeeman. His name is rarely mentioned in the *Globe* for the Second Session of the 39th Congress. He did propose an appropriation for the Marine Hospital in Louisville and he reported on behalf of the

Committee on Military Affairs in favor of a pension increase for Walter C. Whitaker of Louisville, based on his service as Colonel of the 6th Kentucky Infantry in late 1861. And, he took a small part on the discussion of how officials might be removed from office—a question that turned out to have historic ramifications in the other House as the Tenure of Office Act. This was a Radical measure which prohibited the removal of an official without Senate approval, if, by the Constitution, the appointee required Senate confirmation.

However, he was not present in March 1867 when two other transformative Reconstruction acts were passed over the president's veto. The first was the Command of the Army Act, which mandated that all orders from the commander in chief, President Johnson, go through the general in chief, U.S. Grant. Since the Swing Around the Circle, Grant was tilting acutely toward the Radicals.

The second was the Military Reconstruction Act, which ordered that the Southern states must begin the process of Reconstruction all over again. The act divided the South into five military districts, each governed by a high-ranking officer. New state constitutions had to be written providing for universal male suffrage. The constitutions had to be approved by a majority of the state's voters and approved by Congress. The 14th Amendment had to be ratified. Then, the state was eligible for readmission to the Union. Only Tennessee, which had ratified the 14th Amendment, was exempt.

President Johnson would have enjoyed having Rousseau in the House to champion the moderates' arguments against these Radical initiatives, but Rousseau resigned on March 3, 1867, in order to accept a commission in the regular army. His appointment as a brigadier general was narrowly approved by the U.S. Senate on March 28, 1867.

The next several months represent something of a blank spot in the narrative of General Rousseau's life. One trace of his activities that has surfaced was a letter he penned to the *New York Times* on May 11, 1867. Rousseau wrote in response to a comment made during the first week in May by the former abolitionist leader Wendell Phillips. In a speech to the New York Academy of Music, Phillips called Rousseau "the cowardly Kentuckian."[10]

In his letter to the *Times*, Rousseau explained his week-long delay in replying. It was due, he said, to "protracted illness in my family and pressing engagements pertinent to a responsible field of labor," and he confessed that he was "really puzzled, even now" to know whether he should take the time to answer a man such as Phillips, "who, for many years, has considered it his privilege to denounce with very foul breath" whatever or whomever crossed him. Should Phillips be excused "like an old, scolding woman"? Rousseau thought not, especially since others besides himself had been mentioned in Phillip's harangue.[11]

Rousseau wrote that Phillips' characterization of him as a coward was a challenge to his military record and was apparently inspired by his promotion in March to brigadier general of regulars.

Rousseau provided extracts from official army records to demonstrate the esteem in which he was held by his commanding officers. They were so voluminous that the *Times* apologized for not having the space to include them.

Then, Rousseau suggested that perhaps Phillips meant that he was a "moral coward" for not taking the insults of Grinnell, who was "chastised with a little rattan switch for his conduct." Rousseau said that his constituents had made a judgment regarding that matter when they returned him to Congress.[12]

Rousseau said he knew that Phillips and his "school" considered it moral courage to win an argument by resorting to name-calling and then were surprised when the slandered party took action. He thought they wanted to expunge "spirit and manhood ... from man's nature." Rousseau said that he despised "the man who insults another and refuses an apology, and who under circumstances unsexes himself, raises the scream of 'moral courage' and cries out in effect that he has no more physical accountability than an outlawed man or a bad woman."

He closed by saying that his life would be given to army service, henceforth, and he thanked the president and the Senate for "their recognition of my service during the rebellion — this recognition is my pride and glory."[13]

"I have tried to do my duty."[14]

* * *

The next duty awaiting Rousseau, the "responsible field of labor" which he mentioned in his letter, undoubtedly referred to the trip he was about to undertake for the secretary of state. On March 30, William Seward had signed the Treaty of Cession of Russian America to the United States, in which the government agreed to pay the Russian czar $7,200,000 for Alaska. To complete the transaction, some representative of the U.S. government had to go to Sitka. Seward turned to General Rousseau. He arranged for the Kentuckian to be given command of the Department of Oregon, an area that would include Alaska, and ordered him to travel to the far North to formally accept the transfer.

Rousseau had evidently been in Washington during Seward's negotiations with the Russians and had met the czar's representatives in the secretary's office, but when he received the commission, the General left immediately for New York City. He took his son George with him. He planned to sail on

August 21, but was delayed for reasons unknown; perhaps it was to wait on the Russian negotiators whose acquaintance he had made in Washington and who were now making their own trip back to the West Coast, thence to Alaska. In any case, Baron Edouard de Stoeckl, the Russian minister; Captain Aleksei Peshchurov, of the Russian Imperial Navy and Rousseau's opposite number in the transfer; and Captain Koskul, representative of the Russian American Company shared the four-week journey with Rousseau. Their ship sailed on August 31.

It must have been a miserable trip for Rousseau. He suffered violently from seasickness and had not been on the salt water since he crossed the Gulf during the Mexican War. Even crossing the pestilential isthmus of Panama (then a part of Colombia), must have been preferable to what he suffered in his bunk on the steamer from New York City. The isthmus was devilishly narrow, and soon they were on the Pacific, steaming toward San Francisco aboard the *Sacramento*. They arrived on September 22. As their ship entered the harbor, an artillery salute was fired in their honor. Once ashore, Rousseau and Peshchurov were called upon by Captain George F. Emmons of the *Ossipee*, the ship that would carry them to Sitka. Emmons wrote in his *Journal*, "Gen. Rousseau suffered with sea sickness all the way out and is very much opposed to trusting himself in a propeller."[15]

Rousseau and his entourage took rooms at the Occidental Hotel on Montgomery Street. It was one of the premiere lodgings in the greatest city of the West and if he had been a few months earlier, Rousseau might have met Mark Twain, who had checked out of that very hotel the previous December to travel to the East, beginning a journey that was nearly the reverse image of the General's. Twain's fame as a lecturer and writer would grow through the rest of the century. He saw many places, but he never forgot his days as a boarder at the Occidental, which he called "heaven on the half shell." The rooms were elegant and the meals of seafood and cold fowl washed down with chilled champagne were legendary.[16]

Rousseau was no rube. He had seen Mexico and the great cities of the East and had lived a life crowded with varied experiences. Even so, San Francisco must have been a wonderful treat to him as he explored it during the five days before the *Ossipee* weighed anchor. There was no other city in America like it. The climate was invigorating and the vistas unparalleled. Perhaps he toured the city on one of the streetcars that ran from downtown out to the Mission District or to South Park, one of the city's newest and most tony neighborhoods. The streetcar fare was only 10¢, but he might have preferred to hire one of the covered carriages as he took a look around. He would have seen the Montgomery Block, a four-story brick office building at the corner of Montgomery and Washington Streets. Strolling in front of the Block, he might have seen a heavily whiskered man in a gaudy uniform — but not the uniform of any kingdom that existed outside of the excited mind of the man who wore it. This man was Norton, Emperor of the United States and Protector of Mexico. Norton was a beloved local crackpot who lived free of charge in a city that appreciated eccentricity. His palace was a shanty behind the Montgomery Block.

Rousseau would have seen the new neighborhoods crawling up Telegraph Hill, house by house, and would have seen, too, the smaller neighborhood of canvass tents where the men who were about to go up to the gold diggings in the Sierras made their temporary home.

Rousseau would have heard the exotic tongues of the Italians, the Chileans, the Japanese, and the Chinese who made the markets a cacophony and he might have heard of the 1865 Know-Nothing type riot in which several Chinese were murdered.

There was a U.S. Mint in San Francisco, as well as eighteen churches, five theaters, fifteen banks, and saloons beyond counting. There were also nine daily newspapers, one of which ran an item about Rousseau's arrival. It is not known which paper printed the item, but Captain Emmons clipped it and pasted it inside the *Journal of the Ossipee*. After explaining his mission to Alaska, the article reviewed the General's military career and his service in the 39th Congress, told of his recent promotion to the rank of Brigadier and his appointment to command the Department of Oregon. It also named the four staff members who were traveling with him: Captain D. L. Rousseau {presumably the General's nephew}, Lt. George Rousseau, Lt. E.G. Fast, and Lt. T.W. Gibson; and also the U.S. Revenue collector W.S. Dodge.

The article told that the steamer *John L. Stevens* was carrying General Jefferson C. Davis and a contingent of U.S. troops, who would be the new garrison at Sitka, and mentioned the Russian commissioners and a group of businessmen who were going along, expecting to establish commercial connections in the North.

Rousseau may have gone to pay a professional call at the Presidio and Fort Point — four stories of stone and brick mounting 126 guns. The installation stood near land once claimed by John C. Frémont, who had given the whole area its lovely, alliterative name, the Golden Gate.

And always in view was the busy bay, crowded with every sort of vessel, from the long, narrow clippers beneath clouds of white sail to the belching, churning steamers like the *Ossipee*. About 10:00 A.M. on September 27, Captain Emmons welcomed Rousseau's party aboard and pointed the bow north toward Alaska.

The *Ossipee* was a sturdy steam sloop of 1,240 tons. Built in 1862, she had joined the West Gulf Blockading Squadron and fought in the Battle of Mobile Bay in 1864. And in all of her history, it is unlikely that she ever had a sicker man on board than Lovell Harrison Rousseau. The mal de mer began immediately and Captain Emmons included in his log an accounting of General Rousseau's enduring misery. On October 2, nearly a week after leaving San Francisco, he wrote in the ship's log, "General R. on deck for the first time since the first day out." Peshchurov, on the other hand, was "a good sailor and feeling no inconvenience from the ship in motion."[17]

The layover in Victoria, Vancouver Island, October 4 to 6, must have seemed to Rousseau a blessed respite, but it was not for his relief that the *Ossipee* dropped anchor. Victoria was a coal stop and probably a too-short one for the General. Soon after getting underway again, Captain Emmons recorded that a sea swell that met the *Ossipee* from the West as it passed out of Fitzhugh Sound had "obliged Gen Rousseau to take to his cot." The conditions turned worse through the following days as the barometer fell and the ship had to swim through a two-day squall on October 13 and 14. Conditions had moderated only slightly on October 17, when the sea was so choppy that it came over the rails. Emmons described it as only uncomfortable, but it was much worse for Rousseau and his fellow travelers, for Emmons wrote of the landlubbers aboard, "*Gen'l Rousseau and many others toes up.*" He underscored the sentence, emphasizing his amusement, an attitude often felt by the experienced man toward the novice.[18]

On October 18, the *Ossipee* steamed into Sitka Sound. In all of his travels, Rousseau had never seen a place with such dimensions as this. The snow-streaked mountains in the background rose sharply from the water and disappeared into the clouds. One of them, Mt. Edgecumbe, was a dormant volcano. Bald eagles perched in the Sitka spruce, watching for fish at the broad water's edge. Tall, colorful totem poles pierced the sky, joined incongruously by the onion-shaped dome of St. Michael's Cathedral. It was a scene of unique beauty that even the seasick Rousseau had to appreciate. Maybe, though, he was feeling better this day; Captain Emmons recorded that the day was cool but unusually pleasant.

Watching from the beach were heavy-bearded Russians and solemn Tlingits, whose land this had been until 1804 when the Russians took it away from them after a bloody war; now, they were witnessing a second transfer and must have realized that the beautiful land encircling the bay was lost to them forever. A tender brought General Jefferson C. Davis and his battalion ashore "in full uniform, armed, and handsomely equipped."[19]

At about 3:00 P.M., Rousseau and his entourage were ferried to shore from the *Ossipee*. They immediately proceeded, in the company of one hundred Russian soldiers and the American troops, to Castle Hill, where the government house stood. The governor, Prince Dimitri Maksutov, waited there for them. He was a pleasant faced man with a dark fringe of beard and wearing a military coat heavy with medals and gigantic epaulets. Standing by him was his wife, Maria, the Princess Maksutov, a tiny, dark-haired beauty in a gown that gave her the shape of a delicate bell.

A ninety-foot flagpole had been erected at the crest of the hill. At its top, the czar's flag with its curious two-headed eagle design fluttered over Russian Alaska for a few final minutes. The Russians filed to the left, the Americans to the right. The ceremony began.

At a signal, the nine-inch pieces of the *Ossipee* began to fire a salute, alternating with the Russian shore battery, so that the flag of each nation was finally saluted with twenty-one guns.

Up on Castle Hill, as the Russian flag was lowered, it became stuck. A czarist soldier tried to climb the pole to reach it, but he got too tired to continue when only halfway up, so a boatswain's chair was rigged up, a Russian was hoisted up and, rather than respectfully carrying the flag back down, he dropped it. The flag fluttered down like a crippled bird and fell onto the Russian soldiers' upturned bayonets.

Now the American honor guard stepped forward, Lieutenant George Rousseau, a sergeant, and ten enlisted men. Young Rousseau pulled the lanyard to raise the American flag and the artillery of both nations fired another salute, this time with the Russian shore battery going first.

Captain Peshchurov approached Rousseau with his hat in his hand and said, "General Rousseau, by authority from His Majesty the Emperor of Russia I transfer to the United States the Territory of Alaska." General Rousseau said, "I accept it in behalf of the Government of the United States."[20]

Rousseau later reported to Secretary of State Seward, "Three cheers were then spontaneously given for the U.S. flag by the American citizens present, although this was no part of the programme and, on some accounts, I regretted that it occurred."[21]

There is no known photograph of the ceremony or the dignitaries at the time of the event. It all happened too fast. The newspaper reporters who were present were annoyed that the whole thing had concluded so quickly.

The officials retired to a reception that had been prepared for them and drank champagne until sunset. Rousseau was offered and accepted rooms in the government house for himself and his party.

He no longer lived in Sitka, but the presence of one man must have been felt at the reception, Father Ivan Veniaminov, a Russian Orthodox missionary who arrived in Alaska in 1824 and eventually was posted in Sitka, where he directed the building of St. Michael's in 1844. The father was another man always described as Herculean. He was a blacksmith, a clockmaker, a carpenter, a brickmaker, a linguist, and a seaman — a man of action, like Rousseau, and one cannot help but think that the General would have liked him.

On the next Monday, General Rousseau and the Russians began an inventory of Sitka's buildings, distinguishing between the public and the private, and giving certificates of ownership to private owners.

Sitka was a surprisingly busy port while Rousseau and the former owners labored over the finishing-up details of the transfer. Captain Emmons remained on the *Ossipee* and wrote in the *Journal* that, in addition to the Tlingit canoes that crowded around his ship, there were the *Jamestown*, the *Resaca*, the *Lincoln*, the *John L. Stevens*, the *Buena Vista*, the *Milan*, and the *Manaluke*. While at anchor, the *Ossipee* refueled in preparation for the return trip to San Francisco. They would have to start soon; there was a snowstorm on October 21 to remind them that the season was growing late. The Americans did not want a winter's layover in Alaska.

Looking for a more comfortable ship to return on, Rousseau apparently considered going home on the *John L. Stevens*, but when Captain Emmons called on him at the government house on October 25, Rousseau said that he would continue on the *Ossipee*, "if I would return by the inland passage which he much preferred." Emmons was agreeable. They steamed away from Sitka on October 26.[22]

Rousseau's dealings with the Russians had been nothing but pleasant. He later reported to Seward, "You were somewhat particular to impress upon me with your desire that all the intercourse should be liberal, frank, and courteous; I am pleased to say that from the meeting of Captain Pestshuroff [sic] and myself in your office till we parted after our work was ended, all our communication and association with each other, personal and official, were of the friendliest character, just as I am sure you desired."[23]

The weather was ugly on October 26 and was "furious" on the 27th, with a heavy sea "frequently breaking all over the ship and finding its way below and flooding the cabin," Captain Emmons wrote. The ship's four pumps were overworked and could not expel the volume of water that was pouring in, so several crewmen were kept busy with bailing buckets all night. They were working to save their lives, for the storm had swept all the lifeboats from their davits.[24]

Rousseau was sicker than ever. Captain Emmons wrote that "Gen'l Rousseau had gone below to escape the greater motion in the cabin found himself deluged by water in his cot when he retreated back to the cabin where he found himself a little better off in regard to water and much worse off to motion which made him very sick."²⁵

Next morning, the *Ossipee* made its way to shore, dropping anchor at Burk's Island, where they found many boats beached and several buildings wrecked by the storm. Rousseau was eager to get back on land and, apparently, to change boats, for he arranged to continue as a passenger on the *John L. Stevens*— until he went aboard and found it to be a leaking, filthy tub. He returned to the *Ossipee* where he and the captain, both exhausted and in foul moods, argued.

Rousseau told Emmons that he was ready to go, but the captain "gave him distinctly to understand that I was not ready and it might be several days before the ship was in seaworthy condition." Rousseau wanted to hear what repairs were necessary and Emmons gave him a verbal list of what must be done. Rousseau wasn't satisfied and went below where he spoke to some of the other officers who disagreed with their captain's opinion; they believed that the ship could sail immediately. Rousseau reported this to Emmons.²⁶

To Emmons, this sounded very much like he was being second-guessed, not only by his subordinates, but by this green-about-the-gills landlubber, and he responded with some heat. "I then remarked that I was the judge of whether the ship was ready ... I said perhaps I did not wish him to go in the *Ossipee* etc and ... other such remarks that led to some discussion which was not altogether pleasant."²⁷

In fact, the ship was so damaged by the storm that it had to return to Sitka on November 4. The barometer was still falling. That and other signs convinced the Captain that a gale was coming and the *Ossipee* was in no condition to weather another storm at sea. The barometer was still falling on November 5 and Rousseau was joined by twenty others on the sick list. Emmons wrote that all were "painfully anxious to get away from this place," but there was no chance of it until there were more able-bodied hands to complete the repairs and man the ship, and until the weather improved.²⁸

A false start was made on November 6, but on the 7th, the *Ossipee* got fairly away and headed south again. It was, Emmons said, "the best day we have seen since leaving Vancouver." They passed several Indian canoes as they weaved their way through the various straits of the Inner Passage toward Chatham Sound.²⁹

On November 14, the *Ossipee* arrived at Esquimalt Harbor and anchored off Merchants Wharf at Victoria, British Columbia. Rousseau took a final meal with Emmons on November 15 and took his baggage away to the George Hotel. How long he remained is not known, but it was at least until the 19th, when an item appeared in the newspaper announcing that on that night, "under the patronage of General Lovell H. Rousseau, Captain George F. Emmons, and Officers of the *Ossipee*," various acts would appear at the Theater Royal, including Miss Lizzie Yeoman and Miss Sarah J. Von Allman. Emmons permitted "all the officers who could be spared from duty" to attend the gala. On the 26th, the *Ossipee* returned to San Francisco.[30]

On December 5, Rousseau transmitted his report from the Headquarters of the Department of the Columbia in Portland, Oregon, to the secretary of state; Seward acknowledged its arrival on January 24, 1868. The report contained all the pertinent papers (the final document signed by Rousseau and Peshchurov, the inventory of government property, the list of Sitka's private property owners, etc), as well as Rousseau's account of the transfer ceremony, proper, and his evaluation of the accessibility of the Sitka area (which he sometimes called by the Russian name of New Archangel). Considering the agonies he had suffered, it is perhaps surprising that he wrote:

> A steamer of ordinary size and power can go from Victoria to New Archangel by way of the straits.... The passage is a safe one, and amidst scenery as grand and beautiful as there is in the world. The mountains covered with forests, rise almost perpendicularly out of the water to a height of one to three thousand feet, and from the very tops of which gush out foaming waterfalls. In grandeur and sublimity there is nothing like it on this continent.
>
> I have no doubt this passage — about eight hundred and forty miles from Victoria to Sitka — will form a part of the great highway from the United States to the latter place, as it is both safe and delightfully pleasant. The waters are very deep, and anchorages not numerous, but enough. Along the shores are safe land-locked little bays and harbors, formed by notches in the mountain sides, where vessels of any size can anchor in quiet and safety.[31]

Rousseau did not stay in Portland, Oregon, very long. His next assignment required one more voyage and took him to a place about as opposite from the Pacific Northwest as any place in the United States could be. Rousseau was ordered to take command of the Department of Louisiana, with his headquarters in New Orleans.

There, Rousseau would find that the political and racial cross-currents were as treacherous as any he had ever endured.

19

The Department of Louisiana

The Rousseau family closely resembled the more famous Custers — they had the same dash and love of adventure. They were fearless and they tended to stick together. Lovell H. and Richard H. practiced law together and even shared the same residential lot in Louisville. They labored together in 1861 for the Union cause. When Lovell H. began Camp Joe Holt as Colonel of the 5th Kentucky Infantry, his brother David Q. was the First Lieutenant in Company G and it is said that he later became a member of his brother's staff. Before the war, David had worked as an employee along with the youngest Rousseau brother Samuel in the Louisville brickyard which was owned by their older brothers Edmund and William.

However, they were Kentuckians, and like many families in that border state, their sympathies were divided by the Civil War. There were Rousseaus fighting on both sides. The Southern-leaning Rousseaus seemed to gravitate toward New Orleans. The General's brother Samuel (the former brickyard worker) lived there and became a surveyor; he served as a Confederate engineer in the defenses around Richmond during the war. In addition, Rousseau's sister Lucy had married Robert Mahan and moved to New Orleans. Her son, General Rousseau's nephew, was George W. Mahan, a lieutenant in the 1st Louisiana Cavalry, CSA.

Whether either Samuel or Lucy still lived in New Orleans at the time Lovell H. Rousseau was stationed there is unknown, but his nephew George W. Mahan did. Considering the high regard which the Rousseaus had for their own, it is likely that, even though the General was a Union hero during the war, and even though he was busy with his duties as commander of the Department of Louisiana, he must certainly have made time to see his nephew during his time in New Orleans.

In a family that had such a strong sense of the extended clan, it is strange that Rousseau had so few opportunities to be a husband and father to his immediate family. But, he was ambitious, too, and that was a countervailing force that repeatedly disrupted his home life through the years. Rousseau undoubtedly expected his tenure at New Orleans to be an enjoyable domestic interlude. Daughter Mary and her family were already there and Mrs. Rousseau and the other three children could come and join him.

Fate conspired against their happiness. In March 1868, Rousseau's son-in-law, General Louis D. Watkins, suddenly died. He was only thirty-eight years old and he left behind a pregnant widow with two young children, Lovell R. who was not quite three years old, and Eva W. who was only eighteen months. The baby, named Louis D., was born in June, almost exactly three months after his father died.

Fate conspired Rousseau's peaceful enjoyment of a home life in another way, for Louisiana was about to enter one of the most turbulent periods in its history and the General, as department head, was going to be right in the middle.

Fate was fickle, but in this case Rousseau might have had a glimmer of what was coming by the recent history of his new command. Louisiana had been one of the earliest states to come under Union control. In April 1862 Admiral David G. Farragut had steamed up the Mississippi River and captured New Orleans from behind. Major General Benjamin F. Butler became the military commandant of the city, instituting a reign so harsh that he was called "Beast" Butler and so larcenous that he was called "Spoons," a reference to the old family silver that he stole.

After the war's end, Louisiana was part of the Military Division of the Gulf, under General Philip H. Sheridan. His rule resembled that of Butler's in its firmness. Yet, Sheridan's extreme approach to Reconstruction did not work. In the summer of 1866, there was a race riot in New Orleans in which thirty-four blacks and three whites were killed and over one hundred of both races wounded. Sheridan called it a "slaughter" and elsewhere referred to it as "an absolute massacre." It was one of the events which gave the Radicals justification for canceling presidential Reconstruction and replacing it (over President Johnson's veto) with the Military Reconstruction Act. Louisiana reverted to its wartime status and the process leading to re-admission began again. Sheridan enthusiastically embraced the principles of Radical Reconstruction.[1]

In his department, now renamed the 5th Military District, Sheridan was quick to remove from office any elected official who, in his opinion, was not co-operative with Radical Reconstruction. This included the mayor of New Orleans, judges, the attorney general of Louisiana, and the governors of both Louisiana and Texas. Naturally, Radicals were installed to fill the vacancies. He sponsored a vigorous voter registration drive which excluded any man who could not present positive proof that he had been a loyal Union man. It was too strict an interpretation of the law and the U.S. attorney general, Henry Stanbery, ruled so, saying that taking the oath of loyalty was sufficient for a prospective voter to be registered. Sheridan's reply was insubordinate; he said that Stanbery's ruling was an invitation to perjury and fraud. Even the Northern newspapers were shocked at Sheridan's attitude toward the attorney general.

President Johnson removed Sheridan in September 1867 and replaced him with General Joseph A. Mower, a cut-rate version of Sheridan, and then replaced him with General Winfield Scott Hancock, one of the heroes of the Battle of Gettysburg. Hancock, like Sheridan, also pursued a policy of voter sign-ups, but unlike Little Phil, he widened the effort to allow ex–Confederates to register. He also reversed an earlier policy to let blacks serve on juries, since they were not yet citizens under the Constitution, and he removed several Republican appointees from office, putting Democrats in their place. The resulting argument with U.S. Grant, who by now had become a complete tool of the Radicals, caused Hancock to request a transfer. General Robert C. Buchanan was his successor and oversaw the remaining efforts of Louisiana's struggle toward re-admission.

The process was complete by the time Rousseau arrived on September 15, 1868. That is to say, the state had written a new constitution which enfranchised all adult males, regardless of race (save those leading Confederates who were stripped of their citizenship rights). Voters had approved the state constitution, and the 14th Amendment had been popularly ratified in the same April canvass which resulted in the Republican Henry Clay Warmoth becoming Louisiana's new governor. In June, the new state legislature formally approved the 14th Amendment. The U.S. Congress approved Louisiana's actions and seated its senators and representatives, along with those of Florida, Alabama, North Carolina, and South Carolina.

The end of Reconstruction in these states forced a re-drawing of the military district boundaries. Texas alone was now the 5th Military District, severed from Louisiana and Arkansas, which became the Department of Louisiana.

Rousseau made his headquarters in New Orleans, the state capital at the time and, at 144,000 residents, the largest city in the South. Even so, the city was a strangely backward metropolis in a strangely backward state. As Eric Foner pointed out, Louisiana "lacked a hard-surfaced public road, and New Orleans, which contained only two hospitals, had a primitive water system that contributed to regular outbreaks of yellow fever and malaria." New Orleans also had a unique population — half of the white citizens were foreign born and nearly half of its blacks had been born free — and the atmosphere was heavy with pressure between the various groups. There was tension between the whites and the blacks, tension between the born-slave blacks and the born-free blacks (some of whom, like Antoine Dubuclet, had been slave-owners; Dubuclet, though black, owned one hundred slaves), and tension between all three groups and the sizable sub-culture of Italians. There was tension between the Radicals and the conservative groups of pre-war power brokers, and there were various other fault lines that crackled not far beneath the city's surface.[2]

Nerves were drawn tighter in late 1868 as the presidential election drew close. Andrew Johnson was eligible to run for a second term, but he had been impeached in the spring of 1868 and was one of the most unpopular men in America. Mark Twain saw Johnson during the impeachment troubles and wrote, "I never saw any man who looked as friendless and forsaken, and I never felt for any man so much." (Rousseau had been summoned to appear as a witness for Johnson, but the impeachment had ended in an acquittal before he could travel from the West to Washington, D.C.). The 1868 candidates were the Democrat Horatio Seymour and Republican Ulysses S. Grant.[3]

To keep peace between the supporters of the two candidates, across the whole length and breadth of his department, Rousseau had at his command only three regiments of infantry, three companies of cavalry, and one company of artillery, an aggregate of 2,251 men.

As the election approached, the Democrats in New Orleans showed signs of growing stronger. Their rallies equaled those of the Republicans for enthusiasm and, with excitement running high on both sides, it was perhaps inevitable that there would be clashes. The first one occurred on the night of September 22 when two rival parades encountered one another in the narrow streets of New Orleans. In the melee that followed, three blacks were killed and men were wounded on each side. A patrol of soldiers supplemented by city police broke up the fight. The soldiers stayed on hand to watch over a Democratic rally the next day.

The pressures building up in his department were cause for alarm. Rousseau had seen in Louisville in 1855 the devastation which election day violence could bring to a city. It looked as if the same kind of situation might be developing not only in New Orleans but also in far-flung villages and towns across Louisiana. On September 26, Rousseau wrote to President Johnson that the people were like "a volcano ready for an explosion at any moment." The moment came two days later, when there was a violent incident in St. Landry Parish, 150 miles or so northwest of New Orleans. An attack on the Radical newspaper editor there led to a call for members of local Negro political clubs to mobilize. This, in turn, led to a gathering of the whites.

The two groups got into a gun battle that left one dead and several wounded. A number of blacks were arrested and jailed and, the following night, were taken out and killed by vigilantes. More violence followed and over one hundred Negroes were killed. The number of whites who suffered injury or death is uncertain.[4]

Rousseau ordered troops to St. Landry. They found the city of Opelousas and the surrounding parish in control of patrolling bands of whites. St. Landry was locked down — the belligerent whites would not testify as to what had happened there and the blacks were too afraid to.

Violence followed in other parishes and in New Orleans, itself. There, the Italians, who supported the Democrats, were divided into three rival groups; the largest was a group made up of immigrants from Sicily. They called themselves the Innocenti. All three groups were guilty of pre-election violence and had lost members killed. The Innocenti had most recently lost Edward Malone and Listero Barba. The first man had been killed by a Negro and the second, it was originally thought, by one of the rival Italian political clubs led by Raffaele Agnello, a suspected Mafioso. However, as the Innocenti investigated Barba's killing, it became clear to them that he had been murdered by a Negro businessman and Republican legislator named Octave Belot. It was reported that he had gone into hiding. The Innocenti took to the streets, breaking into homes and shops where Belot might be hiding. The chief of police pleaded with them to stop, to no avail.

According to Thomas Hunt and Martha Macheca Sheldon, in their article "America's First Mafia War," this was the moment that Rousseau took personal action. He went before the Innocenti in their clubhouse and, in a speech that was reported in newspapers as far away as New York, "warned them that the responsibility for all outrages and disorders in New Orleans was laid on his shoulders, and he looked to them to keep the peace and encourage others to do the same. He said he felt it his duty to tell them that the laws must be observed and *that everyman who had the right to vote shall vote unmolested on Election Day*" (italics added for emphasis). The Innocenti respected the courage of a man who came into their smoky den to tell them, in person, how things were going to be. The Innocenti would prove to be one group Rousseau did not have to worry about during the November 3 election — they were quiet that day and caused no trouble.[5]

Rousseau appeared before other Democratic-leaning groups to inform them that the army would use its power to put down any disturbance of the peace, whether by the supporters of Seymour or Grant. Invited to speak to a combined rally of Democratic clubs in New Orleans, Rousseau thanked them for their hospitality and then said, "It is, however, a fit occasion to say a word on another matter, induced ... by the passing of a negro procession an instant ago, and the exhibition of some feeling on both sides. Let me tell you, my countrymen, that you cannot afford to have a riot or mob in your city, let who will begin it.... The man, white or black, who induces a riot here deserves instant death, and I trust will receive what he merits."[6]

A political creature always, Rousseau was able to gauge the growing power of the Democratic Party in Louisiana and he foresaw that a victory for the Democrats was likely on November 3. Rousseau had never been a Democrat, so it may be that he was predicting an outcome that, though probable, was not altogether pleasing when he wrote the President, saying: "The ascendance of the negro in this state is approaching its end.... A fair vote will give the state to the democrats."[7]

Rousseau might have appeared before this gathering and that, but he could not be everywhere before the election and could not personally appeal to every group. He requested his superiors to order two more regiments to New Orleans and also to send two Gatling guns.

There was more mob violence on October 23, across the Mississippi from New Orleans in Gretna. Rousseau stopped civilian travel between the two towns and ordered two companies across the river to restore order.

On October 24, six more blacks were killed in New Orleans. During these many and widely-scattered disturbances, Rousseau had been working closely with Republican governor Henry C. Warmoth. Warmoth later remembered that his relationship with Rousseau was good, despite the differences in their political views, and that they frequently conferred as to the most effective way to preserve the peace in New Orleans and the outlying district.

However, the two men sometimes had different ideas about how to calm the situation and Rousseau did not always follow the governor's suggestions. When Warmoth advised that a black regiment be brought into New Orleans to help keep the peace, Rousseau tentatively agreed. Later, he changed his mind, having decided that the sight of black troopers would anger the people and make an incident all the more likely. Anyway, he had little faith that the black troops would stand firm against an armed mob. Perhaps he was thinking of the two black garrisons' performance at Elk River Bridge during Forrest's 1864 raid.

Neither did Rousseau support Governor Warmoth's plan to form his own state militia. In this instance, Warmoth out-flanked Rousseau. He petitioned the state legislature to create the Metropolitan Police Force, a band of 375 men. The Republican legislature accommodated their governor. In spite of the group's name, the Metropolitans were not confined to New Orleans city limits; Warmoth used them like a militia and dispatched them to outlying parishes to put out the brush fires of trouble, wherever they might be. Rather than calm the situation, it further inflamed it, because the local authorities resented these cocky outsiders. Rousseau, too, held them in contempt, citing their unprofessionalism as an ersatz militia. To gain some measure of control over the Metropolitans, Rousseau appointed his war time associate, the capable General James Steedman, to be their chief until after the election. Rousseau promised Steedman the support of the army. Meanwhile, he renewed his call for those two previously requested infantry companies.

On October 26, a small riot broke out in St. Bernard Parish. White Democrats murdered two blacks. The Negroes responded by killing three whites, a baker and his sons, and setting fire to their home while a woman and other children were inside. Two hundred revenge-seeking New Orleans whites made ready to cross the Mississippi, but Rousseau prevented it by sending troops to take away their boat. They had to limit their mischief to New Orleans — widespread vandalism ensued, and some shootings. It was more than Warmoth could bear and he wilted, admitting that events were out of control. He asked Rousseau to assume control of the municipal police, as well as the military, and to restore order. Rousseau telegraphed Secretary of War John Schofield for instructions. Schofield told him in plain language to do whatever was necessary to keep the peace and protect the people's lives and property.

A rare piece of good luck occurred about this time when a portion of the reinforcements which Rousseau had asked for arrived in the city, not two regiments but five infantry companies. Now, the immediate force available to the General — exclusive of the police — numbered slightly over five hundred.

The arrival of these reinforcements still did not give Rousseau the numbers he needed, but the public had seen all the new troopers disembark and perhaps could be persuaded that there was now too much fire power behind Rousseau to be challenged. That hope led Rousseau to issue a proclamation from his headquarters on October 28. Addressing the citizens of New Orleans, Rousseau stated that his orders from Washington were to maintain order and that he was authorized to use the necessary force to do so. He called upon the people to help him by not congregating in the streets. Further, he requested them to refrain from language that would incite violence. He advised the people to go about their usual business.

All of this was in the form of a request, but the language of the proclamation was harder near the end. The General warned the people of New Orleans that the police had the power of the army behind them and that public political demonstrations were temporarily banned. Furthermore, squads of armed men roaming the streets would not be tolerated.

Rousseau made his meaning and his intentions clear, but there was a certain percentage of bluff in the confident tone of his proclamation. The situation was fragile, so fragile that General Robert C. Buchanan suggested to Rousseau that if he were to pull back his meager forces, it would be as justifiable as a battlefield retreat.

Governor Warmoth did not like Buchanan, but in this, he essentially agreed — Rousseau's declaration would not forestall violence. Rousseau asked, in that case, that Warmoth issue a statement of his own in which he advised blacks "to remain away from the polls in the interest of peace and civil order."[8]

The moment Rousseau made that statement to Warmoth became the single most controversial moment of the General's public life. Later observers of the events of 1868 in New Orleans have not been generous in their evaluation of Rousseau as department commander and they use this suggestion of his — that blacks be encouraged not to vote — to buttress the argument that he had no sympathy for the blacks, that he was a party operative in a position of power where he could finesse the situation to favor the Democrats. Certainly, the suggestion that blacks voluntarily stand back during the election was not a perfect solution, but in this case, the perfect was truly the enemy of the good. To Rousseau, the greater good was the preservation of order and the protection of life and property. His orders from Washington were not to guarantee black suffrage but to keep the peace and, like the soldier he was, this was his goal.

And — this is very important — Governor Warmoth, a Republican, agreed that the situation was so volatile that he readily issued the proclamation which Rousseau suggested.

Still worried about the uncertainty of the situation, Rousseau wired more questions to Schofield about the exact parameters of his authority. One senses that Schofield was exasperated, for he forwarded the wires to President Johnson who, for the time being, was still commander in chief. He replied directly to Rousseau in unmistakable language, "You are expected and authorized to take all legitimate steps necessary and proper to prevent breaches of the peace or hostile collisions between citizens."[9]

Meanwhile, Governor Warmoth and General Steedman quarreled over the governance of the Metropolitans and the courts were considering the question of whether the special force was even legal. Steedman had had enough, and on October 31, he resigned, leaving the multiple aggravations of the position to a subordinate.

On election day, November 3, Rousseau deployed his troops to best advantage as he had done when trouble was anticipated in his department back in 1864. He ordered them to protect the polls and to help local officers. Then, he held his breath.

By the end of the day, it was clear that Rousseau's efforts had paid off. Disturbances were minimal; in fact, the *New Orleans Times* reported a "Sabbath-like stillness." That the Democrat Horatio Seymour carried Louisiana was largely due to the lack of widespread Negro participation in the election. But that was not the only factor. Joseph G. Dawson pointed out in his article "General Lovell H. Rousseau and Louisiana Reconstruction" that it was shown in a "subsequent congressional investigation of election violence that the Democrats were better organized." They had been ascendant in the several months preceding the election and, therefore, it is not entirely surprising that Seymour won. It became convenient, though, to blame President Johnson and his allies, including Rousseau, after the Republican hero Grant lost the Pelican State.[10]

Rousseau was in a position that was a lightning rod for criticism. If his performance in 1868 was not satisfactory to some at the time (and to some modern observers) then he was in the company of Philip Sheridan, whose oppressive style of departmental command depended on the bayonet, and whose time in command was so ineffective that a race riot broke out that was the disgrace of the era and in which thirty-four blacks had been killed. Sheridan, too, drew his share of criticism, arguably with more justification than General Rousseau. Rousseau did have some admirers. One newspaper, the *Republican*, editorialized, "Through the leaders of the different parties, he made constant efforts to quiet club and faction justice ... he was earnest and true in his efforts to protect life and prevent a riot."[11]

Rousseau (with the cooperation of Governor Warmoth) had undoubtedly suppressed the black vote by suggesting that African Americans stay away from the polls on November 3, but the General and the Governor had spared lives, and life trumped suffrage. Another day to vote would come. Nevertheless, the incident was, and still remains, controversial and Rousseau has always come under more criticism than Governor Warmoth for the suppression of the black vote.

It was unfortunate for Rousseau's reputation that this was the last page of both his service and his life. On January 4, 1869, the General became suddenly and violently ill with what has been described after the fact as appendicitis, inflammation of the bowels, and congestion of the lower intestinal tract. A precise diagnosis is impossible at this late day, but the "insidious disease" progressed. Three days later, on January 7, 1869, General Rousseau died. He was fifty years old.

Since his boyhood, Rousseau had been continually at war. From an unfortunate beginning, he had fought his way out of ignorance and poverty to a respectable and lucrative life in the law. In the courtroom, he had fought for those who had no other voice to defend them. He had fought the Know-Nothings in Louisville and had made war against his country's enemies in Mexico and, later, in Kentucky and Alabama and Tennessee. He had fought in defense of his honor and had ended his life warring against the forces of civil disorder. Sometimes the cost might have been higher than he had expected — certainly in terms of a normal family life it had been — but Rousseau had been true to his nature and faithful to his duty as he understood it.

Now, he had transcended to that plane where understanding was perfect and his struggles were at an end.

Afterword

The winter season had always been dangerous for Rousseau. He had suffered many serious illnesses in winter, but had always pulled through The odds caught up with him in New Orleans on January 7, 1869.

His funeral was at Christ Church in New Orleans two days later. His body was taken afterward to Lafayette Cemetery. The day was gloomy, but the sidewalks were full of people watching the procession: companies of infantrymen, a regimental band, an artillery battery, and mounted cavalry. Rousseau's Masonic Lodge brothers followed, then the departmental officers, and the casket containing the General's body. Behind it were the local Democratic Party leaders and Rousseau's led horse. Next came the carriage with Rousseau's widow and four children. Rousseau's brother Richard, with whom he had shared so much of his life, would have been there, but he had been appointed U.S. minister to Honduras in 1866 and would not return to the U.S. for another eight months, in August.

Bringing up the rear were more state and local dignitaries, including Governor Warmoth, fire companies, employees in the various city agencies, and plain citizens. Businesses along the funeral route closed their doors out of respect, as the procession passed. More than one newspaper reported that it was the largest funeral the city had ever seen.

The day of the funeral, General U.S. Grant issued General Orders No. 2. It was a complimentary review of Rousseau's career followed by the order: "As military honors appropriate to the memory of the deceased, thirteen minute guns will be fired, commencing at meridian, and the national flag will be displayed at half-staff from the same hour till sunset on the day after the receipt of this order at each post within the Department of Louisiana. Officers of the Army serving in the Department will wear the prescribed badge of mourning for thirty days."[1]

Obituaries were generous to Rousseau's memory. The *Lafayette* (Louisiana) *Advertiser* called him "a most great and good man," and "a departed Hero, Statesman, and Christian."[2]

In his hometown, the *Louisville Daily Democrat* ran the news of his illness and of his sudden death in the same edition on January 9. It said:

> This will be sad news to thousands of people in Kentucky, who held General Rousseau in the highest esteem. Thousand of people, too, throughout the whole South will hear of his death with sincere regret, for he was their friend when they stood in greatest need of friends. He fought them as a brave soldier — and only as a brave soldier fights — and when the conflict had ceased to rage and peace was said to have come, he went among them to calm and to pacify with the olive branch and not to overawe and to terrify with the sword and the bayonet.[3]

Rousseau's death had left his family in difficult financial circumstances. As the head of the Department of Louisiana, with his headquarters in New Orleans, Rousseau had found himself in the center of a region and a city where graft was an expected way of doing business. Few men, from "Spoons" Butler on, had had the strength or the will to resist. Governor Warmoth was among those later accused of making money out of Louisiana's misfortunes. In Rousseau's case, it was a different story. Family researchers say that he died with so little in the way of savings that his staff raffled off his horses for the immediate relief of his widow. Of course, she did later receive his pension.

Rousseau's death was the second in his family in less than a year. It was tragedy enough, but it was not the end. Daughter Mary's newborn, Louis D. Watkins, died two months later, in March 1869, in New Orleans. Mary, who suffered from tuberculosis, traveled to Saint Paul, Minnesota, in search of a cure. She died there on July 8, 1869.

Marie Antoinette Rousseau became the guardian of her two surviving grandchildren, Lovell R. Watkins (called Rousseau) and Eva. Neither one lived long. Eva died of spinal meningitis in 1875. Rousseau died in 1882, at age 26, while a corporal in the U.S. Army.

By the time of Rousseau Watkins' death, Marie had lost her son George. After accompanying his father to Alaska in 1867, he had pursued an army career. While serving as a 2nd Lieutenant in the 20th U.S. Infantry, he killed a man and was arrested and tried. The trial ended in an acquittal, but also in his dismissal from the service. He became an opium addict and committed suicide by a gunshot wound to the head in 1881. He was buried in Laredo, Texas.

The other son, Richard, died the same year. He had gone to sea, but died in June 1881 in a Maine poorhouse, unmarried, drunken and destitute. He filled a pauper's grave.

The remaining Rousseau child, the mysterious daughter known only as "B," may have moved to Europe and may have had a child, but it is only supposition. There is no definite knowledge of "B" or her life. Considering the fate of her brothers and her sister, the odds of her having found happiness are not good.

* * *

General Rousseau's body, along with that of his son-in-law Louis D. Watkins, was moved from New Orleans to Louisville in the spring of 1870. They arrived by river transport and were taken to the city hall, where the two generals lay in state until they were taken to Cave Hill Cemetery for burial.

Still, their travels were not done. In September 1892, Marie Rousseau, who had lost all of her family, came from her home in Arlington, Virginia, to oversee the removal of the bodies of Generals Rousseau and Watkins to Arlington National Cemetery.

Lovell Harrison Rousseau was interred for the third and final time in site 1047. His son George Lovell Rousseau was brought from Texas and buried next to his father, and son-in-law Louis Watkins was buried a few paces away. Marie Antoinette Rousseau joined them there when she died in March 1898.

* * *

A man without descendents has no one to perpetuate his memory. His wife and children all dead, and with no surviving grandchildren, memories of Lovell Harrison Rousseau began quickly to fade. Not that there were not some honors, both then and now. The Grand Army of the Republic held its annual convention in Louisville in September 1895 and the local newspapers ran special sections telling about the early days of the war in Louisville. For a few days, General Rousseau's name was once again prominent in the papers, but then the old soldiers went back home to their homes to await the last bivouac. The stories died with them.

The sculptor Vinnie Ream executed a bust of the General. The GAR post in Greeneville, Indiana, where he had practiced law as a young man, was named in his honor. In modern times, the Perryville Battlefield Preservation Association named its lecture series The General Lovell H. Rousseau Civil War Lecture Series. The association has sponsored the series since 2006.

Yet, Rousseau is not well known. There are many who believe that he is still buried in Cave Hill Cemetery in Louisville. There are no heroic statues of him on the battlefields where he led his men so well. And there is no great archive of his papers. The presumption is that, with no descendants to take an interest in them, all but a few of his papers were destroyed. If a collection exists, it is in some dusty attic trunk and has never come to light. Where are his swords, his shoulder-boards, and his spurs? No one knows.

The evidence of Rousseau's life is skimpy and it must be searched for and tediously brought out. But, like seams of gold painfully extracted from hard granite, the result justifies the effort. As in the case of all men, he had his flaws, but in Rousseau, the researcher finds many of the *best* qualities of the nineteenth century man — honor, courage, a devotion to duty, and a willingness to serve. And, in the end, one feels that Rousseau himself would agree that he needed no monuments of marble and bronze. One needs only to look at the map of a free, united country stretching from the Gulf of Mexico to the Bering Sea to see the best monument to the life and service of Lovell Harrison Rousseau.

Chapter Notes

Introduction

1. W. F. G. Shanks, "Recollections of General Rousseau," *Harper's New Monthly Magazine*, November 1865, 768 (first quote); 765 (second quote).

Chapter 1

1. Lewis Collins, *History of Kentucky* (Lexington: Henry Clay Press, 1968), 402.
2. Ibid., 404.
3. Lovell H. Rousseau, letter to Charles Lanham, 23 October 1866. Charles Lanham Collection, Filson Historical Society, Louisville, KY.
4. Edmund Thickstun, "A Bluegrass Lassie." Unpublished manuscript, collection of Linda Smetzer.
5. Ibid.
6. Ibid.
7. Ibid.
8. Ibid.

Chapter 2

1. Lowell H. Harrison and James C. Klotter, *A New History of Kentucky* (Lexington: University Press of Kentucky, 1997), 127.
2. William Sumner Dodge, *History of the Old Second Division, Army of the Cumberland* (Chicago: Church and Goodman, 1864), 291.
3. Ibid., 293.
4. Rousseau to Lanham.

Chapter 3

1. James Whitcomb, *Indiana in the Mexican War*, compiled by Oren Perry (Indianapolis: Burford, 1908), 16.
2. Ulysses, letter to Benjamin F. Scribner, 26 October 1846. Benjamin F. Scribner Papers, Folder 2. Collection of the Eugene and Marilyn Glick History Center, Indiana Historical Society, Indianapolis, IN.
3. Benjamin F. Scribner, *Camp Life of a Volunteer: A Campaign in Mexico* (Philadelphia: Grigg, Elliott, 1847), 47.
4. Ibid., 56.
5. Zachary Taylor, "Battle of Buena Vista, Official Report," http://www.dmwv.org/mexwar/documents/bvista.htm (accessed May 31, 2008).
6. Cadmus Marcellus Wilcox, *History of the Mexican War*, Mary Rachel Wilcox, ed. (Washington, D.C.: Church News, 1892), 215 (first quote); Scribner, 59 (second quote).
7. Taylor, "Official Report."
8. Scribner, 60.
9. Whitcomb, 161.
10. Taylor, "Official Report."
11. Center of Military History, U.S. Army, *American Military History* (Washington, D.C.: Center of Military History, 1988), 171 (first quote); Taylor, "Official Report" (second quote).
12. Whitcomb, 179.
13. Ibid., 167.
14. Ibid., 186.
15. Ibid., 334.
16. Scribner, 74.

Chapter 4

1. David Evans, *Sherman's Horsemen* (Bloomington: Indiana University Press, 1966), 32.
2. Kay Gill, "Galt House," *The Encyclopedia of Louisville* (Lexington: University Press of Kentucky, 2001).
3. William Fontaine Bullock, letter to John L. Helm, 25 April 1851. Collection of the Filson Historical Society, Louisville, KY.

4. "The Reign of Terror: Louisville Under Mob Law," *Louisville Daily Courier*, 8 August 1855, 2.
5. James Speed, letter to W. R. Thompson, 8 September 1855. Quoted in Tom Stephens, "Annotated Notes on Bloody Monday, Louisville, August 6, 1855," *Kentucky Ancestors: Genealogical Quarterly of the Kentucky Historical Society*, Summer 2006, 180.
6. "Reign of Terror," 2.
7. Ibid.
8. "The Case Stated," *Louisville Daily Journal*, 9 August 1855, 2 (first quote); "Who is Responsible for the Riot?" *Louisville Daily Courier*, 9 August 1855, 2 (second quote).
9. "The Result in the City," *Louisville Daily Courier*, 5 November 1856, 2.
10. Samuel W. Thomas, "An Enduring Folly: The Jefferson County Courthouse," *Filson Club Historical Quarterly*, October 1981, 333.

Chapter 5

1. Shanks, 763.
2. Rousseau to Lanham.
3. Shanks, 764.
4. Alfred W. Harris, "Rousseau's Louisville Legion," Louisville *Commercial*, 11 September 1895, Section 2, 3.
5. Ibid.
6. "Abraham Lincoln Papers." http://memory.loc.gov/cgibin/query/P?mal:5:./temp/-ammem_v5N4::@@@mdb+mcc,gott (accessed April 2, 2009).
7. Shanks, 764.
8. Dodge, 43.
9. Ibid., 303.
10. "Stirring Scenes at Camp Jo [sic] Holt," *Louisville Courier-Journal*, 11 September 1895, Section 2, 7.
11. Shanks, 765.
12. U.S. War Department, *The War of the Rebellion: A Compilation of the Official Records of the Union and Confederate Armies* (Washington, D.C.: Government Printing Office, 1880–1901), Vol. 4, 264. Hereafter cited as *OR*.
13. Shanks, 765.
14. Co. C, 3rd Kentucky Regiment, "To the Editors of the *Daily Journal*," *Louisville Daily Journal*, 5 October 1861, 1 (first quote); *OR*, Vol. 4, 279 (second quote).
15. "Brig.-Gen. W. T. Sherman," *Louisville Daily Journal*, 27 September 1861, 3.

16. Larry J. Daniel, *Days of Glory: The Army of the Cumberland, 1861–1865* (Baton Rouge: Louisiana State University Press, 2004), 16.
17. William T. Sherman, *Memoirs of W. T. Sherman* (New York: Appleton, 1891), Vol. I, 227.
18. *OR*, Vol. 4, 299.
19. Dodge, 69.

Chapter 6

1. J. W. Leonard, "Letter from Kentucky," *Hancock Jeffersonian*, 1 November 1861, 2. Collection of Bowling Green State University, Bowling Green, OH.
2. William C. Robinson, letter to Charlie, 13 October 1861. Collection of the Abraham Lincoln Presidential Library, Springfield, IL.
3. Ibid.
4. Bell I. Wiley, *The Life of Billy Yank* (Baton Rouge: Louisiana State University Press, 1989), 55.
5. "Letter from Camp Nevin," *Louisville Daily Journal*, 16 October 1861, 3.
6. Shelby Foote, *The Civil War, a Narrative: Fredericksburg to Meridian* (New York: Vintage Books, 1986), 726 (first quote); Shelby Foote, *The Civil War, a Narrative: Fort Sumter to Perryville* (New York: Vintage Books, 1986), 728 (second quote); Daniel, 286 (third quote); Daniel, 18 (fourth quote).
7. Alexander McDowell McCook, letter to William Dennison, 15 November 1861. Collection of the Ohio Historical Society, Columbus, OH.
8. Ibid.
9. "The Rebellion in Kentucky," *The New York Times*, 21 October 1861, 1 (first quote); "Our Camp Nevin Correspondence," *The New York Times*, 24 October 1861, 1 (second quote).
10. Basil Duke, *A History of Morgan's Cavalry* (Bloomington: Indiana University Press, 1960), 129.
11. "The War in Kentucky," *The New York Times*, 28 October 1861, 1.
12. *OR*, Vol. 7, 480.
13. Amos Glover, "Diary," Harry J. Carmen, ed. http://publications.ohiohistory.org/hostemplate.cfm?action+dated&page=00442 58.html&s. (accessed January 29, 2008).
14. Dodge, 83.
15. "Affairs in Kentucky," *The New York Times*, 11 October 1861, 2.

Chapter 7

1. Sherman, Vol. 1, 228.
2. Alexander K. McClure, *Recollections of Half a Century* (Salem: Salem Press, 1902), 332.
3. Lyman S. Widney, *Campaigning with Uncle Billy*, Robert I. Girardi, ed. (Victoria, BC: Trafford, 2008), 36.
4. Walter T. Durham, *Nashville: The Occupied City* (Nashville: Tennessee Historical Society, 1985), 89.
5. Ibid., 56.
6. N. G. Markham, letter to Eunice Markham, 27 March 1864. N. G. Markham Papers. Collection of the Filson Historical Society, Louisville, KY.
7. Durham, *The Occupied City*, 71.
8. Foote, *Fort Sumter to Perryville*, 331.
9. Mark W. Johnson, *That Body of Brave Men: The U.S. Regular Infantry and the Civil War in the West* (Cambridge, MA: Da Capo Press, 2003), 98.
10. *OR*, Vol. 10, Pt. 1, 303.
11. Ibid., 308.
12. Johnson, 121.
13. *OR*, Vol. 10, Pt. 1, 303.
14. Johnson, 121.
15. *OR*, Vol. 10, Pt. 1, 310.
16. Ibid., 305.

Chapter 8

1. *OR*, Vol. 10, Pt. 1, 672.
2. Ibid.
3. Bruce Catton, *Grant Moves South* (Boston: Little, Brown, 1960), 270.
4. *OR*, Vol. 10, Pt. 1, 679.
5. James Lee McDonough, *War in Kentucky: From Shiloh to Perryville* (Knoxville: University of Tennessee Press, 1994), 31.
6. Foote, *Fort Sumter to Perryville*, 385.
7. Ibid., 389.

Chapter 9

1. *OR*, Vol. 16, Pt. 1, 351.
2. Dodge, 302.
3. Ibid.
4. Ibid., 303.
5. Alfred Pirtle, "Journal, 1859–1862," 16 April 1862. Alfred Pirtle Papers, 1847–1924. Collection of the Filson Historical Society, Louisville, KY (first quote); Pirtle, "Journal," 27 May 1862 (second quote).
6. *OR*, Vol. 16, Pt. 1, 350.
7. *OR*, Vol. 7, 669.
8. *OR*, Vol. 16, Pt. 1, 350.
9. McDonough, 98.
10. *OR*, Vol. 16, Pt. 1, 352.
11. Kenneth Noe, *Perryville: This Grand Havoc of Battle* (Lexington: University Press of Kentucky, 2001), 25.
12. *OR*, Vol. 16, Pt. 2, 390.
13. Ibid., 395 (first quote); 398 (second quote).
14. Ibid., 419 (first and second quotes); *OR*, Vol. 16, Pt. 1, 611 (third and fourth quotes).
15. *OR*, Vol. 16, Pt. 2, 425.
16. Durham, *The Occupied City*, 117.
17. *OR*, Vol. 16, Pt. 2, 451.
18. Ibid.
19. Ibid., 462.
20. Daniel, 115.
21. *OR*, Vol. 16, Pt. 1, 88.
22. Daniel, 121.
23. "Gen. Buell's Department," *The New York Times*, 2 October 1862, 8.
24. Untitled, undated newspaper clipping from the *Louisville Daily Journal*.
25. Robert E. McDowell, *City of Conflict: Louisville in the Civil War, 1861–1865* (Louisville, KY: Louisville Civil War Roundtable, 1962), 89.
26. Ibid., 93.
27. Ibid., 100.
28. Ibid., 101.
29. Ibid.

Chapter 10

1. *OR*, Vol. 16, Pt. 2, 565.
2. David Claggett, "Civil War Diary of Major David Claggett," *Ancestral News, Quarterly of the Ancestral Trails Historical Society*, Summer 1979, 69.
3. Ibid.
4. Philip H. Sheridan, *Personal Memoirs of P. H. Sheridan* (New York: Webster, 1888), Vol. 1, 118.
5. *OR*, Vol. 16, Pt. 1, 1038.
6. Daniel, 148.
7. *OR*, Vol. 16, Pt. 1, 557.
8. Ibid., 1046.
9. Ibid.
10. Shanks, 767 (first quote); *OR*, Vol. 16, Pt. 1, 1046–47 (second quote).
11. Noe, 274.

12. *OR*, Vol. 16, Pt. 1, 1047.
13. McDonough, 281 (first quote); 282 (second and third quotes); Shanks, 766 (fourth quote).
14. *OR*, Vol. 16, Pt. 1, 1047.
15. Ibid., 349.
16. Ibid., 1042 (first quote); 345 (second quote).

Chapter 11

1. Dodge, 309.
2. Daniel, 177.
3. *OR*, Vol. 16, Pt. 1, 11.
4. Ibid., 8–9.
5. *OR*, Vol. 20, Pt. 2, 75,
6. Ibid., 117.
7. Ibid., 118.
8. Peter Cozzens, *No Better Place to Die: The Battle of Stones River* (Urbana: University of Illinois Press, 1990), 46.
9. Ibid., 58 (first quote); Alfred Pirtle, letter to Jane Pirtle, 27 December 1862. Alfred Pirtle Letters, 1859–1862, Alfred Pirtle Papers, 1847–1925. Collection of the Filson Historical Society, Louisville, KY (second quote).
10. Pirtle Letters, 27 December 1862.
11. *OR*, Vol. 20, Pt. 2, 279.
12. Robert E. Denney, *Civil War Medicine* (New York: Sterling, 1994), 183.
13. Johnson, 274.
14. Daniel, 213.
15. Johnson, 280.
16. Ibid. (first quote); 281 (second quote).
17. Foote, *Fredericksburg to Meridian*, 91.
18. Ibid.
19. *OR*, Vol. 20, Pt. 1, 378.
20. Ibid., 381 (first quote); 222 (second quote).
21. Ibid., 379.

Chapter 12

1. Pirtle, letter to Henry Pirtle, 3 January 1863.
2. Johnson, 309.
3. *OR*, Vol. 16, Pt. 1, 345.
4. Ibid., 347 (first quote); 357 (second quote).
5. Ibid., 355.
6. Ibid., 357.
7. Ibid., 351.
8. Ibid.
9. Earl J. Hess, *Banners to the Breeze: The Kentucky Campaign, Corinth, and Stones River* (Lincoln: University of Nebraska Press, 2000), 231.
10. James R. Gilmore, *Personal Recollections of Abraham Lincoln* (Boston: Page, 1898), 146.
11. Johnson, 331.
12. *OR*, Vol. 23, Pt. 1, 434.
13. Ibid., 435–36.
14. Ibid., 436.
15. Ibid.
16. *OR*, Vol. 23, Pt. 2, 518.
17. Ibid., 552.
18. Ibid.
19. Ibid., 592.

Chapter 13

1. Daniel, 280.
2. David Evans, *Sherman's Horsemen* (Bloomington: Indiana University Press, 1996), 34 (first quote); Daniel, 280 (second quote).
3. *OR*, Vol. 30, Pt. 3, 62.
4. William Shakespeare Hays, "The American Flag." http://www.pdmusic.org/hays/wsh63taf.txt (accessed November 23, 2008).
5. Isaac Funk and Lovell Harrison Rousseau, *The Loyalist's Ammunition* (Philadelphia, 1863), cover.
6. Ibid., 14.
7. Foote, *Fredericksburg to Meridian*, 717.
8. Peter Cozzens, *This Terrible Sound: The Battle of Chickamauga* (Urbana: University of Illinois Press, 1992), 294.
9. Ibid., 498.
10. *OR*, Vol. 30, Pt. 1, 279.
11. Ibid. (first quote); *OR*, Vol. 30, Pt. 2, 762 (second quote).
12. *OR*, Vol. 30, Pt. 4, 60.
13. Johnson, 409.
14. Daniel, 352.
15. *OR*, Vol. 30, Pt. 1, 211.
16. Daniel, 354.
17. Shanks, 766.
18. *OR*, Vol. 30, Pt. 1, 220 (first quote); *OR*, Vol. 31, Pt. 1, 69 (second quote); *OR*, Vol. 30, Pt. 1, 211 (third quote).
19. Dodge, 313.

Chapter 14

1. John H. Ward, letter to John G. Foster, 19 January 1864. Speed Family Papers—Farmington Collection. Collection of the Filson Historical Society, Louisville, KY.

2. William T. Ward, letter to John H. Ward, 5 February 1864. Speed Family Papers — Farmington Collection. Collection of the Filson Historical Society, Louisville, KY.
3. Lovell H. Rousseau, postscript to William T. Ward letter, 5 February 1864.
4. Ibid.
5. *OR*, Vol. 31, Pt. 3, 326.
6. *OR*, Vol. 38, Pt. 4, 167.
7. Felix Prince Salm-Salm, letter to Lovell H. Rousseau, 10 June 1864. John A. McAllister Collection. Collection of the Library Company of Philadelphia, Philadelphia, PA.
8. Robert H. Milroy, letter to Lovell H. Rousseau, 20 June 1864. John A. McAllister Collection. Collection of the Library Company of Philadelphia, Philadelphia, PA.
9. Dodge, 306.
10. *OR*, Vol. 38, Pt. 4, 530–31.
11. Ibid., 531.
12. Ibid., 638.
13. Ibid., 648.
14. *OR*, Vol. 38, Pt. 5, 19.
15. Ibid., 41.
16. Ibid., 82.
17. Shanks, 768.
18. Evans, 101.
19. "What Gen. Rousseau Did," *The New York Times*, 7 August 1864, 8.
20. James Q. Chenoweth, "The Rangers' Last Campaign," in Adam Johnson, *The Partisan Rangers of the Confederate States Army*, William J. Davis, ed. (Utica: McDowell, 1979), 176.
21. Ibid., 177.
22. *OR*, Vol. 38, Pt. 1, 905.
23. Ibid., 906.
24. Evans, 116.
25. Ibid., 117.
26. Walt Whitman, "Cavalry Crossing a Ford," in *Leaves of Grass*, "Book 21: Drum Taps" (New York: Modern Library, 1950), 241–42.
27. Evans, 118.
28. Ibid., 126.
29. *OR*, Vol. 38, Pt. 1, 907.
30. Ibid.
31. "Gen. Rousseau's Raid," *The New York Times*, 3 August 1864, 8.
32. "The Alabama Raid," *The New York Times*, 7 August 1864, 2.
33. *OR*, Vol. 38, Pt. 1, 908.
34. Shanks, 767.
35. Evans, 152.
36. Isabelle W. J. Shacklette, "Narrative." Collection of the Filson Historical Society, Louisville, KY.
37. Ibid.
38. Ibid.
39. William D. Hamilton, *Recollections of a Cavalryman of the Civil War after Fifty Years, 1861–1865* (Columbus: Heer, 1915), 139.
40. Shacklette.
41. Evans, 169.
42. Ibid., 172.
43. Ibid., 174.

Chapter 15

1. Sherman, Vol. 2, 69–70.
2. Ibid., 69.
3. Shelby Foote, *The Civil War, a Narrative: Red River to Appomattox* (New York: Vintage Books, 1986), 486 (first quote); Mark E. Fretwell, "Rousseau's Alabama Raid," *Alabama Historical Quarterly*, Winter 1956, 547 (second quote); Edwin C. Bearss, "Rousseau's Raid on the Montgomery and West Point Railroad," *Alabama Historical Quarterly*, Spring–Summer 1963, 47 (third quote).
4. Evans, 173.
5. Ibid., 474.
6. Verna Rosecrans, e-mail to the author, November 21, 2008.
7. *OR*, Vol. 38, Pt. 5, 666.
8. *OR*, Vol. 38, Pt. 2, 911.
9. *OR*, Vol. 38, Pt. 5, 778–79.
10. Ibid., 826.
11. Ibid., 839 (first quote); Ibid., 850 (second quote).
12. William S. Rosecrans, letter to Lovell H. Rousseau, 14 September 1864. John A. McAllister Collection. Collection of the Library Company of Philadelphia, Philadelphia, PA.
13. *OR*, Vol. 39, Pt. 2, 859.
14. *OR*, Vol. 39, Pt. 1, 537.
15. Ibid.
16. Ibid., 505 (first quote); *OR*, Vol. 39, Pt. 3, 81 (second quote); 83 (second quote).
17. *OR*, Vol. 39, Pt. 2, 486.
18. Ibid., 879.
19. Ibid., 504.
20. Ibid., 523 (first quote); 535 (second quote).
21. *OR*, Vol. 39, Pt. 3, 21 (first quote); 18, (second quote).
22. *OR*, Vol. 39, Pt. 1, 546.

23. *OR*, Vol. 39, Pt. 3, 152.
24. Ibid., 259.
25. *OR*, Vol. 39, Pt. 1, 507.
26. Ibid.
27. Rosecrans, letter to Rousseau.
28. James Speed, letter to Lovell H. Rousseau, 26 October 1864. John A. McAllister Collection. Collection of the Library Company of Philadelphia, Philadelphia, PA.
29. *OR*, Vol. 45, Pt. 1, 32 (first quote); *OR*, Vol. 39, Pt. 3, 589 (second quote).
30. Foote, *Red River to Appomattox*, 667.
31. *OR*, Vol. 45, Pt. 1, 1153.
32. Ibid.
33. *OR*, Vol. 45, Pt. 1, 744.
34. Ibid.
35. Ibid., 745.
36. *OR*, Vol. 45, Pt. 1, 613.
37. Ibid., 745.
38. Ibid.
39. Ibid., 617.
40. Ibid.
41. Ibid., 618.
42. Ibid. (first quote); Ibid., 755 (second quote).
43. Ibid., 613.
44. Ibid.
45. *OR*, Vol. 45, Pt. 2, 152.
46. *OR*, Vol. 45, Pt. 1, 619.

Chapter 16

1. *OR*, Vol. 45, Pt. 2, 435.
2. Stephen G. Burbridge, letter to Lovell H. Rousseau, 13 February 1865. John A. McAllister Collection. Collection of the Library Company of Philadelphia, Philadelphia, PA.
3. *OR*, Vol. 49, Pt. 1, 785.
4. *OR*, Vol. 49, Pt. 2, 346.
5. Ibid., 419.
6. Ibid., 806.
7. Ibid., 753.
8. Ibid., 960.
9. J. F. Speed, letter to James Speed, 28 June 1865. Speed Family Papers, 1813–1981. Collection of the Filson Historical Society, Louisville, KY.
10. J. F. Speed, letter to James Speed, 11 July 1865. Speed Family Papers, 1813–1981. Collection of the Filson Historical Society, Louisville, KY.
11. "General Rousseau on the Stump," *The New York Times*, 14 July 1865, 2.
12. Ibid.
13. "August Election," *Louisville Daily Democrat*, 7 August 1865, 3.

Chapter 17

1. George Brown Tindall, *America: A Narrative History* (New York: Norton, 1988), 705.
2. Ibid., 705–06.
3. "Appendix to the Congressional Globe, House of Representatives, 39th Congress, 1st Session," in "A Century of Lawmaking for a New Nation: U.S. Congressional Documents and Debates," http://memory.loc.gov/cgi-bin/ampage, 69 (accessed June 16, 2008).
4. Ibid., 70.
5. Ibid.
6. Ibid.
7. Ibid.
8. Ibid., 74.
9. Ibid., 72.
10. Ibid., 74.
11. "The Congressional Globe, House of Representatives, 39th Congress, 1st Session," in "A Century of Lawmaking for a New Nation: U.S. Congressional Documents and Debates," http://memory.loc.gov/cgi-bin/ampage, 652 (accessed June 16, 2008).
12. Ibid., 3875.
13. Ibid., 688.
14. Ibid.
15. Ibid.
16. Ibid.
17. Ibid., 754.
18. Ibid.
19. Bertram Wyatt Brown, *Southern Honor: Ethics and Behavior in the Old South* (Oxford: Oxford University Press, 1982), 34–61.
20. Lovell H. Rousseau, letter to W. S. Bodley, 16 March 1866. Bodley Family Papers. Collection of the Filson Historical Society, Louisville, KY.
21. *Congressional Globe*, 3091.
22. Ibid., 3093.
23. Ibid., 3094–95.
24. Ibid., 3095.
25. Ibid., 3096.
26. Ibid.
27. Ibid.
28. Ibid.
29. Ibid., 3097.
30. Ibid., 3822–23.
31. Ibid., 3823.

32. Ibid., 3544.
33. Ibid., 3884.
34. Ibid., 3544.
35. Ibid., 4010.
36. Ibid., 4017.

Chapter 18

1. Lovell H. Rousseau, *Address of Hon. Lovell H. Rousseau to His Constituents* (Philadelphia, 1866), 1.
2. Ibid., 1–2.
3. Ibid., 1–4.
4. Ibid., 5–6.
5. Ibid., 7.
6. "Radical Infamy," *Daily Courier*, 11 September 1866, 2 (first quote); "The Presidential Visit," *Daily Courier*, 11 September 1866, 2 (second quote).
7. "The Presidential Visit," 2 (first quote); "Our President: His Arrival and Reception," *Daily Courier*, 12 September 1866, 2 (second quote).
8. "The Presidential Visit," 2.
9. "Arrival and Reception," 2.
10. Lovell H. Rousseau, "Reply of Gen. Rousseau to Wendell Phillips," *The New York Times*, 10 May 1867, 2.
11. Ibid.
12. Ibid.
13. Ibid.
14. Ibid.
15. "Journal of the *Ossipee*," http://vilda.alaska.edu:80/cgibin/docviewer.exe?CISOROOT+cdmg22&CSIOPTR+3394, 135 (accessed May 15, 2008).
16. Justin Kaplan, *Mr. Clemens and Mark Twain* (New York: Simon & Schuster, 1966), 15.
17. "Journal of the *Ossipee*," 138.
18. Ibid., 141 (first quote); 146 (second quote).
19. Thomas Donaldson, *The Public Domain* (Washington, D.C.: Government Printing Office, 1881), 143.
20. Ibid., 144.
21. Ibid.
22. "Journal of the *Ossipee*," 150.
23. *The Public Domain*, 144.
24. "Journal of the *Ossipee*," 151.
25. Ibid.
26. Ibid., 154.
27. Ibid.
28. Ibid., 156.
29. Ibid., 157.
30. Ibid., 161.
31. http://memory.loc.gov/servicerbc/rbcmisc/mtfrb/1000/0080008.txt (accessed April 12, 2009).

Chapter 19

1. Philip H. Sheridan, *Personal Memoirs of P. H. Sheridan* (New York: Webster, 1888), Vol. 2, 235 (first quote); Eric Foner, *Reconstruction: America's Unfinished Revolution, 1863–1877* (New York: Harper Collins, 2002), 263 (second quote).
2. Foner, 364.
3. Kaplan, 68.
4. Joseph G. Dawson III, "General Lovell H. Rousseau and Louisiana Reconstruction," *Louisiana History*, Fall 1979, 380.
5. Thomas Hunt and Martha Macheca Sheldon, "America's First Mafia War: New Orleans, 1868–1872," http://www.onewal.com/aol6/f_nolafeud.html (accessed May 26, 2008).
6. "Another Speech by Gen. Rousseau in New-Orleans," *The New York Times*, 6 October 1868, 2.
7. Dawson, 381–82.
8. Ibid., 385.
9. Ibid., 386.
10. Ibid., 388.
11. "Gen. Rousseau at New-Orleans — Defence of His Conduct," *The New York Times*, 8 November 1868, 1.

Afterword

1. General Orders, 9 January 1869. Collection of the Filson Historical Society, Louisville, KY.
2. "Gen. Rousseau," *Lafayette Advertiser*, 16 January 1869, 1.
3. "Lovell H. Rousseau," *Louisville Daily Democrat*, 9 January 1869, 2.

Notes on Selected Sources

Chapter 1

The principal sources for Rousseau's parentage and early life were the unpublished biographical sketch written by Linda Smetzer and "A Bluegrass Lassie" by Rousseau's nephew Edmund Thickstun, which Ms. Smetzer generously shared. Useful information was also found in the Rousseau Family File, collection of the Kentucky Historical Society, Frankfort, Kentucky. See also William Sumner Dodge, *History of the Old Second Division, Army of the Cumberland* (Chicago: Church and Goodman, 1864), which contains a great deal of biographical information gathered by one of Rousseau's contemporaries.

Lincoln County, Kentucky, is discussed in Lewis Collins, *History of Kentucky* (Lexington: Henry Clay Press, 1968). The cholera outbreaks in 1832 through 1835 are best described in Nancy D. Baird, "Asiatic Cholera's First Visit to Kentucky: A Study in Panic and Fear" (*Filson Club Historical Quarterly* 48, No. 3, July 1974) and in John E. Kleber, ed., *The Kentucky Encyclopedia* (Lexington: University Press of Kentucky, 1992).

Rousseau's handwritten 1866 autobiographical sketch is found in the Charles Lanham Collection at the Filson Historical Society, Louisville, Kentucky.

Chapter 2

A good discussion of Kentucky's road building efforts in the early 1800s is found in Kleber, *The Kentucky Encyclopedia*, and also Lowell H. Harrison and James C. Klotter, *A New History of Kentucky* (Lexington: University Press of Kentucky, 1997). The history of Bloomfield and Greene County, Indiana, is found in Jack Baber, *The Early History of Greene County, Indiana* (Worthington, IN: Worthington Press, 1875). Details of Rousseau's legislative career in Indiana are to be found in *Journal of the House of Indiana, 29th Session, March-December 1844*, collection of the Eugene and Marilyn Glick History Center of the Indiana Historical Society, Indianapolis, Indiana. Rousseau's marriage to Marie Antoinette Dozier and his relationship with his brother Richard are primarily found in Ms. Smetzer's unpublished sketch.

Chapter 3

Two useful overviews of the Mexican War are Center of Military History, U.S. Army, *American Military History* (Washington, DC: Center of Military History, 1989) and Donald Barr Chidsey, *The War with Mexico* (New York: Crown, 1968). See also, Vincent J. Esposito, editor, *The West Point Atlas of American Wars* (New York: Praeger, 1978).

For the deadly efficiency of Mexican lancers in battle, see the excellent *Blood and Thunder*, by Hampton Sides.

For the role of the 2nd Indiana Volunteers in the Mexican War, two primary sources are highly recommended: Benjamin F. Scribner, *Camp Life of a Volunteer: A Campaign in Mexico* (Philadelphia: Grigg, Elliott, 1847) and Isaac Smith, *Reminiscences of a Campaign in Mexico* (Indianapolis: Chapman and Spann, 1848). Additional material was found in Folders 2 through 5, *Benjamin Franklin Scribner Papers, 1846–1850*, in the collection of the Indiana Historical Society, Indianapolis.

For the Battle of Buena Vista, see Zachary Taylor, "Battle of Buena Vista, Official Report," available online at http://www.dmwv.org/mexwar/documents/bvista. See also Ora Perry, compiler, *Indiana in the Mexican War* and Grigg, Elliott, and Company, *The Mexi-*

can War and Its Heroes (both published Whitefish, MT: Kessinger, 2007).

Chapter 4

The collection of the Indiana Historical Society does not include the journal from the Indiana Senate for the years during which Rousseau served; one may not exist. However, useful information about the time when Rousseau was a state senator is found in *The Report of the Agent of the State to the General Assembly, December 1848* (Indianapolis: Defrees, 1848), which is in the IHS collection.

Louisville in the 1850s is well described in Collins *History of Kentucky*, and John Kleber, editor, *The Encyclopedia of Louisville* (Lexington: University of Kentucky Press, 2001).

Mr. Kleber also wrote an admirable account of the Know-Nothing Riot of 1855 in "August 6, 1855: Bloody Monday" (*Courier-Journal*, July 31, 2005). See also Wallace S. Hutcheon, "The Louisville Riots of August 1855" (*Register* of the Kentucky Historical Society 69, No. 2, April 1971), and Tom Stephens, "Annotated Notes on Bloody Monday, Louisville, August 6, 1855" (*Kentucky Ancestors: Genealogical Quarterly of the Kentucky Historical Society* 41, No. 4, Summer 2006).

Invaluable, of course, were the contemporary newspaper reports which appeared in the *Louisville Daily Courier* and the *Louisville Daily Journal*, August 5 through 9, 1855, available on microfilm at the Louisville Free Public Library.

Chapter 5

For Rousseau's service in the stormy session of the Kentucky General Assembly in 1861, see *Kentucky Senate Journal, 1861* (Frankfort, KY: Yeoman Office, 1861). A wider view of events in Kentucky on the eve of war is found in Lowell H. Harrison, *The Civil War in Kentucky* (Lexington: University Press of Kentucky, 1975), and Harrison and Klotter, *A New History of Kentucky*.

For Rousseau's preparations to defend Louisville against Confederate incursions, see the wonderful book by Robert E. McDowell, *City of Conflict: Louisville in the Civil War, 1861–1865* (Louisville, KY: Louisville Civil War Roundtable, 1962), and Dodge, *History of the Old Second Division*.

The events of April through September 1861 are covered in Alfred W. Harris, "Rousseau's Louisville Legion" (*Louisville Commercial*, September 11, 1895).

Chapter 6

For an overview of the formative events in the Army of the Cumberland, two books come highly recommended. One is Larry J. Daniel, *Days of Glory: The Army of the Cumberland* (Baton Rouge: Louisiana State University Press, 2004). The other is Mark W. Johnson, *That Body of Brave Men: The U.S. Regular Infantry and the Civil War in the West* (Cambridge, MA: Da Capo Press, 2003).

See also R. M. Kelly, "Holding Kentucky for the Union," *Battles and Leaders of the Civil War: The Opening Battles*, Robert Underwood Johnson and Clarence Clough Buel, eds. (Edison, NJ: Castle Books, 1995).

For the creation of Camp Nevin and the experiences of the soldiers there, see Dan Lee, *Camp Nevin: Hardin County's Contribution to Victory in the War of the Rebellion* (by the author, 2008) and Dan Lee, *Always Ready: the Campaigns of the 2nd Kentucky Cavalry, USA* (by the author, 2008).

For the history of those regiments that came to Camp Nevin, see *Report of the Adjutant General of the State of Kentucky* (Frankfort, Kentucky, 1866–1867); Thomas Speed, *The Union Regiments of Kentucky* (Louisville, KY: Courier-Journal Job Printing Co., 1897), and Frederick H. Dyer, *A Compendium of the War of the Rebellion* (Dayton, OH: Broadfoot, 1994). Three very useful primary sources were the 2nd Kentucky Cavalry file, the 5th Kentucky Infantry file, and the 6th Kentucky Infantry file (Collection of the Kentucky Military History Museum, Frankfort, Kentucky).

For the life of the common soldier in camp, the most useful single volume is by Bell I. Wiley, *The Life of Billy Yank* (Baton Rouge: Louisiana State University Press, 1989).

John Hunt Morgan, the "Thunderbolt of the Confederacy," was the terror of the soldiers at Camp Nevin. Two books describe his exploits with particular style. The first, written by Morgan's brother-in-law and second in command, is Basil Duke, *A History of Morgan's*

Cavalry (Bloomington: Indiana University Press, 1960). The second Morgan book is a modern study by James A. Ramage, *Rebel Raider: The Life of General John Hunt Morgan* (Lexington: University Press of Kentucky, 1986).

The *Chicago Tribune*, *The New York Times*, and the *Louisville Journal* all had correspondents at Camp Nevin and their reports from the field in October, November, and December 1861 are both enjoyable and informative to read. However, the letters from the solders who were at Camp Nevin were often repeated in their hometown newspapers and they were indispensable. Especially useful in the preparation of this volume were: William C. Robinson Letters (Collection of the Abraham Lincoln Presidential Library, Springfield, Illinois), J.W. Leonard "Letter from Kentucky." (*Hancock* [Ohio] *Jeffersonian*. November 1, 1861. Collection of Bowling Green State University, Bowling Green, Ohio); Samuel O. Thomas "Letter from Kentucky." (*Hancock* [Ohio] *Jeffersonian*, November 15, 1861. Collection of Bowling Green State University, Bowling Green, Ohio); and Samuel O. Thomas "Letter from Kentucky." (*Hancock* [Ohio] *Jeffersonian*, November 28, 1861. Collection of Bowling Green State University, Bowling Green, Ohio). Also useful was Harry J. Carmen, editor, "Diary of Amos Glover," found online at http://publications.ohiohistory.org/hostemplate.cfm?action=dated&page=0044258.html&s, January 29, 2008.

Three more sources must be mentioned. The first is Alexander McDowell McCook, Letter of November 15, 1861 (Collection of the Ohio Historical Society, Columbus, Ohio). The second is the vividly written autobiography of William T. Sherman, *Memoirs of W. T. Sherman* (New York: Appleton, 1891). The Library of America published a modern reprint of this Civil War classic in 1990.

The third of these sources represents one of the wisest projects ever funded by the U.S. government and is the single greatest source of information available to the student of the Civil War: United States War Department, *The War of the Rebellion: A Compilation of the Official Records of the Union and Confederate Armies*. 129 volumes. (Washington, DC, 1880–1901), usually just referred to as the *ORs*. In studying the early days of the war in Kentucky, Volume 4 of the *ORs* is most useful.

Chapter 7

For the moves of the army after Camp Nevin, see Johnson, *That Body of Brave Men*; Daniel, *The Army of the Cumberland*; Sherman, *Memoirs*; and the *ORs*, Volumes 7 and 10.

Conditions at Nashville at the time of the arrival of Buell's army are described with great skill in Johnson, *That Body of Brave Men*. See also Walter T. Durham, *Nashville: The Occupied City, 1862–1863* (Nashville: Tennessee Historical Society, 1985)

For the Battle of Shiloh, see Wiley Sword, *The Battle of Shiloh*. (Jamestown, VA: Eastern Acorn Press, 1982); Shelby Foote, *The Civil War, a Narrative: Fort Sumter to Perryville* (New York: Vintage Books, 1986); and O. Edward Cunningham, *Shiloh and the Western Campaign of 1862*, Gary D. Jones and Timothy B. Smith, eds. (New York: Savas Beatie, 2007).

Chapter 8

For the aftermath of the Battle of Shiloh and the march on Corinth, see Johnson, *That Body of Brave Men*; Daniel, *The Army of the Cumberland*; Sherman, *Memoirs*; Foote, *The Civil War, a Narrative: Fort Sumter to Shiloh*; and the *ORs*, Volume 16.

Chapters 9 and 10

For the chase after Braxton Bragg into Kentucky and the Battle of Perryville, see Kenneth Noe, *Perryville: This Grand Havoc of Battle* (Lexington: University Press of Kentucky, 2001); Shelby Foote, *The Civil War, a Narrative: Fort Sumter to Perryville* (New York: Vintage Books, 1986); James Lee McDonough, *War in Kentucky: From Shiloh to Perryville* (Knoxville: University of Tennessee Press, 1994); Johnson, *That Body of Brave Men*; and the *ORs*, Volume 16.

See also W.F.G. Shanks, "Recollections of General Rousseau," *Harper's New Monthly Magazine*, November 1865. In addition, readers are referred to Charles C. Gilbert, "On the Field of Perryville," *Battles and Leaders of the Civil War: The Opening Battles*, Robert Underwood Johnson and Clarence Clough Buel, eds. (Edison, NJ: Castle Books, 1995) and Stuart W. Sanders, "The 1862 Kentucky Campaign and the Battle of Perryville," *Blue and Gray Magazine*, Holiday 2005.

For conditions in Louisville in September 1861 and the murder of General Nelson, see McDowell, *City of Conflict*.

Chapter 11

For the transition from General Buell to General Rosecrans, see Daniel, *The Army of the Cumberland*, and Johnson, *That Body of Brave Men*.

For conditions in Nashville in late 1862, see Durham, *Nashville: The Occupied City*.

For the Battle of Stones River, see Earl J. Hess, *Banners to the Breeze: The Kentucky Campaign, Corinth, and Stones River* (Lincoln: University of Nebraska Press, 2000); Stanley F. Horn, "The Battle of Stones River," *The Battle of Stones River* (Jamestown, VA: Eastern Acorn Press, 1987); and Esposito, *The West Point Atlas of American Wars*. As always, Shelby Foote is a joy to read; for Stones River, see *The Civil War, a Narrative: Fredericksburg to Meridian* (New York: Vintage Books, 1986).

However, for both scholarship and high quality of writing, the most highly recommended treatment of Stones River is Peter Cozzens, *No Better Place to Die: The Battle of Stones River* (Urbana: University of Illinois Press, 1990). Of course, the *ORs*, Volume 20, is indispensable.

Chapter 12

For the Tullahoma Campaign, see Shelby Foote, *The Civil War, a Narrative: Fredericksburg to Meridian*; the *ORs*, Volume 23; and Daniel, *The Army of the Cumberland*.

For Rousseau's testimony before the Buell Commission, see the *ORs*, Volume 16.

Chapter 13

For the events leading up to and during the Battle of Chickamauga, see Peter Cozzens, *This Terrible Sound: The Battle of Chickamauga* (Urbana: University of Illinois Press, 1992). and Foote, *The Civil War, a Narrative: Fredericksburg to Meridian*. For an understanding of the geography of this confusing battle, see Esposito, *The West Point Atlas of American Wars*. As always, readers are directed to the *ORs*—see Volume 30.

For the Siege of Chattanooga, see Peter Cozzens, *The Shipwreck of Their Hopes: The Battles for Chattanooga* (Urbana: University of Illinois, 1994), and Glenn Tucker, *The Battles for Chattanooga* (Jamestown, VA: Eastern Acorn Press, 1987).

The lyrics of the patriotic song dedicated to Rousseau in 1863 can be found online at http://pdmusic.org/hays/wsh63taf.txt.

Excerpts from the pamphlet *The Loyalist's Ammunition* came from Isaac Funk and Lovell Harrison Rousseau, *The Loyalist's Ammunition* (Philadelphia, 1863).

Chapter 14

For an overview of wartime Nashville, see Robert Durham, *Reluctant Partners: Nashville and the Union, 1863–1865* (Nashville: Tennessee Historical Society, no date), and James B. Jones, Jr., "A Tale of Two Cities," *North and South* 10, No. 5 (March 2008).

See the *ORs*, Volumes 32 and 39, for events in Tennessee and Alabama in 1864.

The correspondence to Rousseau while he was commander of the District of Nashville is found in the John A. McAllister Collection of the Library Company of Philadelphia, Philadelphia, Pennsylvania, one of the best repositories of Rousseau material.

For Rousseau's Alabama Raid, there are two journal articles that were of particular value: Edwin C. Bearss, "Rousseau's Raid on the Montgomery and West Point Railroad," *Alabama Historical Quarterly* 25, Nos. 1 & 2 (Spring-Summer 1963), and Mark E. Fretwell, "Rousseau's Alabama Raid," *Alabama Historical Quarterly* 18, No. 4 (Winter 1956). However, the most comprehensive account of Rousseau's celebrated raid is found in David Evans, *Sherman's Horsemen: Union Cavalry Operations in the Atlanta Campaign* (Bloomington: Indiana University Press, 1996). Isabelle Wood Johnston Shacklette's eyewitness account of Rousseau's Raiders' visit to Auburn, Alabama, is in the collection of the Filson Historical Society, Louisville, Kentucky.

See also "What General Rousseau Did," *The New York Times*, August 7, 1864 and "The Alabama Raid," *The New York Times*, August 7, 1864.

Walt Whitman's poems are in the public

Notes on Selected Sources

domain, including "Cavalry Crossing a Ford." Its use in this volume was encouraged by Ms. Cynthia Shor, the pleasant and helpful curator of the Walt Whitman Birthplace, West Hills, New York. The poem is found in many collections and anthologies; this one comes from the Modern Library edition of *Leaves of Grass* (New York: Modern Library, 1950).

Chapter 15

Rosecrans' letter of congratulations to Rousseau after the Alabama raid (the same one in which he mentioned Rousseau's vice-presidential bid) is in the McAllister Collection of the Library Company of Philadelphia. Other evaluations of Rousseau's raid are found in Sherman, *Memoirs*; Evans, *Sherman's Horsemen*; Fretwell, "Rousseau's Alabama Raid"; and Shelby Foote, *The Civil War, a Narrative: Red River to Appomattox* (New York: Vintage Books, 1986).

Foote was also a useful source for the raids of Wheeler and Forrest into Middle Tennessee in late summer 1864, and Hood's invasion in December 1864 as were the *ORs*, Volumes 38, 39 and 45. See also Edward G. Longacre, *A Soldier to the Last: Major General Joseph Wheeler in Blue and Gray* (Washington, DC: Potomac Books, 2007) and Jack Hurst, *Nathan Bedford Forrest* (New York: Knopf, 1993).

James Speed's letter to Rousseau regarding the presidential election of 1864 is found in the McAllister Collection of the Library Company of Philadelphia.

Chapter 16

James Speed's letters regarding Rousseau's race for the House of Representatives are found in the Speed Family Papers, collection of the Filson Historical Society. Rousseau's letter to W.S. Bodley predicting the success of Andrew Johnson's Reconstruction policies are found in the Bodley Family Papers, which are also in the collection of the Filson. Rousseau's campaign speech was reported in "General Rousseau on the Stump," *The New York Times*, July 14, 1865.

Military conditions in Tennessee in late 1865 are described in the *ORs*, Volumes 49 and 52. The depredations of Champ Ferguson are recounted in a fine article by Thomas D. Mays, "I Took Time By the Forelock: Champ Ferguson's War," *North and South* 11, No. 1 (September 2008).

Chapter 17

We live in a wonderful age, when so many resources can be found online. One of the best is the *Congressional Globe*, the predecessor of the *Congressional Record*. The debates and speeches are a revealing and delightful look at the tone and substance of Congress in the nineteenth century, and all available at the click of a key. The *Congressional Globe* is found at the Library of Congress Web site, http://memory.loc.gov/cgi-bini/ampage. For Rousseau's congressional quarrel with Grinnell (and his subsequent reprimand) and his re-election, see the volumes from 39th Congress, 1st and 2nd Sessions.

See also "Appendix to the Congressional Globe: Speech of Hon. L. H. Rousseau," in A Century of Lawmaking for a New Nation: U.S. Congressional Documents and Debates. http://memory.loc.gov/cgi-bin/ampage.

For an insightful examination of the prickly attitude of Southern men toward all questions involving honor, see Bertram Wyatt Brown, *Southern Honor* (Oxford: Oxford University Press, 1982).

Chapter 18

Rousseau's explanation of the Grinnell affair is found in Lovell H. Rousseau, *Address of Hon. Lovell H. Rousseau to His Constituents* (Philadelphia, 1866). The continuing ill-will felt by some Northerners toward Rousseau over the Grinnell affair is shown in "Reply of Gen. Rousseau to Wendell Phillips," *The New York Times*, May 10, 1867.

President Johnson's visit to Louisville during the ill-conceived and poorly executed Swing Around the Circle was covered extensively in the local papers. See "The Presidential Visit," *Louisville Daily Courier*, September 11, 1866, and "Our President: His Arrival and Reception," *The Louisville Daily Courier*, September 12, 1866. A later review of the events of September 11, 1866, is Bill Weaver, "That Brief But Pleasant Kentucky Interlude: Andrew Johnson's 'Swing Around the Circle,' 1866," *Filson Club Historical Quarterly*, July 1979.

The documents relating to the purchase and transfer of Alaska are found in Thomas Donaldson, *The Public Domain*. (Washington, DC: Government Printing Office, 1881). For Rousseau's torturous journey to Sitka see "Journal of the *U.S.S. Ossipee*," http://vilda.alaska.edu:80/cgibin/docviewer.exe?CISOROOT+cdmg22&CSIOPTR+3394.

San Francisco in the 1860s is described in Justin Kaplan, *Mr. Clemens and Mark Twain* (New York: Simon & Schuster, 1966), Milton Meltzer, *Mark Twain Himself* (New York: Bonanza Books, 1960), and Louise E. Taber, *Gold Rush Days* (by the author, 1936).

Chapter 19

For a broad understanding of Reconstruction, readers are directed to Eric Foner, *Reconstruction: America's Unfinished Revolution, 1863–1877* (New York: Harper Collins, 2002).

The standard account of Rousseau's short tenure as the commander of the Military District of Louisiana is found in Joseph G. Dawson, "General Lovell H. Rousseau and Louisiana Reconstruction," *Louisiana History* 20, No. 4 (Fall 1979).

Tensions between blacks and Italians in New Orleans and Rousseau's response is found in the online article by Thomas Hunt, and Martha Macheca Sheldon called "America's First Mafia War: New Orleans," http://www.onewal.com/ao16/f_nolafeud.html.

See Gov. Warmoth's letter recounting the situation in New Orleans at http://gunshowonthenet.com/AfterTheFact/GovWarmothLetter1868.html.

Afterword

Of special interest regarding Rousseau's death and the final disposition of his body are "Lovell H. Rousseau," *Louisville Daily Democrat*, January 9, 1869, and "General Rousseau's Remains," *Louisville Courier-Journal*, March 30, 1870. Other obituaries were provided by Linda Smetzer. The U.S. Army's response to Rousseau's death is shown in U.S. Grant, General Orders No. 2, July 9, 1869, collection of the Filson Historical Society.

Bibliography

"The Abraham Lincoln Papers." http://memory.loc.gov/cgibin/query/P?mal:5:./temp/~ammem_v5N4::@@@mdb+mcc,gott. Accessed on April 2, 2009.

Alabama Historic Ironworks Commission. *Alabama Ironworks Source Book*. "Cane Creek Furnace." http://www.alaironworks.com/furnace/cane-creek.htm. Accessed on October 11, 2007.

"The Alabama Raid." *The New York Times*, August 7, 1864.

"Another Speech by Gen. Rousseau in New-Orleans." *The New York Times*. Accessed on October 6, 1868.

"Appendix to the Congressional Globe, 39th Congress, 1st Session, House of Representatives." A Century of Lawmaking for a New Nation: U.S. Congressional Documents and Debates. http://memory.loc.gov/cgi-bin/ampage. Accessed on June 16, 2008.

"The Assault on Mr. Grinnell." *The New York Times*, June 23, 1866.

"August Election." The *Louisville Daily Democrat*. August 7, 1865.

Baber, Jack. *The Early History of Greene County, Indiana*. Worthington, IN: The Worthington Press, 1875.

Baird, Nancy D. "Asiatic Cholera's First Visit to Kentucky: A Study in Panic and Fear." *Filson Club Historical Quarterly*, July 1974.

Barrett, Betty. "'Cavalry Crossing a Ford': Walt Whitman's Alabama Connection." *Alabama Heritage*, Fall 1998.

Batliner, Doris J. "Tragedy's Stigma Affected City's Reputation, Prosperity." *Louisville Courier-Journal*, July 31, 2005.

Bearss, Edwin C. "Rousseau's Raid on the Montgomery and West Point Railroad." *Alabama Historical Quarterly*, Spring–Summer 1963.

Beauregard, P.G.T. "The Campaign of Shiloh." *Battles and Leaders of the Civil War: The Opening Battles*. Robert Underwood Johnson and Clarence Clough Buel, eds. Edison, NJ: Castle Books, 1995.

Bishop, Jim. *The Day Lincoln Was Shot*. New York: Harper and Brothers, 1955.

"Brig. Gen. W. T. Sherman." *Louisville Daily Journal*, September 27, 1861.

Brown, Bertram Wyatt. *Southern Honor: Ethics and Behavior in the Old South*. Oxford: Oxford University Press, 1982.

Buell, Don Carlos. "East Tennessee and the Campaign of Perryville." *Battles and Leaders of the Civil War: The Opening Battles*. Robert Underwood Johnson and Clarence Clough Buel, eds. Edison, NJ: Castle Books, 1995.

_____. "Shiloh Revisited." *Battles and Leaders of the Civil War: The Opening Battles*. Robert Underwood Johnson and Clarence Clough Buel, eds. Edison, NJ: Castle Books, 1995.

Bullock, William Fontaine. Letter to Governor John L. Helm, April 25, 1851. Collection of the Filson Historical Society, Louisville, KY.

"The Campaign in Kentucky." *The New York Times*, December 3, 1861

"The Campaign in Kentucky." *The New York Times*, January 21, 1862.

Catton, Bruce. *Grant Moves South*. Boston: Little, Brown, 1960.

Center of Military History, U.S. Army. *American Military History*. Washington, DC: Center of Military History, 1988.

Chenoweth, James Q. "The Rangers' Last Campaign." *The Partisan Rangers of the Confederate States Army*. Adam Johnson, ed. Utica, KY: Cook and McDowell, 1979.

Chidsey, Donald Barr. *The War with Mexico*. New York: Crown, 1968.

Claggett, David M. "Civil War Diary of Major David McKee Claggett." *Ancestral News: Quarterly of the Ancestral Trails Historical Society*, Summer 1979.

Collins, Lewis. *History of Kentucky*. Lexington, KY: Henry Clay Press, 1968.

Company C, 3rd Kentucky Infantry. "To the Editors of the Daily Journal." *Louisville Daily Journal*, October 5, 1861.

The Congressional Globe, House of Representatives, 39th Congress, 1st Session. http://memory.loc.gov/cgi-bini/ampage. Accessed on June 17, 2008.

The Congressional Globe, House of Representatives, 39th Congress, 2nd Session. http://memory.loc.gov/cgi-bini/ampage. Accessed on June 17, 2008.

Cozzens, Peter. *No Better Place to Die: The Battle of Stones River*. Urbana: University of Illinois Press, 1990.

_____. *The Shipwreck of Their Hopes: The Battles for Chattanooga*. Urbana: University of Illinois Press, 1994.

_____. *This Terrible Sound: The Battle of Chickamauga*. Urbana: University of Illinois Press, 1992.

Cunningham, O. Edward. *Shiloh and the Western Campaign of 1862*. Gary D. Jones and Timothy B. Smith, eds. New York: Savas Beatie, 2007.

Daniel, Larry J. *Days of Glory: The Army of the Cumberland*. Baton Rouge: Louisiana State University Press, 2004.

Davis, William C. *The Battlefields of the Civil War*. London: Salamander Books, 2003.

Dawson, Joseph G. "General Lovell H. Rousseau and Louisiana Reconstruction." *Louisiana History*, Fall 1979.

DeArmond, Bob. "Around and About Alaska: Peschurov and Rousseau." *The Daily Sitka Sentinel*, October 17, 1991.

"Death of L. H. Rousseau." *Louisville Daily Democrat*, January 9, 1869.

Denney, Robert E. *Civil War Medicine: Care and Comfort of the Wounded*. New York: Sterling, 1994.

"Department of the Ohio." *The New York Times*, October 6, 1862.

"Diary of Amos Glover." Harry J. Carmen, ed. http://publications,ohiohistory.org/ohstemplate.cfm?action+dated&page=0044258.html&s. Accessed on January 29, 2008.

Dodge, William Sumner. *History of the Old Second Division, Army of the Cumberland*. Chicago: Church and Goodman, 1864.

Donaldson, Thomas. *The Public Domain*. Washington, DC: Government Printing Office, 1881.

Duke, Basil. *A History of Morgan's Cavalry*. Bloomington: Indiana University Press, 1960.

Durham, Walter T. *Nashville: The Occupied City*. Nashville: Tennessee Historical Society, 1985.

_____. *Reluctant Partners: Nashville and the Union*. Nashville: Tennessee Historical Society, 1987.

Dyer, Frederick H. *A Compendium of the War of the Rebellion*. Dayton, OH: Broadfoot, 1994.

"Election Returns." *Louisville Daily Democrat*, August 8, 1865.

"The Election Saturday." *Louisville Daily Courier*, September 17, 1866.

Esposito, Vincent J., ed. *The West Point Atlas of American Wars*. New York: Praeger, 1978.

Evans, David. *Sherman's Horsemen: Union Cavalry Operations in the Atlanta Campaign*. Bloomington: Indiana University Press, 1996.

Fifth Kentucky Infantry Files. Collection of the Kentucky Military History Museum. Frankfort, KY.

Foner, Eric. *Reconstruction: America's Unfinished Revolution, 1863–1877*. New York: Harper Perennial Classics, 2002.

Foote, Shelby. *The Civil War, a Narrative: Fort Sumter to Perryville*. New York: Vintage Books, 1986.

_____. *The Civil War, a Narrative: Fredericksburg to Meridian*. New York: Vintage Books, 1986.

_____. *The Civil War, a Narrative: Red River to Appomattox*. New York: Vintage Books, 1986.

Fretwell, Mark E. "Rousseau's Alabama Raid." *Alabama Historical Quarterly*, Winter 1956.

"From GNN [sic] McCook's Division." *The New York Times*, February 23, 1862.

"The Funeral of Gen. Rousseau in New-Orleans — An Imposing Procession." *The New York Times*, January 10, 1869.

Funk, Isaac, and Lovell Harrison Rousseau. *The Loyalist's Ammunition*. Philadelphia, 1863.

"Gen. Buell's Department." *The New York Times*, October 2, 1862.

"Gen. Rousseau at New-Orleans — Defence of His Conduct." *The New York Times,* November 8, 1868.
"General Rousseau on the Stump." *The New York Times,* July 14, 1865.
"General Rousseau's Raid." *The New York Times,* August 3, 1864.
"General Rousseau's Remains." *Louisville Courier-Journal,* March 30, 1870.
Gilbert, Charles C. "On the Field of Perryville." *Battles and Leaders of the Civil War: The Opening Battles.* Robert Underwood Johnson and Clarence Clough Buel, eds. Edison, NJ: Castle Books, 1995.
Gilmore, James R. *Personal Recollections of Abraham Lincoln.* Boston: Page, 1898.
Grant, U.S. General Orders No. 2. January 9, 1869. Collection of the Filson Historical Society, Louisville, KY.
Grigg, Elliott, and Co. *The Mexican War and Its Heroes.* Whitefish, MT: Kessinger, 2007.
Hamilton, William D. *Recollections of a Cavalryman of the Civil War after Fifty Years, 1861–1865.* Columbus, OH: Heer, 1915.
Harper's Weekly, December 7, 1861.
Harris, Alfred W. "Rousseau's Louisville Legion." *Louisville Commercial,* September 11, 1895.
Harrison, Lowell H. *The Civil War in Kentucky.* Lexington: University Press of Kentucky, 1975.
_____, and James C. Klotter. *A New History of Kentucky.* Lexington: University Press of Kentucky, 1997.
Hays, William Shakespeare. "The American Flag." *Public Domain Music.* http://www.pdmusic.org/hays/wsh63taf.txt. Accessed on November 23, 2008.
Hess, Earl J. *Banners to the Breeze: The Kentucky Campaign, Corinth, and Stones River.* Lincoln: University of Nebraska Press, 2000.
Hollis, J. T. Letter to Lovell H. Rousseau, March 25, 1864. John A. McAllister Collection. Collection of the Library Company of Philadelphia, Philadelphia, PA.
Horn, Stanley F. "The Battle of Stones River." *The Battle of Stones River.* Jamestown, VA: Eastern Acorn Press, 1987.
"How the Bridge Across Nolin Was Burned One Night." *Elizabethtown News,* August 15, 1890.
Hunt, Thomas, and Martha Macheca Sheldon. "America's First Mafia War: New Orleans, 1868–1872." http://www.onewal.com/ao16/f_nolafeud.html. Accessed on May 26, 2008.
Hurst, Jack. *Nathan Bedford Forrest.* New York: Knopf, 1993.
Hutcheon, Wallace S. "The Louisville Riots of August, 1855." *Register* of the Kentucky Historical Society, April 1971.
Indiana. *Journal of the House of Representatives, 29th Session, March-December, 1844.* Collection of the Eugene and Marilyn Glick History Center, Indiana Historical Society, Indianapolis, IN.
_____. *Report of the Agent of State to the General Assembly, December 1848.* Indianapolis: Defrees, 1848.
"Janney Furnace." http://JanneyFurnace.org/history/html. Accessed on October 11, 2007.
Johnson, Adam. *The Partisan Rangers of the Confederate States Army.* William J. Davis, ed. Utica, KY: Cook and McDowell, 1979.
Johnson, Mark W. *That Body of Brave Men: The U.S. Regular Infantry and the Civil War in the West.* Cambridge, MA: Da Capo Press, 2003.
Jones, James B., Jr. "A Tale of Two Cities." *North and South,* March 2008.
Jones, Mary Josephine. *The Civil War in Hardin County, Kentucky.* Utica, KY: McDowell, 1995.
"Journal of the U.S.S. *Ossipee.*" http://vilda.alaska.edu:80/cgibin/docviewer.exe?CISOROOT+cdmg22&CSIOPTR+3394. Accessed on May 15, 2008.
Kaplan, Justin. *Mr. Clemens and Mark Twain.* New York: Simon & Schuster, 1966.
Kelly, R. M. "Holding Kentucky for the Union." *Battles and Leaders of the Civil War: The Opening Battles.* Robert Underwood Johnson and Clarence Clough Buel, eds. Edison, NJ: Castle Books, 1995.
Kentucky. *Report of the Adjutant General of the State of Kentucky.* 2 vols. Frankfort, KY: Kentucky Yeoman Office, 1866–1867.
_____. *Senate Journal, 1861.* Frankfort, KY: Yeoman Office, 1861.
Kleber, John E. "August 6, 1855: Bloody Monday." *Louisville Courier-Journal,* July 31, 2005.
_____, editor-in-chief. *The Encyclopedia of Louisville.* Lexington: University Press of Kentucky, 2001.
_____, editor-in-chief. *The Kentucky Encyclo-*

pedia. Lexington: University Press of Kentucky, 1992.

Kniffin, G. C. "The Battle of Stone's River." *Battles and Leaders of the Civil War: The Tide Shifts.* Robert Underwood Johnson and Clarence Clough Buel, eds. Edison, NJ: Castle Books, 1995.

Lee, Dan. *Always Ready: The Campaigns of the 2nd Kentucky Cavalry, USA.* Private publication, 2008.

———. *Camp Nevin: Hardin County's Contribution to Union Victory in the War of the Rebellion.* Private publication, 2008.

———. *The 26th Kentucky Infantry.* Private publication, 2009.

———. *Your Son Until Death: The Boys of the 27th Kentucky Infantry.* Private publication, 2007.

Leonard, J. W. "Letter from Kentucky." *Hancock* [Ohio] *Jeffersonian,* November 1, 1861. Collection of Bowling Green State University, Bowling Green, OH.

"Letter from Camp Nevin." *Louisville Daily Journal,* October 16, 1861.

"Letter of Governor Warmoth, of Louisiana to Senator Kellogg on the Subject of the Late Elections in That State." http://gunshowonthenet.com/AfterTheFact/GovWarmothLetter1868.html. Accessed on January 6, 2009.

Longacre, Edward G. *A Soldier to the Last: Major General Joseph Wheeler in Blue and Gray.* Washington, DC: Potomac Books, 2007.

"Louis Douglass Watkins." Arlington National Cemetery Website. http://arlingtoncemetery.net/ldwatkins.htm. Accessed on June 13, 2008.

"Louisiana: Continued Difficulty in the Police Department of New-Orleans — Address of Gen Rousseau Before the 'Innocents.'" *The New York Times,* November 1, 1868.

"Louisiana: The Political Disturbances — Action of Gen. Rousseau — The Excitement in New Orleans." *The New York Times,* October 28, 1868.

"Lovell H. Rousseau." *Louisville Daily Democrat,* January 9, 1869.

"Lovell Harrison Rousseau." Arlington National Cemetery Website. http://arlingtoncemetery.net/lrousseau.htm. Accessed on June 13, 2008.

Magoffin, Susan Shelby. *Down the Santa Fe Trail and into Mexico.* Stella M. Drumm, ed. Lincoln: University of Nebraska Press, 1982.

Markham, N. G. *Papers, 1854–1905.* Collection of the Filson Historical Society, Louisville, KY.

Mays, Thomas D. "I Took Time By the Forelock: Champ Ferguson's War." *North and South,* September 2008.

McClure, A. K. *Colonel Alexander K. McClure's Recollections of Half a Century.* Salem, MA: Salem Press, 1902.

McCook, Alexander McDowell. Letter of November 15, 1861. Collection of the Ohio Historical Society, Columbus, OH.

McDonough, James Lee. *War in Kentucky: From Shiloh to Perryville.* Knoxville: University of Tennessee Press, 1994.

McDowell, Robert E. *City of Conflict: Louisville in the Civil War, 1861–1865.* Louisville, KY: Louisville Civil War Roundtable, 1962.

Meltzer, Milton. *Mark Twain Himself.* New York: Bonanza Books, 1960.

Milroy, Robert H. Letter to Lovell H. Rousseau, June 21, 1864. John A. McAllister Collection. Collection of the Library Company of Philadelphia, Philadelphia, PA.

National Cyclopedia of American Biography. New York: White, 1904.

Ninety-Eighth Congress. *The Capitol: A Pictorial History of the Capitol and of the Congress.* Washington, DC: Government Printing Office, 1988.

Noe, Kenneth. *Perryville: This Grand Havoc of Battle.* Lexington: University Press of Kentucky, 2001.

Nye, Wilbur S. "Cavalry Operations Around Atlanta." *The Campaign for Atlanta.* Conshohocken, PA: Eastern Acorn Press, 1986.

O'Connor, Richard. *Sheridan.* New York: Konecky & Konecky, 1993.

"Obituary." *Lafayette Advertiser,* January 16, 1869.

"Obituary." *Memphis Daily Appeal,* January 16, 1869.

"Our Camp Nevin Correspondence." *The New York Times,* October 24, 1861.

"Our Louisville Letter." *Chicago Tribune,* December 27, 1861.

"Our President: His Arrival and Reception." *Louisville Daily Courier,* September 12, 1866.

Perret, Geoffrey. *Lincoln's War.* New York: Random House, 2004.

Perry, Oran, comp. *Indiana in the Mexican War*. Whitefish, MT: Kessinger, 2007.
Pirtle, Alfred. *Journal, 1859–1862*. Alfred Pirtle Papers, 1847–1924. Collection of the Filson Historical Society, Louisville, KY.
———. Letter to Henry Pirtle. January 3, 1863. Alfred Pirtle Papers, 1847–1924: Letters, 1862–1863. Collection of the Filson Historical Society, Louisville, KY.
———. Letter to Jane Pirtle. December 27, 1862. Alfred Pirtle Papers, 1847–1924: Letters, 1862–1863. Collection of the Filson Historical Society, Louisville, KY.
Pontiac. "Affairs in Kentucky." *The New York Times*, October 11, 1861.
"The Presidential Visit." *Louisville Daily Courier*, September 11, 1866.
"Radical Infamy." *Louisville Daily Courier*, September 11, 1866.
Ramage, James A. *Rebel Raider: The Life of General John Hunt Morgan*. Lexington: University Press of Kentucky, 1986.
"The Rebellion in Kentucky." *The New York Times*, October 21, 1861.
"The Reign of Terror: Louisville Under Mob Law." *Louisville Daily Courier*, August 8, 1855.
Reinhart, Joseph R. *A History of the 6th Kentucky Volunteer Infantry, U.S.: The Boys Who Feared No Noise*. Louisville, KY: Beargrass Press, 2000.
"Reply of Gen. Rousseau to Wendell Phillips." *The New York Times*, May 10, 1867,
"The Result in the City." *Louisville Daily Courier*, November 5, 1856.
"The Riots Yesterday." *Louisville Daily Journal*, August 7, 1855.
Robinson, William C. Letters. Collection of the Abraham Lincoln Presidential Library, Springfield, IL.
Rosecrans, Verna. E-mail to the author, November 11, 2008.
Rosecrans, William S. Letter to Lovell H. Rousseau, September 14, 1864. John A. McAllister Collection. Collection of the Library Company of Philadelphia, Philadelphia, PA.
Rousseau, Lovell H. *Address of Hon. Lovell H. Rousseau to His Constituents*. Philadelphia, 1866.
———. Enclosure in William T. Ward letter of February 5, 1864. Speed Family Papers—Farmington Collection. Collection of the Filson Historical Society. Louisville, KY.

———. Letter to Charles Lanham, October 23, 1866. Charles Lanham Collection. Collection of the Filson Historical Society, Louisville, KY.
———. Letter to W. S. Bodley, March 16, 1866. Bodley Family Papers. Collection of the Filson Historical Society, Louisville, KY.
———. "Reply of Gen. Rousseau to Wendell Phillips." *The New York Times*, May 10, 1867.
Rousseau Family File. Kentucky Historical Society. Frankfort, KY.
Sanders, Stuart W. "The 1862 Kentucky Campaign and the Battle of Perryville." *Blue and Gray Magazine*, Holiday 2005.
Scribner, Benjamin F. *Camp Life of a Volunteer: A Campaign in Mexico*. Philadelphia: Grigg, Elliot, 1847.
———. Papers, Folders 2–4, SC 1322. Collection of the Eugene and Marilyn Glick History Center, Indiana Historical Society, Indianapolis, IN.
Second Kentucky Cavalry Files. Collection of the Kentucky Military History Museum. Frankfort, Kentucky.
Shacklette, Isabelle W. J. *Narrative, 1864*. Collection of the Filson Historical Society, Louisville, KY.
Shanks, W.F.G. "Recollections of General Rousseau." *Harper's New Monthly Magazine*, November 1865.
Sheridan, Philip Henry. *Personal Memoirs of P. H. Sheridan*. 2 vols. New York: Webster, 1888.
Sherman, William T. *Memoirs of W. T. Sherman*. 2 vols. New York: Appleton, 1891.
Sides, Hampton. *Blood and Thunder*. New York: Doubleday Books, 2006.
Sixth Kentucky Infantry Files. Collection of the Kentucky Military History Museum. Frankfort, KY.
Smetzer, Linda. E-mail to the author, October 7, 2008.
———. E-mail to the author, October 8, 2008.
Smith, Isaac. *Reminiscences of a Campaign in Mexico*. Indianapolis: Chapmans and Spann, 1848.
Spalding, Lieutenant Colonel George. Letter to Captain W. Nevin, February 18, 1864. John A. McAllister Collection. Collection of the Library Company of Philadelphia, Philadelphia, PA.
Speed, J. F. Letter to James Speed, June 28, 1865. Speed Family Papers. Collection of

the Filson Historical Society. Louisville, KY.

———. Letter to James Speed, July 11, 1865. Speed Family Papers. Collection of the Filson Historical Society. Louisville, KY.

Speed, James. Letter to Lovell H. Rousseau, October 26, 1864. John A. McAllister Collection. Collection of the Library Company of Philadelphia, Philadelphia, PA.

Speed, Thomas. *Letterbook, 1863–1896.* Collection of the Filson Historical Society, Louisville, KY.

———. *The Union Regiments of Kentucky.* Louisville, KY: Courier-Journal Job Printing Co., 1897.

Stephens, Tom. "Annotated Notes on Bloody Monday, Louisville, August 6, 1855." *Kentucky Ancestors: Genealogical Quarterly of the Kentucky Historical Society*, Summer 2006.

Sword, Wiley. *The Battle of Shiloh.* Jamestown, VA: Eastern Acorn Press, 1982.

Taber, Louise E. *Gold Rush Days,* 1936.

Taylor, Zachary. "Battle of Buena Vista, Official Report." http://www.dmwv.org/mexwar/documents/bvista.htm. Accessed on May 31, 2008.

"Terrible Tragedy—Negroes Executed by Mob." *Louisville Daily Courier,* May 15, 1857.

Thickstun, Edmund. "A Bluegrass Lassie." Unpublished mss. Collection of Linda Smetzer.

"Thirty-Ninth Congress." *The New York Times,* July 3, 1866.

"Thirty-Ninth Congress." *The New York Times,* July 18, 1866.

Thomas, Samuel O. "Letter from Kentucky." *Hancock* [Ohio] *Jeffersonian,* November 15, 1861. Collection of Bowling Green State University, Bowling Green, OH.

———. "Letter from Kentucky." *Hancock* [Ohio] *Jeffersonian.* November 28, 1861. Collection of Bowling Green State University, Bowling Green, OH.

Thomas, Samuel W. "An Enduring Folly: The Jefferson County Courthouse." *The Filson Club Historical Quarterly,* October 1981.

Tindall, George Brown. *America: A Narrative History.* New York: Norton, 1988.

Townsend, E. D. Assistant Adjutant-General, Kentucky. General Orders No. 2, January 9, 1869. Collection of the Filson Historical Society, Louisville, KY.

Tucker, Glenn. *The Battles for Chattanooga.* Jamestown, VA: Eastern Acorn Press, 1987.

Ulysses. Letter to Benjamin F. Scribner, October 26, 1846. Benjamin F. Scribner Papers, Folder 2, Collection of the Eugene and Marilyn Glick History Center, Indiana Historical Society, Indianapolis, IN.

United States Census Bureau. Indiana Census, 1850.

———. Kentucky Census, 1810.

———. Kentucky Census, 1820.

———. Kentucky Census, 1860.

United States Congress. *Biographical Dictionary of the United States Congress, 1774–1989.* Washington, DC: Government Printing Office, 1989.

United States War Department. *The War of the Rebellion: A Compilation of the Official Records of the Union and Confederate Armies.* 129 vols. Washington, DC: Government Printing Office, 1880–1901.

"A Visit Among the Kentucky Camps." *Chicago Tribune,* January 1, 1862.

"The War in Kentucky." *Chicago Tribune,* November 5, 1861.

Ward, John H. Letter of January 19, 1864. Speed Family Papers—Farmington Collection. Collection of the Filson Historical Society, Louisville, KY.

Ward, William T. Letter of February 5, 1864. Speed Family Papers—Farmington Collection. Collection of the Filson Historical Society, Louisville, KY.

Warmoth, Henry Clay. *War, Politics and Reconstruction: Stormy Days in Louisiana.* Columbia: University of South Carolina Press, 2006.

Warner, Ezra J. *Generals in Blue.* Baton Rouge: Louisiana State University Press, 1992.

"Washington." *The New York Times,* September 29, 1868.

"Washington News." *The New York Times,* July 18, 1866.

Watkins, Sam. *Company Aytch.* New York: New American Library, 1999.

Weaver, Bill. "That Brief But Pleasant Kentucky Interlude: Andrew Johnson's 'Swing Around the Circle,' 1866." *The Filson Club Historical Quarterly,* July 1979.

"What General Rousseau Did." *The New York Times,* August 7, 1864.

Wheeler, Joseph. "Bragg's Invasion of Kentucky." *Battles and Leaders of the Civil War: The Tide Shifts.* Robert Underwood Johnson and Clarence Clough Buel, eds. Edison, NJ: Castle Books, 1995.

Whitman, Walt. "Cavalry Crossing a Ford." *Leaves of Grass*, "Book 21: Drum Taps." New York: Modern Library, 1950.

"Who Is Responsible for the Riot?" *Louisville Daily Courier*, August 9, 1855.

Widney, Lyman S. *Campaigning with Uncle Billy*. Robert I. Girardi, ed. Victoria, BC: Trafford, 2008.

Wilcox, Cadmus Marcellus. *History of the Mexican War*. Mary Rachel Wilcox, ed. Washington, DC: Church News, 1892.

Wilcox, Timothy. "Army Correspondence." *Fremont* [Ohio] *Journal*, November 8, 1861. Collection of Bowling Green State University, Bowling Green, OH.

Wiley, Bell I. *The Life of Billy Yank*. Baton Rouge: Louisiana State University Press, 1989.

Williams, John S. Letter to Brigadier General W. D. Whipple, May 21, 1865. John A. McAllister Collection. Collection of the Library Company of Philadelphia, Philadelphia, PA.

Winn-Cook Family Papers, 1861–1875. Collection of the Filson Historical Society, Louisville, KY.

Woodworth, Steven E. *Nothing but Victory: The Army of the Tennessee, 1861–1865*. New York: Knopf, 2005.

Index

Acworth, Georgia 164
Adams, John Quincy 184
Address of Hon. Lovell H. Rousseau to His Constituents 190–191
Aggie (slave) 8–10
Agnello, Raffaele 207
Agua Nueva, Mexico 22, 26
Alabama & Tennessee Railroad 156
Alabama Troops: 6th Infantry (CSA) 142; 8th Infantry (CSA) 142
Alexander, E.P. 125
Allatoona, Georgia 164
"The American Flag" 119–120, 143
American (Know-Nothing) Party 31–36, 197, 212
Anderson, J.B. 73
Anderson, Robert 42, 43
Anderson's Crossroads, Tennessee 125
Apache Indians 48
Appomattox Courthouse, Virginia 172, 173, 174
Arkansas Mtd. Infantry (Battle of Buena Vista) 24
Arlington National Cemetery 215
Ashville, Alabama 140
Ashville Vidette 140
Athens, Alabama 70, 74, 164
Athens, Tennessee 155, 156, 157, 158, 161
Atlanta, Georgia 136, 137, 145, 150, 153, 154, 155, 157, 163, 164
Auburn, Alabama 149, 151
Augusta, Georgia 174

Bacon Creek (Bonnieville), Kentucky 51–52, 79, 96
Baird, Absalom 121, 122, 123, 124
Baltimore, Maryland 162, 173
Banks, Nathaniel P. 185, 187, 190
Barba, Listero 207
Barbee, John 32, 33, 34
Bardstown, Kentucky 79
Bass, Sion S. 47
Bate, William B. 166, 167
Baton Rouge, Louisiana 17
Battle Creek, Tennessee 69, 71
Beasley's Station, Alabama (Fight at) 147–148, 186

Beatty, John 95, 98, 101, 105, 127
Beauregard, P.G.T. 65, 66
Becker, Charles 33
Bedini, Gaetano 31
Belot, Octave 207
Berry, William W. 40
Bethlehem, Alabama 151
Big Hill, Kentucky (Fight at) 76
Big Shanty, Georgia 164
Big Spring, Tennessee 113
Blaser, David 111
Bloody Monday 32–34, 36
Bloomfield, Indiana 12, 13–14, 15, 27
Bloomfield, Kentucky 83
Bloomfield Comet 13
Bloomington, Indiana 12
Blountsville, Alabama 140
Blue Licks, Kentucky 5
Board, Buckner 42, 47, 80
Bobo Crossroads, Tennessee 114
Bodley, W.S. 183
Boone, William P. 39
Booth, John Wilkes 130, 172, 192
Bottoms, Henry 87
Bowles, W.A. 17, 18, 23, 26, 27
Bowling Green, Kentucky 56, 77, 78, 94, 95, 107, 135
Boyle, Jeremiah 49, 95
Boyle County, Kentucky 84
Bradyville, Tennessee 112
Bragg, Braxton 22, 24, 25, 66, 72–73, 74, 75, 76, 77, 78, 79, 80, 84, 85, 90, 92, 93, 94, 96, 97, 98, 102, 103–104, 105, 106, 107, 109, 112, 114, 115, 121–122, 124, 137, 146
Bramlette, Thomas E. 135
Brannan, John M. 113, 122
Brazos Santiago, Texas 18
Breckinridge, John C. 59, 104, 122
Brentwood, Tennessee 97
Bridgeport, Alabama 121, 124, 128, 134
Brooks, Preston 188
Brown, James 140
Brownlow, William "Parson" 171, 173
Brownsville, Kentucky 78
Bruge, George 32
Buchanan, Robert C. 205, 210

239

Buckley, Harvey M. 40, 47, 51, 60
Buckner, Simon Bolivar 42, 55
Buell, Don Carlos 54, 56, 57, 59, 62, 63, 64, 67, 68–69, 70–71, 72, 73–74, 75–76, 77–79, 80, 82, 83, 84, 85, 90–91, 92, 93–94, 95, 107, 108, 115, 116, 124, 127
Buell Commission 93, 106, 107–08, 127, 130
Buena Vista, Mexico (Battle of) 22–25, 26, 27, 28, 29
Buffalo, Kentucky 51
Buford, Abraham 160, 168
Buford, John 127
Bull Run, Virginia (1st Battle of) 48
Bullock, William F. 30
Burbridge, Stephen G. 135, 170
Burghold, Fred 33
Bush, Asahel K. 88
Butler, Benjamin 162, 204, 214

Calhoun, Georgia 155
Camargo, Mexico 19, 21
Cameron, Simon 54
Camp Belknap, Texas 18–19
Camp Joe Holt, Indiana 40–42, 69, 139, 203
Camp Muldraugh 43
Camp Nevin, Kentucky 44, 45, 47–48, 49, 50–51, 52, 54, 55, 79, 91, 99
Camp Watts, Alabama 149
Camp Whitcomb, Indiana 17, 18
Campbell, Wallace 157–158
Campbellsville, Tennessee 156
Canby, Edward R.S. 138
Cane Creek Furnace, Alabama 143
Carlin, Daniel 13
Carpenter, Arthur 106, 125
Carrico, Thomas 15
Carrollton, Georgia 151–152
Cass, Lewis 29
"Cavalry Crossing a Ford" 142
Cave City, Kentucky 79
Cerralvo, Mexico 19
Cerro Gordo, Mexico (Battle of) 28
Chalmers, James R. 77, 107
Chalmette Plantation, Louisiana 17
Chapultepec, Mexico (Battle of) 28
Charleston Railroad 67
Chattanooga, Tennessee 67, 68, 72, 73, 114, 121, 123, 124–125, 126, 128, 137, 155, 174
Cheatham, Benjamin F. 166
Cheatham, R.B. 56
Chehaw Station, Alabama 147–148
Chenoweth, James Q. 141
Cherokee County, Alabama 154
Cherokee Indians 133
Chicago, Illinois 191
Chickamauga, Georgia (Battle of) 121–124, 125, 126, 128, 130, 137, 163
Chihuahua, Mexico 22
cholera 5, 6, 9, 31
Churubusco, Mexico (Battle of) 28

Cincinnati, Ohio 76
Cincinnati Enquirer 76
Civil Rights Act 179, 191
Claggett, David McKee 84
Clanton, James H. 138
Clarksville, Tennessee 134, 172
Clay, Henry 11, 37
Cleburne, Patrick 165, 172
Cleveland, Ohio 162, 192
Colfax, Schuylar 162, 179, 184, 185, 186, 189
Columbia, Tennessee 58, 74, 156, 160, 161, 164
Columbus, Georgia 150, 152
Columbus, Kentucky 42
The Congressional Globe 180, 190, 193
Coolidge, Sidney 113
Corinth, Mississippi 56, 58, 63, 64, 65, 66, 67, 75, 78, 81
Cotter, Charles S. 49, 64
Covington, Georgia 155
Crab Orchard, Kentucky 92
Craddock, A.G. 77
Crittenden, Thomas L. 73, 79, 80, 81, 83, 86, 90, 91, 92, 94, 97, 98, 99, 102, 103, 110, 112, 120, 122, 123, 128
Crittenden, Thomas T. 47
Crook, George 191, 192
Croxton, John T. 122, 162
Culpeper County, Virginia 6
Curl, William 140–141
Custer, George A. 191, 192
Cynthiana, Kentucky 5, 135

Dalton, Georgia 164
Dana, Charles A. 127
Danville, Kentucky 7, 80, 84, 92
Darr, Francis 74
Daviess, Samuel 7
Daviess County, Indiana 13
Davis, Garrett 40
Davis, Jefferson 24, 26, 163, 180, 186
Davis, Jefferson C. 80–81, 98, 99, 100, 123, 197, 198
Decatur, Alabama 74, 138, 139, 155, 157, 161, 162, 164, 172
Dechard, Tennessee 71, 73, 75, 114, 160
Delph, John M. 68
Democratic Party 20, 37, 162, 170, 175, 206, 207, 208, 209, 210, 211
Dennison, William 49
Department of Louisiana 3, 203, 205, 213, 214
Department of Oregon 195, 196
Department of the Columbia 202
De Soto, Alabama 146
Dibrell, George 156
Dickens, Charles 30
Dickey, Moses R. 47
Dodge, William S. 12, 40, 52, 136
Dodge, W.S. 197
Donelson, Andrew Jackson 171
Doran, James 144–145

Dorsey, John 85, 86, 90
Dozier, James I. 13, 14
Dozier, Marie Antoinette *see* Rousseau, Marie Antoinette
Dozier, Mary 14
Drout, Charles 33
Drum Taps 143
Dubuclet, Antoine 206
Duke, Basil 51
Dunlop, Tennessee 125

Early, Jubal 136
East Tennessee Railroad 67
Eastaboga, Alabama 144
Eastport, Alabama 161
Edgefield, Tennessee 56, 95
Edgerton, George 33
Elizabethtown, Kentucky 42, 43, 44, 45, 78, 79, 80
Elk Creek, Tennessee 3
Elk River Bridge, Tennessee (Fight at) 158
Elkin, Thomas 148
Elliott, Jonas D. 158
Emancipation Proclamation 108, 127, 132
Emmons, George F. 196–198, 200–202
Engels, Friedrich 31
Ewell, Richard 136
Ezra Church, Georgia (Battle of) 163

Fairfield, Tennessee 113
Fairplay, Indiana 13
Farragut, David G. 191, 192, 204
Fast, E.G. 197
Fayette County, Kentucky 6
Fayetteville, Tennessee 121, 159
Feller, John 33
Fentress County, Tennessee 174
Ferguson, Champ 174
Fifth U.S. Congressional District, Kentucky 175, 193
Florence, Alabama 158, 160, 164
Forrest, Nathan Bedford 71, 72, 74, 75, 96, 97, 122, 135, 138, 157–161, 166, 167–68, 169, 172, 208
Fort Brown, Mexico 19
Fort Donelson, Tennessee 134
Fort Donelson, Tennessee (Battle of) 55, 56, 63
Fort Henry, Tennessee (Battle of) 56
Fort Negley, Tennessee 172, 173
Fort Pillow, Tennessee 65
Fort Sumter, South Carolina (Battle of) 38, 42, 80, 172
Fortress Rosecrans, Tennessee 109, 164, 167, 169
Foster, John G. 132, 133
Fourteenth Amendment 191, 194, 205
Francis, T.H. 149
Frankfort, Kentucky 37, 79
Franklin, Tennessee 58, 109, 155, 160, 162, 165, 166
Free Soil Party 29

Freedman's Bureau Bill 179, 180, 183, 191
Frémont, John C. 41, 162, 197
Friedlander, A. 135–136
Funk, Isaac 120

Gallatin, Tennessee 72, 74, 75, 96, 135
Garesché, Julius P. 102, 107
Garfield, James A. 106–107, 188, 190
Gatch, Asbury 150
Gay, Ebenezer 85
Gettysburg, Pennsylvania (Battle of) 114, 125, 127, 136, 163
Gibson, Mary Jane 87
Gibson, T.W. 197
Gibson, William H. 48, 60
Gilbert, Charles C. 82, 83, 84, 85, 86, 87, 89, 90, 91, 92
Gilfillen, James 172
Gilman, Captain 47
Gilmore, James R. 110
Glasgow, Kentucky 172
Glover, Amos 52
Gooding, Michael 89–90
Gorman, Willis A. 24
Graham, Thomas 141, 142, 143
Granger, Gordon 112, 121, 123
Granger, Robert S. 111, 130–131, 132, 134, 155, 156, 157, 162, 164, 172
Grant, U.S. 3, 55, 56, 58, 60, 63, 115, 128, 136, 172, 173, 191, 194, 206, 207, 213
Greeley, Horace 110
Greene County, Indiana 12, 13, 14, 15, 16, 29
Greeneville, Indiana 215
Greeneville, Tennessee 157
Gretna, Louisiana 208
Grierson, Benjamin H. 154
Grinnell, Josiah B. 181, 182, 183, 184, 185–187, 188, 190, 191, 195
Griswold, Roger 188
Guadalupe-Hidalgo, Mexico 28
Guenther, F.L. 104
Guntersville, Alabama 141
Guthrie, James 39, 40, 47, 69, 170, 192

Haldeman, Walter N. 35
Hale, Robert 188
Halleck, Henry W. 63, 64, 65, 66, 67, 68, 115, 118, 156
Hambright, Henry A. 49, 108, 109, 110, 113, 114
Hamilton, William 145, 149, 150, 151
Hamlin, Hannibal 162
Hancock, Winfield Scott 205
Hardee, William J. 98
Harding, Abner C. 185
Harper, Green 151
Harper's New Monthly Magazine 139
Harris, George C. 58
Harris, Leonard A. 80, 85, 87, 88, 90
Harrison, Thomas J. 47, 137, 148
Harrodsburg, Kentucky 5, 92

Hartsville, Tennessee 96
Hawkins, Enos 80
Hays, William Shakespeare 119–120, 143
Hazen, William B. 102
Helm, John L. 30
Henry County, Kentucky 175
Herra, José 16
Heybach, Charles 33
Hinkley, Otis 13
Hodgenville, Kentucky 79, 80
Hogan, John 187
Hollis, J.T. 135
Holt, Joseph 162
Hood, John Bell 122, 155, 162, 163–165, 166, 169
Hook, Joseph 33
Hooker, Joseph 128
Hoover's Gap, Tennessee (Fight at) 112–113
Horner, John W. 174
Horse Cave, Kentucky 55
Hotchkiss, William 85
Houston, Sam 1, 2, 188
Humphrey, George 105
Huntsville, Alabama 68, 69–70, 71, 72, 73, 74, 79, 121, 160, 161, 164, 174

Illinois Troops: 1st Volunteer Infantry (Mexican War) 22, 24; 2nd Volunteer Infantry (Mexican War) 22, 24; 14th Cavalry 152; 34th Infantry 45, 48, 55
Indiana Democrat 16, 28
Indiana Sentinel 23, 28
Indiana Troops: 2nd Volunteer Infantry (Mexican War) 16, 17–19, 21–22, 23–26, 27, 29, 40; 3rd Cavalry 49; 3rd Volunteer Infantry (Mexican War) 24; 6th Infantry 44, 47, 59; 8th Cavalry 137, 138, 141, 142, 143, 148; 9th Cavalry 159; 10th Cavalry 159; 29th Infantry 47, 64; 30th Infantry 44, 47, 52; 32nd Infantry 48; 38th Infantry 44, 47, 52; 39th Infantry 45, 47, 50, 51; 42nd Infantry 85, 86; 88th Infantry 104
Indianapolis, Indiana 13, 27, 192
The Innocenti 207
Iowa Troops: 5th Cavalry 138, 140, 142, 145, 147–148, 149, 186

Jackson, Andrew 1, 2, 11, 17, 133, 171
Jackson, James S. 85, 86, 87, 90
Jackson, John 123
Janney Furnace, Alabama 143
Jasper, Tennessee 73
Jefferson, Tennessee 98
Jefferson County, Kentucky 6, 81, 175
Johnson, Adam "Stovepipe" 141
Johnson, Andrew 57, 75, 76, 134, 162, 171, 173, 175, 178, 179, 181, 183, 184, 191–193, 194, 204, 205, 206, 210, 211
Johnson, Edward 136
Johnson, Richard W. 47, 55, 64, 65, 98, 99, 100, 128, 172, 175

Johnston, Albert Sidney 66
Johnston, Joseph E. 115, 137, 163, 169, 173
Jones, Fielder 142, 148
Jonesboro, Georgia (Battle of) 163

Kennesaw Mountain, Georgia 137, 152
Kentucky Cavalry (Battle of Buena Vista) 22, 24
Kentucky County 6
Kentucky Troops: 1st Battery (Stone's) 44, 47, 95; 1st Cavalry (CSA) 112; 2nd Cavalry 42, 43, 44, 47, 50, 51, 80, 85, 86, 95, 98, 99, 100, 137, 138, 139, 142, 147, 149, 151; 2nd Volunteer Infantry (Mexican War) 22, 24; 3rd Infantry 42; 5th Infantry 41, 44, 47, 59, 60, 203; 6th Infantry 42, 44, 47, 194; 15th Infantry 88; 17th Infantry 84; 27th Infantry 132, 134
Key, John J. 40
Kilpatrick, Judson 154
King, John H. 108, 113, 123
Kingston, Tennessee 132
Kingston Springs, Tennessee 172
Kirk, Edward N. 48, 60, 64, 99
Kitzler, Conrad 32
Knoxville, Tennessee 132, 155
Koskul, Captain 196

La Angostura, Mexico (Battle of) *see* Buena Vista (Battle of)
Lafayette Advertiser 213
Lancaster, Kentucky 5, 11
Lancaster, Pennsylvania 120
Landrum, George 89
Lane, Joseph 17, 23, 26
Laredo, Texas 214
LaVergne, Tennessee 155
Lawrenceburg, Tennessee 156, 160
Lawson, O.A. 104
Lebanon, Kentucky 44
Lebanon Junction, Kentucky 42–43
Lee, Phillip 44
Lee, Robert E. 114, 115, 127, 172, 173
Leitchfield, Kentucky 78
Leonard, J.W. 45
Lexington, Kentucky 5, 11, 76, 79, 104
Liberty, Tennessee 110
The Lightning Brigade 109, 112–113, 114, 117, 122
Lincoln, Abraham 3, 27, 38, 40, 45, 76, 93, 110, 118, 125, 127, 136, 162, 172–173, 178, 179, 184, 192
Lincoln County, Kentucky 5, 6, 9, 10, 92
Loachapoka, Alabama 146–147
Logan, Benjamin 7
London, Kentucky 76, 92
Long, Eli 109
Longstreet, James 122, 123, 125
Lookout Mountain, Tennessee 124, 125, 128
Loomis, Cyrus O. 85, 86, 89, 101, 104–105, 108, 113, 164
Loudon, Tennessee 132
Louisiana Troops: 1st Cavalry (CSA) 203

Louisville, Kentucky 2, 12, 17, 29, 30, 31, 32, 34, 35, 37, 38, 39, 40, 41, 42, 43, 44, 45, 47, 48, 49, 52, 53, 54, 68, 69, 71, 77, 78, 79, 80, 81, 82, 83, 93, 95, 106, 130, 131, 134, 135, 162, 170, 176, 177, 192, 193, 194, 203, 212, 214, 215
Louisville & Nashville Railroad 39, 42, 44, 47, 51, 56, 68, 69, 72, 77, 95, 96, 109, 130, 170
Louisville and Nashville Turnpike 44, 51, 55, 78, 79
Louisville Anzeiger 31
Louisville Courier-Journal 41
Louisville Daily Courier 33, 34, 35, 192, 193
Louisville Daily Journal 32, 34, 35, 39, 43, 48, 53, 79
Louisville Democrat 39, 175, 214
The Loyalist's Ammunition 120
Lumley's Stand, Tennessee 112
Lynchburg, Tennessee 160
Lyon, Hylan B. 160
Lyon, Matthew 188
Lytle, William H. 74, 80, 85, 86, 87, 88, 90

Mackville, Kentucky 84
Madison & Indianapolis Railroad 14
Magoffin, Beriah 38
Mahan, George W. 203
Mahan, Robert 203
Maksutov, Prince Dimitri 199
Maksutov, Princess Maria 199
Mallory, Robert 175
Malone, Edward 207
Manchester, Tennessee 112, 156
Maney, George 123
Mardisville, Alabama 145
Marietta, Georgia 152
Markham, N.G. 57
Martin's Mill, Alabama 144
Marx, Karl 31
Mason County, Kentucky 6
Massachusetts Troops 54th Colored Infantry 3
Matamoros, Mexico 18, 19
Matz, John 144
Maysville, Kentucky 5, 6, 11
McCaleb, Major 180, 181, 182
McCallum, D.C. 161
McClellan, George B. 40, 162, 163
McCook, Alexander McDowell 48, 49, 50, 52, 55, 56, 57, 59, 60, 61, 62, 64, 65, 68, 69, 73, 77, 79, 80, 83, 84, 85, 86, 87, 88, 89, 90, 92, 94, 97, 98, 99, 100, 101, 102, 103, 107, 111, 112, 121, 122, 123, 128
McCook, Daniel 84, 104
McCook, Edward 154
McKinney, Patrick 145–146
McMinnville, Tennessee 110, 112, 113, 114
McMinnville & Manchester Railroad 110
McPherson, James B. 136
Meade, George Gordon 114, 115, 127
Meier, Chris 32
Memphis, Tennessee 56, 65, 158

Memphis & Charleston Railroad 65, 67, 68, 72
Mendenhall, John 104
Mexico City, Mexico 20, 28
Michigan Troops: 1st Engineers and Mechanics 80; 1st Light Artillery 95, 139; 18th Infantry 57, 158
Middle Tennessee, District of 172
Military Reconstruction Act 194
Mill Springs, Kentucky 5, 9
Miller, John F. 47, 134, 171, 172
Millerstown, Kentucky 51
Milroy, Robert H. 136, 155, 162, 164, 166, 167–169, 171, 172, 174
Minty, Robert H.G. 124
Missionary Ridge, Tennessee 124, 128
Mississippi Rifles (Battle of Buena Vista) 24, 25, 26
Mitchel, Ormsby 55, 70, 74, 128
Mitchellsville Depot, Tennessee 95, 172
Mobile & Ohio Railroad 65
Mobile Bay, Battle of 198
Monin, Adam 44
Monterrey, Mexico (Battle of) 19–20, 21
Montgomery, Alabama 145, 152
Montgomery Advertiser 147
Montgomery & West Point Railroad 146–147, 154
Montgomery County, Tennessee 174
Moorhead, James K. 187
Morgan, John Hunt 50–51, 52, 71, 72, 74, 75, 96, 97, 135, 157
Morton, Oliver P. 49, 81
Mount Pleasant, Tennessee 160
Mower, Joseph A. 205
Mueller, Michael 49
Mulberry, Tennessee 160
Muldraugh Hill, Kentucky 43, 45, 96
Mundy, Marc 176
Munfordville, Kentucky 52, 55, 77, 78, 94, 107, 109
Murfreesboro, Tennessee 72, 77, 97, 98, 99, 105, 106, 108, 109, 110, 115, 117, 133, 134, 155, 164, 165, 166–168
Muscroft, Charles S. 103

Nashville, Tennessee 56, 57, 71, 72, 73, 74, 75, 76–77, 78, 95, 96, 97, 100, 106, 117, 128, 129–132, 134, 135, 138, 154, 155, 156, 159, 160, 161, 165, 166, 169, 170, 171, 172, 173, 174, 175, 176
Nashville & Chattanooga Railroad 67, 98, 100, 109, 155, 159, 160, 161, 169
Nashville Daily Union 71
Nashville Turnpike 98, 100, 101, 102
National Union Party 162
Negley, James 49, 55, 98, 101, 112, 114, 121, 122, 128
Nelson, William "Bull" 65, 78, 80, 81, 82, 98
Nevin, David 44, 48
New Albany, Indiana 17, 27, 40, 130

New Orleans, Louisiana 17, 133, 138, 202, 203–204, 205–206, 207, 208, 209, 210, 213, 214, 215
New Orleans Times 211
New York City 31, 184, 195, 196, 207
New York Times 50, 51, 53, 79, 140, 147, 194–195
New York Tribune 110
Nolensville, Tennessee 97
Nolin, Kentucky 44, 47, 48, 51, 79, 96
Norton, Emperor 197
Notasulga, Alabama 147, 149, 151

O'Brien, John Paul Jones 22, 23, 24
Ohio Troops: Battery A, Light Artillery 49, 64; 1st Infantry 48, 59, 60; 2nd Infantry 89; 3rd Infantry 104; 9th Cavalry 138, 145, 149, 150; 10th Infantry 69, 85; 15th Infantry 45, 47, 52; 21st Infantry 74; 32nd Infantry; 49th Infantry 45, 48, 50, 52; 59th Infantry 58; 102nd Infantry 158
Oldham County, Kentucky 175
Opelika, Alabama 138, 151, 152
Opelousas, Louisiana 207
Orange County, Indiana 27
The *Ossipee* 196–202
Overall Creek, Tennessee (fight at) 166
Overton, John, Jr. 171
Overton County, Tennessee 174
Owen County, Kentucky 29, 175
Owen's Store, Tennessee 47
Owensburg, Indiana 17

Pace, Thomas N. 158
Paducah, Kentucky 44
Paine, E.A. 74
Pakenham, Edward 17
Palmer, John M. 98, 102, 126, 128
Palo Alto, Mexico (Battle of) 19
Paris, Kentucky 5
Passmore, Augustine 13
Peachtree Creek, Georgia (Battle of) 163
Pennsylvania Troops: Battery B, Light Artillery 49, 52; 77th Infantry 49; 78th Infantry 49; 79th Infantry 49, 91; 115th Infantry 120
Pensacola, Florida 138
Perryville, Kentucky (Battle of) 83–90, 92, 93, 94, 95, 105, 107, 111, 126, 133
Peshchurov, Aleksei 196, 198, 200, 202
Phelps, A.J. 100
Phillips, Wendell 194–195
Pilcher, William S. 36
Pirtle, Alfred 69, 70, 97, 100, 101, 106
Pittsburg Landing, Tennessee 56, 58, 59, 60, 62, 63, 90
Pittsburgh, Pennsylvania 49
Polk, James K. 16, 20, 28, 57, 188
Polk, Leonidas 42, 123
Polk, Lucius 123
Polk, Sarah 57

Pope, John 63
Portland, Oregon 202
Powder Springs, Georgia 152
Powell, Lazarus W. 170
Prentice, George D. 32, 34, 35
Prime, Frederick E. 44
Pulaski, Tennessee 158, 159, 160, 161–162, 169, 172
Pulaski County, Kentucky 5, 6

Quincy, Josiah 184
Quinn, Francis 34

Ramsey, Robert 168
Raymond, Henry J. 187, 188
Ream, Vinnie 245
Republican Party 37, 162, 179, 206, 207, 208, 210, 211
Resaca de Palma, Mexico (Battle of) 19
Reynolds, Joseph J. 109, 110, 112, 113
Richmond, Kentucky 76, 80
Richmond, Virginia 66, 203
Robinson, William C. 47
Rock Mills, Alabama 151
Roddey, Phillip 153, 157
Rosecrans, William S. 93, 94, 95–96, 97–98, 99, 102–103, 104, 106, 107, 108–109, 110–111, 112, 114, 115–116, 117, 118, 119, 121, 122, 123, 124, 125, 126, 157, 162
Rough and Ready, Alabama 151
Rousseau, B. (daughter) 29, 177, 213, 214–215
Rousseau, Catherine Gaines (mother) 6, 8
Rousseau, D.L. 197
Rousseau, David (father) 5–6, 8–9
Rousseau, David Q. (brother) 8, 40, 203
Rousseau, Edmund P. (brother) 8, 10, 203
Rousseau, Elizabeth B. (sister) 8
Rousseau, George (son) 36, 177, 195, 196, 213, 214, 215
Rousseau, John (uncle) 6, 8
Rousseau, John A. (brother) 6, 8
Rousseau, Lovell Harrison: Alabama Raid 137–154; in Alaska 198–201; appearance of 11, 37; at Battle of Perryville 85–91; at Battle of Shiloh 58–61; at Battle of Stones River 98–105; birth and early life 3–10; in Bloody Monday 33, 35; at Camp Joe Holt 40–42; at Camp Nevin 44–51, 52; at Chickamauga and Chattanooga 123–129; in command at Huntsville 69–72; as commander of Dept. of Louisiana 203–211; as commander of District of Middle Tennessee 172–176; as commander of District of Nashville 130–137; as commander of District of Tennessee 137–172; death and funeral of 211–214; during Tullahoma Campaign 112–115; family life of 14, 16, 36, 79, 177, 203; Grinnell incident 181–183, 184–189; illnesses of 12, 18, 48, 95, 97, 154, 170, 196, 198, 200, 211, 213; in Indiana House of Representatives 14–15; in Indiana Senate

28–29; in Kentucky Senate 37–38; legal career of 14, 30, 35–36; as manual laborer 11–12; in Mexican War 16–27;move to Indiana 12, 14; move to Louisville 29–30; personality of 1, 2, 12, 44, 59, 88, 89, 100, 111, 127, 139, 143–144, 148, 153, 183, 187, 190–191, 194–195, 199, 201, 216; promotions of 43, 93; racial attitudes of 175, 179–180, 207, 208; relations with troops 88, 106, 126, 140, 151, 185; return to military service 194; special mission to Washington, D.C. 117–119; testimony at Buell Commission 94, 107–108; in U.S. House of Representatives 3, 175–189, 193–194
Rousseau, Lucy Ann (sister) 8, 203
Rousseau, Marie Antoinette (nee Dozier, wife) 14, 16, 29, 177, 204, 213, 214, 215
Rousseau, Mary (daughter) 16, 29, 177, 204, 213, 214
Rousseau, Mary G. (sister) 8, 9–10
Rousseau, Nancy M. (sister) 8
Rousseau, Richard (son) 16, 29, 177, 213, 214
Rousseau, Richard H. (brother) 6, 8, 12–13, 14, 29, 41, 203, 213
Rousseau, Samuel D. (brother) 8, 203
Rousseau, William C. (brother) 8, 203

St. Asaph's (Standing Fort), Kentucky 7
St. Louis, Missouri 31
St. Paul, Minnesota 214
Salem, Indiana 13
Salm-Salm, Felix Prince 135
Saltillo, Mexico (Battle of) 20, 21, 23, 25
Saltville, Virginia (Battle of) 174
Sampson (slave) 8, 9
Sanderson, Ellen 183–184
Sanderson, John 117, 118
Sanderson, John P. 184
Sanderson, W.L. 17, 18
San Luis Potosi, Mexico 22
San Pasqual, California (Battle of) 25
Santa Anna, Antonio Lopez de 22, 28
Savannah, Georgia 169
Savannah, Tennessee 58, 62, 63
Schofield, John 137, 164, 209, 210
Scott, Thomas 54
Scott, Winfield 20, 28
Scribner, Benjamin F. 18, 21, 23, 27, 47, 48, 95, 98, 101, 108, 109, 113, 123
Selma, Alabama 137, 143
Seminole Indians 19
Sequatchie Valley, Tennessee 73, 124, 125
Seward, William 191, 192, 195, 199, 202
Seymour, Horatio 206, 207, 211
Shacklette, Isabelle Wood Johnston 149, 150, 151
Shanklin, George S. 181
Shanks, W.F.G. 2, 88, 89, 139, 143, 148
Shaw, Robert Gould 3
Shawnee Indians 7, 133
Shelbyville, Tennessee 112
Shepherd, Oliver L. 95, 98, 101, 106

Sheridan, Philip H. 84, 85, 87, 90, 98, 99, 100, 102, 103, 110, 123, 125, 204–205, 211
Sherley, Zack 41, 69
Sherman, Thomas W. 22, 23, 24
Sherman, William T. 3, 42, 43, 45, 48, 49, 54, 58, 70, 136, 137, 138, 152, 153, 154, 155, 156, 157, 163, 164, 173
Shiloh, Tennessee (Battle of) 58–62, 64, 66, 69, 81, 90, 126
Sidell, W.H. 42
Sill, Joshua 83
Simonson, Peter 86
Sirwell, William 49
Sitka, Alaska 195, 196, 197, 198–200, 201, 202
Smith, A.A. 172
Smith, A.J. 138
Smith, Charles 144
Smith, Edmund Kirby 73, 76, 78, 79, 92
Smook, Daniel 33
Socopatoy, Alabama 145
Somerville, Alabama 139
Spalding, George 131, 135, 158
Spalding, Rufus P. 187
Spears, James G. 104
Speed, James 39, 162, 175
Speed, Joshua F. 39, 40, 175
Speed, Thomas 33, 35
Sportsman Hill, Kentucky 7
Spring Hill, Tennessee 58, 96, 160, 161, 165, 172
Springfield, Indiana 17
Stalcup, Isaac 13
Stanbery, Henry 205
Stanbery, William 188, 205
Stanford, Kentucky 6, 7, 92
Stanley, David S. 94, 103, 105, 110, 112, 121
Stanton, Edwin M. 115, 118–119, 127, 128
Starkweather, John C. 80, 84, 85, 86, 87, 88, 90, 95, 98
Steedman, James B. 123, 155, 156, 191, 192, 209, 210
Stevens, Thaddeus 180
Stevenson, Alabama 71, 72, 121, 135, 161
Stevenson's Depot, Virginia (Fight at) 136
Stoeckl, Edouard de 196
Stone, David C. 47, 55, 88
Stoneman, George 152, 154
Stones River (Battle of) 97–106, 108, 109, 126
Stowe's Ferry, Alabama 146
Stumbaugh, Frederick S. 49, 64, 65
Sullivan County, Indiana 13
Sulphur Branch, Tennessee 158
Summit, Alabama 139
Sumner, Charles 188
Swift, Ebenezer 103
The Swing Around the Circle 191–193, 194
Sylacauga, Alabama 145

Talladega, Alabama 144, 145, 150, 153
Taylor, Zachary 16, 19, 20, 21–22, 23, 24, 25, 26, 29, 30

Taylorsville, Kentucky 83
Ten Islands Ford, Alabama (Fight at) 141–142, 143
Tennessee & Alabama Railroad 161
Tennessee, District of 137, 154, 169
Tennessee Troops: 4th Cavalry 138, 140, 142; 21st Infantry (CSA) 158
Terrill, William R. 86, 87
Texas Rangers (Mexican War) 19
Thames, Battle of (War of 1812) 7
Thickstun, Edmund 8, 9
Thirteenth Amendment 2, 171, 175
Thomas (slave) 8, 9, 10
Thomas, Bryan M. 147, 148
Thomas, George H. 63, 77, 78, 93, 94, 95, 97, 98, 99, 100, 102, 103, 104, 105, 108, 112, 121, 122, 123, 124, 126, 128, 136, 137, 138, 152, 155, 156, 159, 161, 161, 164, 165, 166, 168, 169, 170, 171, 172, 173, 174
Thomas, Lorenzo 54
Thomas, Samuel O. 50
Thomasson, Charles L. 39
Thompson, C.R. 172
Thompson, W.R. 33, 35
Thornburgh, Duff G. 137
Tilton, Georgia 155
Tlingit Indians 198, 200
Torrejon, Anastasio 24, 25
Trabue, Robert P. 59
Treaty of Cession of Russian America to the United States 195
Triune, Tennessee 109
Tullahoma, Tennessee 112, 114, 115, 120, 155, 159, 160, 162, 164, 172, 174
Tupelo, Mississippi 65
Turchin, John B. 70
Tuscumbia, Alabama 68, 157
Twain, Mark 196, 206

Unconditional Unionist Party 175, 178, 179, 181
United States Colored Troops: 110th Infantry 157
United States Troops Battery H 95; 2nd Infantry (Post 1865) 192; 5th Infantry (Mexican War) 19; 15th Infantry 44, 47, 59, 117; 16th Infantry 44, 47, 59; 19th Infantry 59, 60; 20th Infantry (Post 1865) 214
Upton, Kentucky 51, 56, 79

Van Buren, Martin 29
Van Cleve, Horatio 98
Vandyke, Augustus C. 50
Vanslyke, Peter 13
Vanverse, John 13
Veniaminov, Ivan 199–200
Veracruz, Mexico 28
Vicksburg, Mississippi (Siege of) 115
Victoria, British Columbia 198, 201, 202
Villa Ricca, Georgia 152

Vogt, John 33
Von Allman, Sarah J. 202

Wabash & Erie Canal 14, 15
Wade, Benjamin 178
War Trace, Tennessee 112
Ward, John H. 132–134
Ward, William T. 132, 133
Warmoth, Henry C. 205, 208–209, 210, 211, 213, 214
Washington, John 22, 23
Washington, D.C. 30, 39, 40, 41, 43, 93, 96, 109, 112, 115, 116, 117–118, 125, 171, 191, 192, 196, 206, 209, 210
Watkins, Eva W. 204, 214
Watkins, Louis D. 177, 180, 204, 215
Watkins, Louis D., Jr. 204, 214
Watkins, Lovell Rousseau 177, 204, 214
Watts, Elijah S. 147
Wayne County, Kentucky 5, 6, 9
Waynesboro, Tennessee 164
Webster, George P. 86, 87
Webster, J.D. 155, 156
Welles, Gideon 191, 192
West Point, Alabama 149, 152
West Point, Kentucky 78, 79
West Point Military Academy 48, 49
Western & Atlantic Railroad 67, 164
Wharton, John 86–87, 100, 101
Wheeler, Joseph 75, 78, 86, 90, 92, 96, 97, 98, 125, 135, 155, 156, 157, 172
Whig Party 14, 20, 29, 30, 37
Whipple, W.D. 174
Whitaker, Walter C. 39, 47, 48, 194
Whitcomb, James 14
White County, Tennessee 174
White Mills, Kentucky 51
Whitley, William 7
Whitman, Walt 142
Widney, Lyman S. 55
Wilcox, J.C. 140
Wilder, John T. 77, 107, 109, 112, 113, 122
Wilderness Road 7
Williams, John S. 156, 174
Williams, Thomas C. 142, 144
Willich, August 31, 48, 60, 99, 109
Winchester, Tennessee 121
Winchester, Virginia 136, 155
Winterboro, Alabama 145
Wisconsin Troops 1st Infantry 109; 21st Infantry 84
Wood, Thomas J. 47, 55, 77, 98
Woodruff, W.B. 39
Wool, John E. 22, 23, 26
Worth, William 19

Yeoman, Lizzie 202
Young, William P. 150
Youngville, Alabama 146